Alfred Hitchcock

PHILOSOPHICAL FILMMAKERS

Series editor: Costica Bradatan is a Professor of Humanities at Texas Tech University, USA, and an Honorary Research Professor of Philosophy at the University of Queensland, Australia. He is the author of *Dying for Ideas: The Dangerous Lives of the Philosophers* (Bloomsbury, 2015), among other books.

Films can ask big questions about human existence: what it means to be alive, to be afraid, to be moral, to be loved. The *Philosophical Filmmakers* series examines the work of influential directors, through the writing of thinkers wanting to grapple with the rocky territory where film and philosophy touch borders.

Each book involves a philosopher engaging with an individual filmmaker's work, revealing how it has inspired the author's own philosophical perspectives and how critical engagement with those films can expand our intellectual horizons.

Other titles in the series:

Eric Rohmer, Vittorio Hösle
Werner Herzog, Richard Eldridge
Terrence Malick, Robert Sinnerbrink
Kenneth Lonergan, Todd May
Shyam Benegal, Samir Chopra
Douglas Sirk, Robert B. Pippin
Lucasfilm, Cyrus R. K. Patell
Christopher Nolan, Robbie B. H. Goh

Other titles forthcoming:

Leni Riefenstahl, Jakob Lothe
Jane Campion, Bernadette Wegenstein

Alfred Hitchcock

Filmmaker and Philosopher

Mark William Roche

BLOOMSBURY ACADEMIC
LONDON • NEW YORK • OXFORD • NEW DELHI • SYDNEY

BLOOMSBURY ACADEMIC
Bloomsbury Publishing Plc
50 Bedford Square, London, WC1B 3DP, UK
1385 Broadway, New York, NY 10018, USA
29 Earlsfort Terrace, Dublin 2, Ireland

BLOOMSBURY, BLOOMSBURY ACADEMIC and the Diana logo are trademarks of
Bloomsbury Publishing Plc

First published in Great Britain 2022

ISBN: HB: 978-1-4742-2131-3
PB: 978-1-4742-2130-6
ePDF: 978-1-4742-2132-0
eBook: 978-1-4742-2133-7

Series: Philosophical Filmmakers

Typeset by Newgen KnowledgeWorks Pvt. Ltd., Chennai, India
Printed and bound in Great Britain

To find out more about our authors and books visit www.bloomsbury.com
and sign up for our newsletters.

For Susan, Jason, and Michael

Contents

Figures

Acknowledgments

I have benefited from discussions of cinema with many persons over the years, above all with my wife, Barbara, for which I am deeply grateful. Film is a good topic for cross-disciplinary discussion, and I am thankful for many rich conversations. In particular I want to thank Jan Hagens of Yale University, Christian Illies of the University of Bamberg, and Dmitri Nikulin of the New School for Social Research. I also want to remember my deceased colleague Chuck Hoffmann of Ohio State, who was a mentor to me when I first taught German cinema many years ago, and I want to thank Vittorio Hösle, with whom I co-authored two essays on film. Anton Kaes and Eric Rentschler introduced me to the study of film as film at the inaugural German Film Institute in 1985.

At the invitation of Don Crafton, I was able to present an early version of my analysis of *Shadow of a Doubt* to Notre Dame colleagues in Film, Television and Theatre. I am also grateful to Pam Wojcik for inviting me to discuss Hitchcock with her film students at Notre Dame. At the invitation of Gudrun Grabher I was able to explore Hitchcock and America with students and faculty at the University of Innsbruck.

I also want to thank the students with whom I have had the pleasure of analyzing film off and on for thirty-five years. Above all I want to thank my engineering honors students from spring 2014, with whom I discussed multiple Hitchcock films, and my arts and sciences honors students from fall 2020, whose seminar was devoted exclusively to Hitchcock. I agree with Heinrich von Kleist's theory, modeled on Plato's, that one formulates one's best thoughts not in private reflection but in dialogue with others (2.319–23).

I dedicate this book to my siblings, Sue, Jay, and Mike. As Hitchcock knew, family can be a great source of love. Since no one chooses their parents or siblings, one can only be grateful if one is as blessed as I have been.

Introduction

Philosophical categories illuminate films, and cinematic works invite philosophical questions. My students recognize both points immediately, and a favorite director for them is Hitchcock, be it *Blackmail*, with its consistent ambiguity; *Shadow of a Doubt*, with Charlie's identity crisis and battle with her uncle; *Strangers on a Train*, with its diabolically fascinating antihero; *I Confess*, with its tragic structures and hint at reconciliation; *Rear Window*, with its deep self-reflection; or *North by Northwest*, with its combination of adventure, wit, and philosophical resonance. Artistic works give life to philosophical puzzles and often push them forward, offering different perspectives and asking new questions. Hitchcock's favorite cinematic emotion is fear. In an era when fear of an invisible virus has upended countless lives, creating an almost universal sense of uncertainty and vulnerability, Hitchcock's films have even greater resonance.

There are good reasons why Hitchcock is among the most interpreted directors and why he thought good films should be seen more than once (*Alfred* 50). Like Shakespeare, Hitchcock reaches wide audiences, in his case with chase scenes, murder suspicions, and complex human interactions, but with enough depth and nuance to fascinate a smaller set of viewers who recognize an inexhaustible richness of form and content, including ambitious philosophical questions.

My experience of Hitchcock began as a child, before I knew what philosophy was, but over time, as his films continued to fascinate me, I realized that my enduring interest emerged from a mix of entertainment and reflection. Film depicts characters whose thoughts and actions intrigue us for their own sake, but these portrayals also reveal essential aspects of the world. Art is a source of knowledge. In engaging Hitchcock, we encounter themes that are existentially rich. This is another reason why Hitchcock is so popular. Sure, we experience suspense, laden with a sense of unease and often danger, and we laugh, but we also identify with the struggles of characters who undergo challenges that most human beings experience on a less grand scale: unexpected difficulties, uncertainty in knowledge, identity crises, a sense of isolation, wrestling with and combating evil, recognizing deficiencies in ourselves and those we love, and the human desire for some kind of reconciliation.

In fighting the micro-management of his first American producer, David Selznick, Hitchcock found that envisaging every scene in advance, such that Hitchcock could shoot in a targeted and limited manner, creating a distinctive "jigsaw" puzzle, that in the editing room could be combined in just one way, meant that only he—and not the producer—could finalize the film (Bogdanovich 516). The puzzle method enhanced Hitchcock's autonomy. In *Spellbound* Dr. Alex Brulov says that dreams "tell you what you are trying to hide. But they tell it to you all mixed up, like pieces of a puzzle that don't fit. The problem of the analyst is to examine this puzzle and put the pieces together in the right place." In *Vertigo*, Scottie is intertwined in a complex world of yearning that represents longing for love and knowledge, and his face in the crucial dream sequence expresses not so much loss as "puzzlement," as Robert Pippin notes (*Philosophical Hitchcock* 92). Even in Hitchcock's less overtly psychological works, puzzles and mysteries surface. Mystery implies depth and can be alluring, as with Charlie's love for her uncle in *Shadow of a Doubt* or Scottie's fascination with Madeleine in *Vertigo*. Most Hitchcock films have elements of complexity: how to interpret a character who is an enigma to others, if not also themselves. Some of Hitchcock's shots are visual puzzles. Consider the "visual incongruity" of Cary Grant in a business suit waiting at the bus stop while standing in the midst of cornfields (*Hitchcock on Hitchcock* 1.296). In its incongruity the image is almost comical, but it is also unnerving. We as viewers must constantly work to interpret and piece together the various elements of Hitchcock's films in order to grasp their hidden meanings.

Hitchcock's films address a wide array of philosophical puzzles:

- They explore incongruities and ambiguities, which are rich sources of philosophical reflection and essential to both the comic and the horrific.

- The films, which frequently revolve around the difficulty of knowing what is inside the mind of another person and often portray characters who know more than those around them, invite questions about the fragility and complexity of knowledge.
- Identity crises, mistaken identities, and doubles repeatedly surface; these, too, interweave artistic and philosophical questions.
- Many Hitchcock characters are inadvertently thrown into worlds they did not choose. The resulting question, what do they make of their situations, dramatizes ideas at the heart of existentialism.
- Hitchcock's films exhibit fascination with the structures and power of evil. Who is evil, and how does evil shield and reveal itself?
- The topics of knowledge and identity often lead to the question: how should I act in the light of what I know? In this context Hitchcock explores courage. What is at stake when one knows the truth but cannot move others?
- Hitchcock's heroes are often isolated and alone, but they are for that no less desirous of love; his films offer nuanced insights into the dynamics of love.
- An interest in narrative arcs, in the combination of individual action and unanticipated aid, and in gestures to reconciliation raise broader questions of providence.
- By way of self-reflection Hitchcock interrogates the relation of art and reality.
- Hitchcock plays with diverse philosophical genres, including tragedy, but his most distinctive mode may be a fascinating middle ground between acceptance of the world as it is and hatred of that world; his critique of human weaknesses is a loving critique and so embodies what philosophers have called humor, a relatively uncommon comic form.

Hitchcock does not treat these issues in isolation but creatively winds them together. The director has crafted a remarkably coherent philosophical universe; each of these themes is ultimately related to the others. Knowledge of complexities interweaves ambiguities and uncertainties. Such knowledge can also elicit crises of identity, especially when the world as we knew it differs from what we suddenly encounter. Uncertainty in recognizing evil reminds us how thin the line is between goodness and evil. The mystery of evil, which Hitchcock accentuates, forces characters to focus on knowledge and counter-strategies. Knowledge of evil impels otherwise ordinary characters to rise to the occasion. Evil is challenged with courage and often love, at times love of a higher ideal, at times love of another person, occasionally both. These topics also drive Hitchcock's play with genre. Incongruities are essential to horror as well as to tragedy and comedy. Hitchcock recognizes and exposes human weaknesses, including vulnerability to evil from within and without, but he does not hate humanity for this. Despite his engagement with terror Hitchcock almost always concludes his films with a gesture toward reconciliation. The director's focus on original sin does not mean that he has a negative or cynical view of humanity. To say that something is evil is to suggest that it is not as it should be, that is, original sin has meaning only insofar it presupposes deviation from an ideal that we can recognize and seek to realize. Only by knowing evil can we effectively guard against it, and only by knowing evil as part of a larger plan can we feel sympathy for villains even as we challenge them.

Hitchcock affirms American individualism, but tempers it with a Catholic worldview that recognizes the value of transcending individuality.[1] In Hitchcock we encounter isolated characters whose lives are endangered by the collective. Government institutions, including the police, are unreliable, in many cases corrupt. Hitchcock identifies with the modern embrace of autonomy and its skeptical attitude toward tradition, consensus, and authority figures. Yet elevation of individuality is only part of the Hitchcock narrative. Having grown up in Essex, a Catholic enclave within Protestant England, having attended Mass at the church where his father's nephew was a priest, having served as an altar boy himself, having gone to a Jesuit school, where daily Mass and weekly confession were obligatory, having had a private audience with Pope Pius XI, Hitchcock remained a Catholic throughout his life (*Alfred* 12; McGilligan 17–19, 176). He was a donor to Catholic churches and organizations, called himself a Catholic, and was buried as a Catholic (Truffaut 204; McGilligan 440; Hurley, *Soul* xi). Hitchcock recognizes the value of, and need for, help from others; embraces the primary Christian virtue, love; acknowledges moments of grace; and invokes providence. Still, true to his natural irreverence, Hitchcock both developed and questioned Catholic positions.

This book interweaves Hitchcock's layered accounts of philosophical issues with his technical brilliance. Hitchcock experienced film at its origin when it was still a silent medium. He then carried his work forward to the age of talkies, color films, and ever new technical innovations. Like few others, Hitchcock mastered cinematic means of indirect communication: camera angles, framing, light, editing, and sound.

My focus in these pages is artwork aesthetics, that is, a film's ideas and form, the interrelation of the two, and the interrelation of parts and whole. Production and reception aesthetics play minor roles; they interest me here only insofar as they cast indirect light on the works or on the relevance of the films for us today. This is why even when it comes to the topic of women, which has received considerable attention in recent Hitchcock literature, I look primarily at women in the films themselves, not at the director's personal relations with women, which Donald Spoto has harshly criticized in *The Dark Side of Genius*.[2]

In Chapter 1, "Hitchcock's Philosophical Universe," I explore the philosophical questions Hitchcock raises and the positions his films adopt. His integration of incongruities opens up the horrific and the comic. Hitchcock reflects on uncertainty in knowing others, challenges to identity, means of exerting power, and ways of wrestling with evil. He returns again and again to the concepts of courage and love. His critique of human inadequacy, which reinforces his assessment of an impulse toward cruelty, a kind of original sin, is nonetheless compatible with an ultimately affirmative view of humankind, one enhanced by concepts of grace and providence. The topics he explores bring his films into conversation with objective idealists, such as Plato and Hegel; skeptics, such as Nietzsche; and philosophers of art, such as Hermann Cohen, who articulates a theory of humor as the loving critique of an inadequate world.

My second chapter, "Hitchcock as a Master of Form," opens with observations on film as a distinctive art and analyzes some of Hitchcock's film-specific ways of conveying meaning and arousing emotions. The chapter moves on to broader artistic dimensions, including Hitchcock's integration of doubles and symbolic forms, and concludes with his play with genre, from self-reflexive art, which is by nature philosophical, to tragedy, comedy, and a complex third form beyond tragedy and comedy.

Chapter 3 interweaves the themes above with a close analysis of *Shadow of a Doubt*, one of Hitchcock's favorites. The young heroine, Charlie, is bored with the ordinary world and wants to transcend it. What she discovers, however, is horrific. The film explores the dialectic of love and hate and engages a range of genre categories. Here Hitchcock is both critical of the ordinary and aware of its ultimate dignity. Charlie must wrestle with uncertainty in intersubjective relations, esoteric knowledge, and the complexity of evil. We see in this film the ways in which Hitchcock interweaves the universal and the contemporary, which leads me to introduce a new concept, "evocative allusion," a mode of drawing attention to specific historical events without, however, reducing a work to allegory.

Two shorter chapters conclude the work. "Hitchcock's Real and Apparent Gaps" analyzes areas in which Hitchcock can be evaluated for potential weaknesses: his relative neglect of social challenges; his portrayal of women; his unevenness in dealing with psychological issues; and his occasionally implausible plot lines and black-and-white character portrayals. All of these have a moment of truth, but they can also be at least partially countered. "Hitchcock and Beyond" initiates a broader intellectual conversation. Hitchcock's themes shed indirect light on a wide range of contemporary issues, including the dichotomy of superior and inferior beings, opposition between fear and openness, the rise of disinformation, and the advancement of power as an end in itself. Hitchcock's elevation of the unrelenting search for knowledge, his loving critique of contemporary inadequacies, and his hope despite adversity provide unexpected resources as we think through contemporary dilemmas.

The book shows how one can philosophize indirectly by engaging the films of a great director. Via Hitchcock's exemplary case, we see how productive film can be for philosophy and philosophy for film analysis.[3] I am arguing that Hitchcock's films evoke philosophical ideas, not that Hitchcock intended to express them. The meaning of a work is not reducible to the consciousness that created it. Already Plato observed that poets are poor interpreters; they write not so much out of wisdom as out of instinct or inspiration. Great artists may have an unconscious sense of what is fitting, as when they step back to view a canvas before continuing to paint or make revisions after rereading lines of a poem, but they less commonly have the categorical apparatus to describe the value of their works or their meanings. Hitchcock downplays ideas and views himself as a technician: "I am not deeply interested in the moral or the message of the film."[4] By referring to the form and content of a work, we can ferret out meanings of which the director may have been at most only vaguely aware. The trick is not to read into the works but to recognize the patterns, structures, dimensions of the works that allow the viewer to defend this or that interpretation.

The book should interest not only scholars and students in philosophy and film but also educated film connoisseurs. It is not the first book to explore Hitchcock and philosophy, but its style and selection of themes differ from what is otherwise available.[5]

Chapter 1

Hitchcock's Philosophical Universe

Hitchcock's engagement with philosophical questions ranges widely. His films give rise to questions concerning knowledge. They address the value of uncovering contradictions. Of central concern to him are power as the defining element of the social in modernity and the often deceptive ways in which evil surfaces in our world. Hitchcock repeatedly returns to a classical virtue (courage) and a Christian virtue (love). He also shows how love of an ideal can motivate courage. Finally, Hitchcock's extensive portrayals of inhumanity and misfortune are nonetheless complemented by occasional glimpses of benevolence and providence.

Knowledge and Incongruities

What we can know, how we can know, and how we can know that what we think we know is true are significant philosophical questions. Hitchcock places knowledge at the forefront of his films. Often the audience knows more than the figures on the screen, a gap that drives suspense.[1] Knowledge can be knowledge of different spheres: knowledge of an ideal realm, including knowledge of what we should do; knowledge of the physical world; knowledge of self; and knowledge of the social world, including other persons.

Following Vittorio Hösle, who revises Hegel's three realms of reality and Karl Popper's concept of three worlds, I explore Hitchcock in terms of four worlds.[2] The first world is the world of ideal meaning, which includes mathematical truths and valid conceptual and logical arguments. Valid transcendental norms, including those concerning the dignity of the human being, to which Hitchcock affectionately refers, belong to this first realm. The other three realms fall within the spatiotemporal world. The second is the physical world, available to us through experience. It is the focus of the natural sciences, which seek to understand its laws and so its grounding in the first world. The physical world, including non-verbal gestures, provides clues concerning hidden motivations. When nature is prominent, as in the magnificent aged redwood trees in *Vertigo,* the vast fields in *North by Northwest*, or the horror of *The Birds*, film captures this second world as well as or better than any other art. The third world is the interior world, which we access through introspection and which forms the subject of psychology. It presupposes a physical world as its basis and reveals itself indirectly and partially through physical signs. Whereas long shots can evoke the majesty of the physical world, close-ups tend to capture physical representations of the mind, thus interweaving the second and third worlds. For Hitchcock, the "visual image" makes manifest "thought" (*Hitchcock on Hitchcock* 1.296). Reaction shots, "the juxtaposition of imagery relating to the mind of the individual," also illuminate the third world (Bogdanovich 522). Reaction shots dominate in *Rear Window*. An intriguing third-world activity is self-deception, which we see with characters as diverse as Eve in *Stage Fright* and Devlin in *Notorious*. The fourth world is the social world, which involves the interaction of beings with interior dimensions and so builds on the third world as well as the second, where interior dimensions manifest themselves. The fourth world is the subject of both the humanities and the social sciences. This fourth world is the most fascinating, as it involves both interior and exterior realms. We can know the interior depth of other persons only through their physical and social manifestations. The fourth world also relates to the first: social norms, including also laws, seek (or at least should seek) their ultimate grounding in the first world. The fourth world is further related to the second insofar as the collective identity of a culture manifests itself in the natural landscape of a country and its most prominent physical symbols. Consider *Saboteur*, with its trip across the country, culminating at the Statue of Liberty.

Hitchcock's films belong of course to the fourth world, but they are also physical entities, which we experience in the physical world, and they are the result of conscious acts. Moreover, they seek to portray meanings whose validity can be assessed in relation to the first world. Hitchcock engages then all four worlds, though his primary interest is not the first or second world, but the psychological and social realms we find in the third and fourth worlds. Above all his fascination is with subject-subject relations, including how and to what extent a person knows others and how a hero can defend their position against evidence that seems to implicate the hero and against an external consensus that rallies against the hero.

Power and love are the two great intersubjective themes that dominate Hitchcock's immersion in the fourth world. The MacGuffin, a desired object in the physical world, as with the uranium-enriched sand in *Notorious*, or a sought-after intellectual formula, as in *The 39 Steps*, is simply a stratagem to generate intersubjective action involving power, love, or both. In Hitchcock's best films the two themes, power and love, are intertwined, as in *Shadow of a Doubt*, where a love relationship develops into a power struggle, or *Notorious*, where the spy story and love story are so interwoven that love and power are constantly at odds with one another. While power and love are the most important categories of the fourth world, they are also opposites. Power involves treating persons merely as means, whereas love presupposes that persons are also ends. Power is necessarily asymmetrical, whereas love culminates in symmetry. Power is something that in all but the most unusual cases involves will, force, and manipulation, whereas love cannot be forced. It must be a voluntary act and is often undeserved, animated by a kind of grace.

Because Hitchcock trusts in a moral universe and does not often focus on the hero's intellectual anguish, his references to the first world, what transcends us and what we should do, tend to be implicit or given. Note that for a director who works mainly with visuals and wants to avoid photographs of people talking, the first world cannot be a primary focus. Nonetheless, Hitchcock offers a window on to the question, how we might access the first world. Many of his characters trust in goodness and display an intuitive suspicion of evil. Even in a work such as *The Man*

Who Knew Too Much, which brings forward an intellectual quandary, in each version the scream (and thus the resolution of the conflict) comes seemingly from the subconscious. Films such as *Spellbound* and *Rope* give us the language to understand Hitchcock's view of intuition as a mode of accessing a higher realm. Most Hitchcock heroes are intuitively moral and not at all self-reflective. Indeed, when it comes to morality and self-reflection, they tend to be self-deprecating. Self-righteousness surfaces instead among minor, unappealing characters, such as the coroner in *Vertigo*, who at the end of the inquest unleashes a tirade against Scottie, even as he exonerates him and remains oblivious to the truth, or Mr. Struck, who in *Marnie* is not only self-righteous but also lecherous, even as he denies it (which motivates others to roll their eyes). Sophistication, as we see with the villains in *The 39 Steps*, *Saboteur*, *Notorious*, and *Rope*, does not guarantee a moral compass any more than does majority opinion. Often the first world is evoked *ex negativo* by the way in which characters in the fourth world misjudge persons. The attack on consensus is an appeal to what is valid and what transcends what persons recognize—and thereby to what should be recognized because it is valid. The blind man in *Saboteur*, who falls in a long tradition, beginning with Tiresias, of insightful blind persons, states: "one's duties as a citizen sometimes require breaking the law." That is an appeal to the first world. Indeed, the widespread defiance of the law in Hitchcock, which we find with innocent heroes who flout the authorities and with their allies who break the law at some risk to themselves, such as Erica in *Young and Innocent* and Constance in *Spellbound*, underscores the director's recognition that the first and fourth worlds differ.

Though a philosopher might criticize Hitchcock for not grounding his moral norms in reason, Hitchcock is decidedly not seeking to do philosophy but to create art and indeed art that elicits emotions and evokes mystery. Moreover, because his films convey meaning indirectly and integrate emotional motivation, their mode of communication differs radically from philosophical argument. One of Giambattista Vico's insights is that it is not enough to ground philosophically the norms and institutions that give societies and cultures stability; we must also bond with them emotionally. In a society that offers endless reflection on the end of art and on art as negativity, Vico's theory and Hitchcock's works display the advantages of an alternative mode of art, whose emotional power can help bring us closer to values and to one another. The one Hitchcock film in which at the very center is a longing for something like the first world, a yearning for transcendence, for ideal beauty, for a union with what goes beyond everyday, empirical reality is *Vertigo*, which offers a distinctive cinematic achievement, for it is a film about what cannot be visualized. Even here, then, Hitchcock gives us an emotional, not a rational, connection, to the worlds.

Given his fascination with power and evil, Hitchcock dwells less vigorously on the second world, though *The Birds* is an obvious exception, even if in this film the threat from the natural world is another way of opening up human relations. Other exceptions, such as the massive rock formations in *The Manxman* and the rolling autumn landscape in *The Trouble with Harry*, underscore via tragedy and comedy, respectively, that the individual alone is not fully in charge of their fate or destiny.

Identity crises and struggles with how one should relate to the world play roles in many Hitchcock films. A thinker who explores fear is naturally drawn to the unconscious. Take *Notorious*, where after feeling ashamed by her father's postwar adherence to the Nazis, Alicia loses herself in alcohol and then longs for some form of recognition, be it by finding love with Devlin or sacrificing herself for patriotism. Just as Hitchcock shows the value of trusting in the future, even as he makes us aware of evil rampant in the world, so he displays the interpersonal longing for trust, which is often thwarted by egoism, coldness, and cynicism. Each figure, Devlin and Alicia, does not want to be rejected, to land in an asymmetrical position of loving and not being loved, so they protect themselves; each holds back from declaring their love for the other—and so events unfold horrifically. Devlin stays silent and cold, remaining first and foremost a spy and not confessing his love for Alicia or even his faith in her, such that Alicia is reduced to a means; Alicia, in turn, expresses hatred toward Devlin, even as she loves him. This collective silence leads to Alicia's dishonest relationship with Sebastian and eventually her being poisoned by him and her mother. And yet, we see the opposite as well. Sebastian trusts too quickly, too thoughtlessly, and is as a result betrayed by Alicia.

In *Spellbound* the hero suffers an acute identity crisis (he doesn't even know who he is), which derives from his suppressing knowledge that is too difficult to bear. As Constance says to him, "You remain sane by forgetting something too horrible to remember." Here knowledge follows a fascinating dialectic. Alex explains: "The human being very often doesn't want to know the truth about himself, because he thinks it will make him sick. So he makes himself sicker trying to forget." One must fight for knowledge—even about oneself, and gaining that knowledge can involve pain and risk. The hero, John, suffers an extreme version of an identity crisis virtually all persons undergo as they abandon earlier views by gaining a more complex mental framework. Constance herself undergoes a transition from one identity to another, moving from a focus on reason and book learning to an elevation of emotions and personal experience. The dual development is underscored by the two parallel lines that trigger John's disturbances and act as a cinematic leitmotif.

But above all the exploration of intersubjective relations defines Hitchcock's primary focus, the fourth world. Puzzles of knowledge bring together the third and fourth worlds, the relation of inner and outer and the individual's relations to others. These also drive action: the hero's desire for knowledge, the attempt to find exculpatory evidence, and the difficulties and possibilities of deciphering and combating evil. Furthermore, the audience recognizes incongruities as essential elements of cinematic horror and comedy. Knowledge thus drives a certain reception. Rarely does Hitchcock present mere physical power. That is too simple for his sense of nuance, complexity, and development. Instead, we see the search for knowledge and a contest of forces.

Vertigo, which displaced *Citizen Kane* in the most recent *Sight and Sound* ranking of the best films ever made, is arguably Hitchcock's most interpreted film. Primarily *Vertigo* is read in the realm of knowledge and uncertainty, where it certainly at least partially belongs. However, it uses the puzzle of knowledge to reach into cultural commentary, the mystery of love, the nature of evil, and the fascination of necrophilia. These are all related. In ancient cultures, our relationship to the past and to death was very much present, as persons died in their homes, and their orientation was as much to the past and the present as to the future. In modernity, a tendency arises to leave the past behind, which leads to a perverse relationship to time. The film's necrophilia is related to this broader understanding of death as something removed from life. In the second part of the film, Scottie loves Judy because she reminds him of a dead woman. That is psychologically perverse, but it sheds light on modernity's unhealthy relation with the past. A further aspect is that mystery is used strategically for instrumental purposes to gain erotic power. In both cases, we see instrumentalization of the other person. In the first part, Scottie is instrumentalized because of his fascination with dying and his fear of heights. In the second part, Scottie's faithfulness toward Madeleine becomes a moment of instrumentalization toward Judy. Romantic love, which seeks symmetry, is not easily compatible with such asymmetric power relations, and that is part of the film's tragedy: when love is awakened, power and instrumentalization have already destroyed the potential for its realization. Scottie regains Madeleine only to find that she was a fiction. The fascination of *Vertigo* is based partly on an unresolved and unresolvable contradiction: a desire for as yet unrealized love and a recognition of betrayal. The film plays with time not only in evaluating characters' relations to the past, it recognizes the tragedy of time insofar as recognition comes too late. In the first case, love is awakened, but the crime has been arranged. In the second, love is once again awakened, but Judy is an accomplice to the murderer. We see to what extent knowledge already opens up into power and love.

Often knowledge triggers action or omission. What should I do with the knowledge I have? What evil confronts me? How should I engage it? The latter question combines knowledge of the physical and social worlds (second and fourth worlds) with knowledge of the self and one's capacities (the third world) and knowledge of a moral realm (the first world): What should I do? In short, to know in any full sense what we should do, we need to know all four worlds. To know the good but not recognize evil or not know how to realize the good is as deficient a model as is the capacity for action without a guiding moral vision.

Central for Hitchcock is how to recognize evil, how to differentiate it from seeming evil, and how to combat it. He also reflects on how persons, often but not only public officials, fail despite wanting or seeking to counter evil. Enacting evil presupposes power. Hitchcock links mechanisms of power with knowledge. Various characters, such as Charlie in *Shadow of a Doubt* and Bruno in *Strangers on a Train* are able to gain an advantage over their counterparts, to manipulate them, insofar as they do not reveal what they know. Yet knowledge can also be constraining. Because of having heard Keller's truth in the confessional, Fr. Logan in *I Confess* is not allowed to reveal it. In other cases, knowledge is ineffectual because no one will believe the speaker. In *The 39 Steps* no one trusts Hannay, and in *Saboteur* only a few outsiders believe Barry. But Hitchcock reminds us in *Stage Fright* that the seemingly wrong man might well be the criminal himself, so there is on Hitchcock's part no blanket identification with the accused.

Hitchcock's fascination partly lies in his breaking away from the traditional idea that horror and banality are divorced from one another. Hitchcock brings these incongruous worlds together. Fear and danger enter into everyday reality. The extraordinary and the ordinary are woven together, such that our secure understanding of how the world works is torn asunder. An innocent person can be arrested and considered guilty. A seemingly innocent ally, even a family member, can be a spy or a murderer. Such incongruities not only spark our cognitive interest, they also grab us emotionally.

***

One of the oldest ideas of knowledge is that one moves forward in the search for truth by understanding what does not belong together, what is incongruous. Recognizing what is not as it should be helps us on the path to truth. When in Plato's dialogues the interlocutors try to define a virtue, the first task is to give not simply an example, but a broader definition that encompasses all instances. The next step is to assess whether the position is internally consistent. One cannot rationally defend as true a position that contradicts itself, for then one could justify any position. An important chapter in the history of incongruities is Kant's recognition of the four antinomies of pure reason, which address whether the world is spatially and temporally finite or infinite, whether freedom or necessity reigns, and whether God exists. Hegel, who speaks with existential pathos about Plato's Socratic dialogues, also elevated Kant's antinomies, but he criticized Kant for recognizing only four. For Hegel, contradictions are visible in "*all* objects of all kinds, in *all* representations, concepts, and ideas" (8.127–8, emphasis in the original; cf. 20.356). Hegel uses contradictions as a lens to understand history, which moves forward as contradictions are uncovered, contested, and resolved, thus leading to a new stage of development.

Incongruities are also central to art, including comedy. Philosophers and psychologists have developed essentially three theories of laughter: superiority, relief, and incongruity.[3] According to the superiority theory, often associated with Hobbes, we laugh at the misfortunes of others. Laughter arises from a feeling of superiority and a sense of the ridiculous. Consider the German concept of *Schadenfreude*: someone slips harmlessly on a banana peel while a crowd looks on and laughs. According to the relief theory, primarily associated with Freud, laughter arises from our overcoming or circumventing the inhibitions of an internal censor. Laughter is awakened in the light of unconscious desires, urges, and thoughts that otherwise would not make the light of day, what we would otherwise not be allowed to say, what in other contexts we would repress, for example, sexual jokes or jokes of aggression, whereby aggression is to be understood widely and includes not only political criticism but also aggression against persons, institutions, moral values, world views, religion, and even one's own fears, such as the fear of death. The superiority and relief theories have two elements in common: first, they focus not on the object of our laughter, but on its production and reception contexts, what conditions elicit laughter and how we react to a situation; second, they are descriptive and answer the question, what makes us laugh.

The third theory, the incongruity theory, has been associated with various thinkers, including Hegel (10.113–14). Here laughter arises from incongruities in the situation, which trigger our emotional and cognitive recognition. For example, we laugh at the end of the second *Man Who Knew Too Much* when the McKennas' guests, who have spent hours in the suite and have fallen asleep, hear the McKennas arrive with the innocuous line: "I'm sorry we were gone so long, but we had to go over and pick up Hank." Note that the focus in this theory is on the object, the incongruity, not the production or reception contexts. In that sense, it is perfectly compatible with the other two theories, which can be absorbed into it. Indeed, we laugh not only at the incongruity between the horrific situation and the innocuous line, but also at the dichotomy between our knowledge and the guest's lack of knowledge. We are in a position of superior knowledge. Moreover, the line offers welcome comic relief after the extraordinary tension.

Because the incongruity theory focuses on the object, it allows us to evaluate incongruities on a normative level, recognizing that some jokes, some actions, some objects, are not funny, that is, if our laughter is also intelligent, we will not laugh at them. At the end of *Blackmail*, the constable laughs at Alice's allegedly knowing more about the murder than Frank, whereas Frank and Alice can only pretend to laugh. The audience cannot laugh either, for even as we identify with Alice and want her safe, we are partially relieved when she resolves to confess, and thus full of ambivalent sentiments, but certainly not laughter, when she, under Frank's direction, steps back from the truth. If confession represents release, Frank's act of silencing her imprisons her, even as it frees her from a horrendous trial, where she would have been sexualized, much as Crewe and the camera (and thus the viewer) had sexualized her earlier. The only justified laughter comes from the painting of the mocking jester, which passes by in this final scene and points a finger at everyone, including society and the audience (Figure 1).

Even as Hitchcock's comedy is built on incongruities, Hitchcock also plays with comic relief. Consider, for example, the unsatisfying and comically bizarre gourmet meals the Chief Inspector's wife prepares in *Frenzy*. Hitchcock notes, "An audience gets worked up, and they need

Figure 1 In *Blackmail*, the laughing jester is first seen in Crewe's apartment, where Alice initially laughs and is later horrified. It reappears at the end of the film and seems to mock, and point its finger at, everyone, including the audience. *Blackmail* directed by Alfred Hitchcock. © Delta Entertainment 1929. All rights reserved.

relief" (Cavett). Comedy relieves "tension," he notes, because of "the incongruous" (*Hitchcock on Hitchcock* 1.81). Comic relief arises from two factors: the comic moment relieves fear, and the comic incongruity itself is harmless. At times we laugh at characters for their mistakes or triviality, such as when Ben in the second *Man Who Knew Too Much* ends up at the taxidermist or when we look down on the child-like machinations of Herb and Joe in *Shadow of a Doubt*. Hitchcock's comic moments, including his self-deprecating humor, can be understood then via all three theories.

Almost all Hitchcock films include some comic elements. Indeed, they are part of his signature, and actors have consistently commented on his sense of humor (Raubicheck 33–4). The comic incongruities in his works tend to come not from pre-existing material, but from Hitchcock's additions, including his cameos, where we laugh at the dichotomy between art and life (*Hitchcock on Hitchcock* 1.23).[4] In *The 39 Steps*, the minister amuses us, for he is confronted with the salesmen who hold up women's undergarments. We laugh further at their continuing a mundane discussion, while Hannay seeks to learn whether he is being pursued for murder. Hitchcock comically interweaves the ordinary and the weighty. Barry in *Saboteur* is worried about his murder charge, while the long-haul truck driver yaps and yaps. The driver complains about monotony, but we see how a non-routine situation, such as escaping a false charge of espionage, can be a bit less appealing. In *Stage Fright*, Eve plays an absurd number of different roles such that we are amused as well as unnerved that she might be uncovered as she juggles her various parts. At times the incongruity is both funny and ominous, as in *Strangers on a Train* when at the tennis court all heads move back and forth, save Bruno's. In *Notorious* Sebastian realizes that he has married an American spy and returns to his role as the subordinate son, confiding in his mother. Her response ("We are protected by the enormity of your stupidity") is both accurate and funny. The others will not suspect him—at least for a while.

Not only is comedy, with its structural incongruities, already philosophical, Hitchcock uses comedy to raise broader philosophical puzzles. Comic incongruities may derive from the tension between knowledge and lack of knowledge, as with the obliviousness of Herb and Joe, as they discuss murder scenarios. Identity puzzles can be comic; in *North by Northwest* Roger Thornhill, whose life has been empty of substance, is mistaken for a man who doesn't even exist. We may laugh when those destined for love can only express their disdain for one another, a structure we see already in the British films, such as *The 39 Steps* and *The Lady Vanishes*. Even death can be the focus of comedy, as in *The Trouble with Harry* where Harry is dug up and buried multiple times. Power relations, too, can be the subject of comedy, as when Thornhill makes a fool of himself at the auction so as to evade his pursuers. Laughter arises from the incongruity of art and life whenever a character plays a role that is radically counter to their normal self, as when the rich Betty tries to roll out bread in *Champagne* or the leads in *Mr. and Mrs. Smith* pretend to be in love with someone else. An epistemological moment is at play as we recognize, often intuitively, such comic contrasts.

Whereas comedy is harmless and elicits laughter, terror and suspense evoke fear (*Hitchcock on Hitchcock* 1.116–21). Terror is a form of incongruity where pain or the potential for pain is significant. In the *Philebus* Plato argues that harmless ignorance is "ridiculous" (49c), whereas "ignorance in the strong" is "hateful and ugly" (49c). In the wake of this distinction, Aristotle associates harmless ugliness with the comic. Like the comic, the horrific is related to knowledge. In the oscillation between the comic (which is characterized by innocuous incongruities) and horror (which is defined by painful incongruities), we have yet another meta-incongruity, since Hitchcock plays with the two conflicting modes. Consider in *Shadow of a Doubt* the cut from a medium shot of Charlie and Graham laughing together to a close-up of Charlie's horror, as she learns of Graham's deception.

Noël Carroll has argued that horrific subjects fascinate us because they upend traditional concepts of what should be. The unexpectedly threatening violates our categories. Consider, for example, the beloved who is in fact a malicious criminal, as Eve discovers at the end of *Stage Fright*, or consider birds that attack humans, forcing them to huddle in boarded-up houses. The horrific contravenes our concepts, which triggers a desire to comprehend the incongruity. Why do horror films attract so many viewers? How can they be both repulsive and attractive? The answer, according to Carroll, has to do with our desire for knowledge. We are drawn to the question, how will this threatening incongruity play itself out in this particular world. Horror narratives "revolve around proving, disclosing, discovering, and confirming" the existence of "something that defies standing conceptual schemes" (*Philosophy* 181). Horrific incongruities are cognitively disruptive. Horror and suspense films are not so much pleasurable as fascinating. And like horror films, suspense films derive from "contrast" (*Hitchcock on Hitchcock* 1.115), including ordinary persons being placed in dangerous situations.

We desire to understand what is inexplicable. The unknown is mysterious and therefore alluring, as Hitchcock recognizes (*Hitchcock on Hitchcock* 1.140). The terror we experience when the hero knows the truth but cannot reveal it or when the hero encounters a seemingly unimaginable threat is the price we pay to follow the narrative until its resolution. The present, from which we cannot turn away, is riddled with fear, even if the as-yet-to-be unveiled future makes possible hope (*Hitchcock on Hitchcock* 1.141). This is the broad-ranging suspense of Hitchcock. We want to see and understand the danger. We are fascinated as we identify with the hero's horrific situation, are repulsed by the forces against which the hero battles, and remain eager to grasp how the incongruity can be positively resolved. On the narrative level, to see through incongruities is to gain knowledge, which can help thwart a threat. Suspense operates at the dialectic of fear and hope. We are uncertain as to the outcome, fearing for the worst, hoping for the best. We are absorbed in situations that are unusual, repelling, and not easily resolved. Standard categories are applied in vain. The ornithologist in *The Birds*, for example, is at a complete loss.

Hitchcock often underscores tension by juxtaposing music with either images or words. In *Mr. and Mrs. Smith*, the club's joyous dance music conflicts with David's inward feelings of misery and embarrassment. Non-diegetic examples occur in *Shadow of a Doubt*: when Joe and Herb learn that the Merry Widow murderer has been caught and the case closed, we hear "ominous woodwinds," and when Graham expresses his relief, which Charlie says she shares, that Uncle Charlie is no longer the subject of the investigation, we hear "unsettled strings" (Sullivan 93).[5] Incongruities arise between words and image as well: in the bar, Uncle Charlie says that he made some mistakes, nothing serious, as he aggressively twists, one might say, strangles, a napkin, revealing his destructive urges. In *Strangers on a Train,* the diegetic music from the carousel and the voices of the two boys are joyful, even as we observe Miriam's gruesome strangling. *Rear Window* offers a jarring contrast between the composer's romantic music and Thorwald's attacks on Lisa. One must look deeper to find the harmony: Lisa's courageous action, an extension of Jeff's initial concerns, solidifies their relationship, even as she stands in danger.

Hitchcock understood the higher unity of the horrific and the comic. In his interview with Dick Cavett, Hitchcock notes that "there's that fine line between fear and what is comic . . . a fine line between tragedy and comedy." Both elements feature prominently in his works, simultaneously or sequentially. *The Birds* moves from a comic to a horrific mode, but it occasionally interweaves both, as with the religious drunk, the unknowing ornithologist, and the café scene references to eating fried chicken, not to mention the introduction of a literal birds-eye view after the wreckage around the diner, as we and the birds assess the havoc.

***

Knowledge can not only be applied to the worlds of ideas and physical objects, but it can also involve the fourth world. The questions how do we know when another person is being truthful and how do we know when to trust another person are at the core of Hitchcock's films. For Hitchcock ambiguity is a marker of our relation to other persons. Human nature is so complex that we sometimes cannot know whether we are with a lover or a murderer. Hitchcock's single most interesting contribution to human relations may well be his assessment of how difficult achieving absolute certainty is in intersubjective relations and how variously we try to navigate this uncertainty, which can evoke fear, thwart love, enable evil, and hinder the revelation of truth. But uncertainty can also find its truth in trust. Many Hitchcock characters do not know whether they will be able to prove their innocence to others, but they trust all will work out and act to make that vision a reality. Others at times believe in the protagonist's innocence and goodness, which they base on little beyond an intuition. We see both moments in *Young and Innocent*.

In *The 39 Steps* Hannay first mistrusts and then, with modest evidence, trusts a spy. When the spy is murdered, he resolves to continue her mission. To exit his house incognito, he explains his situation to the milkman, asking to borrow his uniform as a disguise. The milkman does not believe Hannay's wild, but true, story of espionage and murder, so

Hannay lies, telling the milkman that he is an adulterer. The milkman immediately believes this more relatable, ordinary story. To be believed, the hero must lie. It is a topsy-turvy world, and of course as funny as it is suspenseful. When Hannay later tells the truth to Pamela, she does not believe him and turns him in to the police. Later he lies, saying that he is the murderer after whom the police are searching, and she believes him. Here the story fulfills her expectations—after all the police are chasing him. When she gains more evidence, she finally believes his original story. Unable to persuade the police, he realizes that the only way to clear his name is to catch the criminals himself even as the police chase him, a common structure in Hitchcock, which Andrew Britton aptly termed the "double chase" (72).

Suspicion revolves around the wife's uncertainty as to whether her husband is a murderer and might be planning to murder her. Even *Spellbound*, which stresses Constance's trust and love in the apparent murderer, offers us moments when her non-verbal expressions radiate fear and uncertainty. Will he kill her too? Other works, such as *Rebecca* and *Lifeboat,* also render uncertainty within the fourth world prominent. The second Mrs. de Winter does not know how to understand her husband. In *Lifeboat* the characters are deceived even as they, especially Kovak, harbor suspicions. In *Stage Fright* Eve discovers her trust in Jonathon was entirely misplaced: she has been working to shield a murderer and is now herself in danger. In *To Catch a Thief* Francie suspects that Robbie, who had already lied about his name and background, is also the jewel thief sought by the police, but she is wrong. The complexity of intersubjective relations also arises in such works as *The Lady Vanishes*, *Foreign Correspondent*, and *Saboteur*. It is one of Hitchcock's most widespread themes.

***

At times heroes do not know themselves and do not grasp the possible consequences of their thoughts. Here knowledge or lack of knowledge relates to the third world. In *Strangers on a Train* Guy wants to be rid of his wife, Miriam. Guy's double in this film, Bruno, senses Guy's subconscious desires and offers to trade murders: Bruno will kill Guy's wife as long as Guy kills Bruno's father. After Bruno has carried out his part, Bruno stands behind a gate, the shadows of which resemble jail bars. After a police car pulls up in front of Guy's house, Guy falls back with the murderer, quickly moving behind the gate: "You've got me acting like I'm a criminal." Guy is also guilty—and may be imprisoned. Ironically, striped shadows cover Guy's face precisely when Bruno tells him he is free. The line separating the ordinary and extraordinary is not wide. Just as ordinary characters can rise to almost heroic stature, so can ordinary characters (consider here the symbolism of the name Guy) succumb to evil temptations and cross the line.

Knowledge, then, can also be directed to oneself, and here, when we add incongruities to the mix, we encounter identity crises, mistaken identities, and doubles. Identity crises increase in modernity. A range of modern works in which identity crises are central—from Goethe's *Faust* to Woody Allen's *Zelig*—would have been inconceivable in earlier eras. Identity, as Hösle notes in his account of identity and identify crises, both individual and collective, should not be at odds with itself, but empirically it often is (*Morals* 222–75). In *Notorious* Alicia's identity crisis, her lack of being at home with her past, is symbolized spatially: she is not at home in her father's Miami residence, at the Rio hotel, or with Sebastian and his mother (Leitch 125–6). Many Hitchcock heroes are on the run; some, such as Thornhill, are never at home. Hitchcock dramatizes the heroes' inner conflicts as they adopt various roles, which only underscores their lack of stable identity. Identity crises can arise from multiple factors and take on various forms, not all of which are mutually exclusive.

- First, in some Hitchcock films the hero is challenged by their environment, such that what one or more other persons think of them—what George Herbert Mead calls the "Me" (175)—differs radically from what the figure knows in terms of the first and third worlds. The difficulties are especially engaging when even the characters' love interest doubts them, as in *The 39 Steps, Saboteur,* and *Notorious.* These conflicts provide the motor for drama and tend to be resolved only after considerable uncertainty or conflict. This widespread dilemma in Hitchcock usually involves not how to think about oneself, but how to act. The model is more social than psychological, more concerned with power than interiority. Whereas in most modern identity crises the hero circles around his own private subjectivity, in tortured self-doubt and self-pity, in Hitchcock we tend to see a sovereign indifference to one's own interests and self-confident readiness to act. The hero trusts that justice will prevail and contributes to its realization. As a result, Hitchcock's crises are more dramatic, involving active engagement in the fourth world. Nonetheless, we do see glimpses of psychological struggle. In *Vertigo* Judy resists being loved for who she is not: Scottie loves not her but the person she pretended to be at an earlier time, the one he thinks she is or should be. Judy desperately asks Scottie, "Couldn't you like me just the way I am?" An obvious antidote arises when someone does trust and love the hero as they are and against the crowd, as in *Young and Innocent*, *Spellbound*, and *Marnie*.

- Second are films where the hero is uprooted from their previous world and enters an entirely new frame in which they must assume a new identity. This can mean playing a new role as well as adopting a new name, as in *Rebecca* and *North by Northwest*. The hero must struggle with new identity and surroundings. Note that the first model often overlaps with the second. In *North by Northwest* the hero must adapt to a new Me, which can require new modes of identity and action. *The Wrong Man* offers a more somber treatment of this overlap. By the end of *Lifeboat* Connie has lost everything associated with her past. The camera and typewriter that mark her as a reporter and the diamond bracelet that signal her rise in society are gone, yet her new identity, minus these trappings, is richer.

- A third scenario arises when the hero weighs whether and to what extent another is no longer the person the hero thought they were. One's worldview begins to crumble under uncertainty and the threat of abandonment or betrayal as well as insecurity and dwindling confidence in one's own judgment. *Rebecca* is a case in point, as is *Suspicion*. In some instances, however, mistrust is justified, as in *Foreign Correspondent*, where the daughter must recognize her father's duplicity. Hitchcock often plays with this kind of uncertainty. Note that this model reverses the first: the crisis is not because of what others think of the hero, but what the hero thinks of others. This third scenario can also overlap with the second, as in *Shadow of a Doubt* when Charlie's knowledge forces her into a new relationship with her uncle. In *Notorious* Alicia's distance from her treasonous father is so great that it triggers a crisis: she hates her father and herself and longs desperately for some kind of redemption. Disgust with one's roots can be the germ of a new identity, but such a transition is rarely without difficulties.

- A fourth scenario arises when the hero wavers between the life they have led until now and their infatuation with an entirely different life or person or set of values. While this is a common identity crisis in modernity (the individual in mental anguish), it is rarer in Hitchcock. We do recognize a kind of self-torment in *The Paradine Case*, where Anthony Keane is torn between his wife, Gay, and the woman he is defending. But it is also typical Hitchcock that Gay, while troubled, is not torn asunder, but in a certain sense confident and sovereign in the situation. She allows her husband to experience negativity, recognizing his need to work through the crisis and reaffirming him despite his faults.
- A final model involves a severed or unhealthy relation to one's past. The identity crisis in *Spellbound* arises from loss of memory. The hero wants to turn himself in for a murder he did not commit, and his lover wants to keep him away from the police, who will only complicate any potential recovery. To rescue him, she must bring back his identity. Until the end Marnie is unable to reconcile with her past, for she hates herself, including her past and her future: "I believe in nothing." When Hitchcock portrays an identity crisis, he usually brings the character not into internal wrangling but toward action, as with *Spellbound*, where the character assumes another's identity, or *Marnie*, where Marnie hectically races around for meaning, moving from location to location and from job to job, even if she finds that she brings herself and her psychoses along with her. These characters burdened by the past have an ambivalent relationship to knowledge: they both seek knowledge of the past and are threatened (and thus repulsed) by it.

Not only are these models not mutually exclusive, but in some of Hitchcock's most complex films, such as *Vertigo* and *Psycho*, elements of every single one of these five scenarios is present.

In the tradition, mistaken identities can be tragic or comic. *Oedipus Rex* is a tragedy of mistaken identity: Oedipus, who solves the riddle of man, does not know himself, or, more precisely, his origins. But mistaken identity can also give rise to comedy; indeed, mistaken identity is central to New Comedy. In Hitchcock's second *Man Who Knew Too Much* mistaken identity results in both horror and comedy. In Morocco the British spy Louis Bernard misreads which couple he should be watching, which brings the American family, Ben and Jo McKenna, into the world of espionage and leads to their son, Hank, being kidnapped. But in the midst of this extreme terror, Hitchcock interlaces one comic moment after another. When trying to find the person McKenna thinks has knowledge of his son, McKenna has to navigate a joyous reunion of stage personalities visiting his wife. He then goes to the wrong location. Upon entering the shop, McKenna meets the older Ambrose Chappell before seemingly being redirected to the right one, his son, but even he is not the one he wants: the younger Chappell knows nothing of the affair, and a ludicrous struggle ensues. This comic iteration (the correction of the first mistaken identity is just another mistaken identity) is the flip side of the confusing and mounting horror. Though the scene is comic, the location, a taxidermy shop, reminds us of the possibility of death. In *Spellbound*, an otherwise serious film, Constance pompously declares love a delusion just before she herself succumbs to love. We can also consider the feigned mistaken identities in *The Birds*, where each hero pranks the other. Here the comic is interwoven with aggression and power play. In *The Trouble with Harry* the major figures, one after another, think, erroneously, that they have killed Harry. More frequently in identity crises, the innocent hero is mistaken for a criminal, as in *The Wrong Man*, which leads to the need for courage in combating evil and in enduring injustice.

Evil and Power

Arguably Hitchcock's most prominent topic is fascination with evil, the way it tempts and attracts us as well as endangers us, the power it has over us, the way it plays with us, behind our backs, and in the end is still not always revealed for what it is. Hitchcock was intrigued with threats to wellbeing. The world is not as it should be. Why? What drives people out of the realm of the ordinary and into evil acts? What makes us susceptible to charismatic but evil figures? These interwoven questions animate his works. Our cognitive interest in them helps drive our fascination even when what we see is morally and emotionally repugnant.

Evil is a form of incongruity: we hate evil actions because they are not as they should be. Hitchcock is well aware of the dangers when evil and power are combined. One need only think of Willie in *Lifeboat*. As captain of a German submarine, Willie shot torpedoes not only at the supply ship but also at the lifeboats. Later he effectively drowns Gus by pushing him overboard. Throughout Willie deceives those who rescued him. He stands far above the American survivors not only in malice but also in brute power and tactics. Even so, Hitchcock portrays him as having a certain charisma. Hitchcock wants to sober Americans to the threats they face. To combat immorality of all kinds, we need to understand it. In *Lifeboat* the repetition of taking on board one German survivor after another, each first visible via their hands, and then using the exact same expression, "Danke schön," has something comic about it, for iteration tends to be comic, but here, it is also horrific, for both Germans are dangerous (the second, though described as a boy, points his pistol at the crew).[6] The repetition suggests that the fight will be long and arduous. Evil is not easily vanquished. Nonetheless, the lesson has been learned: the Americans do not kill this German, as they did Willie, but they are cautious.

Humans are fascinated with horror and death. In the fourth book of *The Republic,* Plato describes the human desire to see something unappealing, such as a corpse, even when we consciously resist the temptation. While walking, Leontius becomes aware of dead bodies that lay at the place of public execution. He is repulsed and at the same time irresistibly drawn to them. He holds back at first, covering his face, but is then overpowered. In a beautiful formulation, Plato has him say that his eyes take over his body: "for a time he resisted and veiled his head, but overpowered in despite of all by his desire, with wide staring eyes he rushed up to the corpses and cried, There, ye wretches, take your fill of the fine spectacle!" (439e–440a). Internally split, Leontius apostrophizes his eyes. His desires violently prevail over his reason, and his involuntary action represents the tension that surfaces between the innate longing simply to know reality and the conscious feeling that we should exhibit restraint. Plato uncovers a feature that belongs to anthropology, the human fascination with physical ugliness and death.

Moral ugliness is even more engrossing, for it engages not only the second world, but also the third and fourth worlds. To combat wickedness, we must seek to understand the mind of another person, the intentions behind evil's realization. How are we to decipher a person's hidden intentions? What physical signs open a window on to the soul? And when we do come to know turpitude, how should we combat it? The complexity of recognizing evil is evident in a short French film *Bon Voyage* that Hitchcock directed to support the war effort. The film has three levels: we see the escape of an RAF pilot from France to England; then we view the same escape with greater information, such that we learn that the pilot's accomplice was in fact a Gestapo agent seeking to ferret out and kill members of the French resistance; a brief third rendition unveils the capturing of Gestapo agents but not before one of them, in a haunting close-up, kills a female member of the resistance. Hitchcock combined the unmistakable horror of evil with the difficulty of uncovering which persons can be trusted (Vest). The second French short film *Aventure Malgache* underscores to what extent the resistance valuably adopts precisely such strategies of deception.

Hitchcock theorizes the human fascination with evil, its enactment, and modes of resistance, some more effectual than others. In doing so, he implicitly offers us a typology, in which he himself identifies with multiple modes of relating to evil.

Theorizing and Enacting Evil

The first mode involves fascination with the power to do evil. We should pause for a moment at the expression 'the power to do evil.' The idea is distinctly modern, for in the Greek and early Christian universe, for Plato in *Gorgias* (467a–b) and Boethius in *Consolatio* (4.2), for example, power is a normative category. If one triggers or enacts evil, one is not being powerful; one is instead succumbing to lower desires. Power is a normative category; therefore, the only power that is truly powerful is power for goodness. Today, in contrast, power is a purely descriptive category. This modern revolution is inaugurated to some extent by Niccolò Machiavelli's bracketing of morality from politics. Hitchcock seems fascinated by the descriptive workings of power, but unlike filmmakers who revel in portrayals of power without a moral frame, Hitchcock not only analyzes power, he seeks a synthesis of normative values and descriptive power.

Hitchcock presents us with diverse motivations for enacting evil. In a few cases we see a partially good intention go awry. In *The Paradine*

Case, Keane is smitten with Maddalena Paradine and prejudges her as innocent. When his infatuation becomes obsessive, he no longer seeks truth or justice, and his cruel courtroom tactics contribute to André Latour's suicide. In *I Confess* Keller wants to free Alma from her hard labor. Intending to steal from Villette, he kills him. Money is a common motivation. In *Sabotage* Verloc gets involved in terrorism in order to support his family. Here, too, we see an escalation. At first Verloc will not participate in any activity that leads to death, but he relents when others can be hired to plant the bomb, and in the end, when he loses his underworld partners and cannot himself act, because the police are on to him, he sends his wife's little brother, Stevie. The eventual killing of Stevie as he enjoys a day of celebration is brutal and horrific. Money is a driving force for Pengallan in *Jamaica Inn*, Flynn in *Saboteur*, and Tony in *Dial M for Murder*. In *Under Capricorn* the servant girl Milly wants to displace the mistress. Sensual desire drives Mrs. Paradine, who wants to be free of her husband, so that she can be with his valet. Others are technicians, fulfilling their roles with little interest in money or power. Consider Mr. Memory in *The 39 Steps*. Motivation can also be intellectual. In *Rope*, Brandon's desire for recognition is interwoven with the dangerous game of trying to outwit and outdo others. A form of recognition is revenge, which seeks to place the other where they belong and restore one's rightful place; consider the mob mentality in *Lifeboat*. Ideology or values (in the descriptive sense associated with the fourth world) can also play a role, as in *Shadow of a Doubt*, *Lifeboat*, and *Rope*. The captain in *Lifeboat* is driven by nationalism (he would prefer that Gus retain his German name "Schmidt,") and by ideology ("A poor cripple dying of hunger and thirst. What good could life be to a man like that?").

One of Hitchcock's goals is to allow us to recognize how close we are to some of these models. Evil figures are in many ways like us; they are part of society. Having intentions that go awry, desiring money and recognition, focusing only on one's own task, sensual longing, susceptibility to aberrant ideas, and discontent with the present are all human traits that can tempt otherwise normal persons into committing horrific acts. And given Hitchcock's manipulation of the camera, we often identify with sinful figures who are otherwise like us or have admirable qualities. Hitchcock foregrounds two modes of engaging evil in order to accentuate the thin line between good and evil. First are those who play with evil, as we do when we watch a Hitchcock film. Second are those who subconsciously desire evil even when they are not fully conscious of their deepest inclinations. In several films Hitchcock also presents on behalf of his characters the idea that harming others is in truth justified and appealing. In other words, Hitchcock also theorizes and shows evil as an end in itself.

Playful Evil

The first mode of engaging evil, including the power to kill another person, is playful, even if dark moments inevitably arise. Innocuous and dallying play with murder drives *The Trouble with Harry*. Harry's corpse is first discovered by a little boy with a toy gun (Figure 2).

That shot, coupled with the lyrical music with which we observe his discovery, sets the tone. Character after character mistakenly confesses that they killed Harry, such that Harry is buried and disinterred three times. The procedures are light and nonchalant. Harry's body has no visible wounds, and the camera dwells, somewhat comically, on his shoes and socks. The entire affair is softened by the surroundings, the beauty of nature, and the bizarre ways in which the characters either

Figure 2 Harry's corpse is first discovered by a little boy with a toy gun, played by Jerry Mathers. The bizarre but harmless image, coupled with lyrical music and beautiful fall colors, helps to set the comic tone. *The Trouble with Harry* directed by Alfred Hitchcock. © Samuel Taylor and Patricia Hitchcock O'Connell as Co-Trustees 1955. All rights reserved.

overplay or ignore the dead body as they continue with their daily lives. In the end all the suspicions of murder turn out to be erroneous.

In *Shadow of a Doubt* the father, Joe, and his neighbor Herb likewise engage murder harmlessly, contemplating one imaginative strategy after another while oblivious to them a real murderer sits at the table. What adds to the comedy is how serious Joe and Herb are in contemplating acts that they would never carry out and which would surely horrify them. The audience is not wildly distant from those who play with evil, for we as film viewers also enjoy, often perversely, the play of murder.

Hitchcock adopts a darkly jolly pose in the cameos for his television shows, first *Alfred Hitchcock Presents* and then the *Alfred Hitchcock Hour*, where his dry wit mocks, even as it introduces and concludes, the chilling episodes, and in his often witty interviews, talks, and short essays, for example, his 1965 "After Dinner Speech at the Screen Producers Guild Dinner" (*Hitchcock on Hitchcock* 1.54–8). Hitchcock recognizes the ways in which comedy and horror play well together, two modes of incongruities, one fearful, the other harmless. He notes his enjoyment in contemplating with others: "Wouldn't it be fun to kill them this way" (*Hitchcock on Hitchcock* 2.207). Hitchcock has compared the making of a film to the design and building of a roller coaster. At this point, he suggests, they'll really get a scream, and eventually they'll leave giggling.

Even sinister Hitchcock films sometimes engage evil playfully, as with Mrs. Cunningham in *Strangers on a Train,* who laughingly admits there are persons she at times would have liked to be rid of: "You know, I read of a case once. I think it would be a wonderful idea! I can take him out in the car, and when we get to a very lonely spot, knock him on the head with a hammer, pour gasoline over him and over the car, and set the whole thing ablaze!" Bruno counters that in such a scenario she would need to walk all the way home. Strangling, he suggests, is best and then proceeds to show her, nearly choking her to death, as he falls into a spell, seemingly driven by his repressed conscience. It is a cruel scene, on which the camera lingers, and we, having been seduced by the playfulness, are forced to witness the repercussions. That a playful attitude toward murder does not easily remain only playful is also underscored in *Secret Agent*, where Elsa finds spy work, even the prospect of murder, thrilling and exciting, but when it becomes a reality, she is devastated at what it really means, and this is before she even realizes that her fellow spies have killed the wrong man.

The macabre humor with which Hitchcock deals with murder reaches arguably its apex in *Rope*. A murder has taken place in the cinematic reality, but Hitchcock still plays with it. Double entendres abound, especially early in the film, with elliptical or unintended references to death, killing, and strangling. For example, after reading his palm, Mrs. Atwater says to Phillip, who plays the piano but who had also, unbeknownst to Mrs. Atwater, strangled David: "These hands will bring you great fame." What makes the viewer wince at these playful lines is that to laugh is to associate oneself with Brandon, who views murder as art, a kind of game, and who announces as the guests arrive, while the dead body is in the trunk, above which is a buffet dinner, "Now the fun begins." Though Hitchcock himself plays with murder, he shows the extreme consequence of viewing murder and art as one and the same. Rupert's playful comments on murder as legitimate are mirrored back to him with a reality he did not imagine. And yet, the entire film is just a film, so the play is genuine: everything is imagined, not real.

Subconscious Evil

Some characters contemplate or pursue evil almost involuntarily. They are unaware of their impulses, which they may seek to repress, even as they are revealed to the audience and in some cases over time to the characters themselves. Hitchcock suggests that just thinking an evil thought can be wicked because of its potential consequences. We should not flirt with temptations but instead reject them. In *Strangers on a Train*. Guy never fully dismisses Bruno's idea of exchanging murders, after which Bruno acts out Guy's unconscious. Bruno's mother is a parallel but unintentionally comic, if complex, figure: she consciously ignores evil (her son is in her eyes wonderful) but expresses violence in her art. In this way she borders two modes, the playful (her violent art is comic) and unconscious (she is oblivious to violence itself).

Hitchcock manipulates us into this subconscious mode. When the corrupt and stupid barrister (and aspiring judge) in *The Lady Vanishes* abandons the others on the train and is shot, we are lulled into not wailing his death. He is so unappealing. The comic tone underscores its harmlessness, but still we are implicated in certainly not rooting for his survival. In *Strangers on a Train* Hitchcock depicts Miriam, Guy's wife, as untrustworthy and promiscuous, such that viewers may not be unhappy at her departure. The director includes us in his accusations. Viewers can easily have subconscious impulses that contradict our normative sense of what is right. On his boat ride before strangling Miriam, Bruno enjoys a bag of popcorn. The implications for the audience, which is entertained by the action, are clear. Bruno eats his popcorn as we sit in the theater, observing his shadow, an echo of Plato's cave allegory. When we identify with Bruno, even vicariously, we succumb to a lower realm of reality. In *Dial M for Murder* we are encouraged to identify with Tony, whose watch has stopped, such that the anticipated murder might not take place (the murderer is about to leave the apartment without having encountered Margot), and that would certainly be less exciting. But the phone eventually does ring, and just before the murder attempt commences, the camera shifts between the perspective of the would-be murderer and shots of Margot's face: we are taken aback as our desire for drama is about to be realized. Hitchcock guides our emotions and reactions, such that we are at times implicated in the unconscious desire for plot, which can also mean the longing for a corpse.

Spoken Evil

A further form of theoretical interest in evil is neither playful nor subconscious but serious and spoken, even if the speaker does not enact the deed. This suggests the danger of an unjust attitude toward human beings that can be realized by other, more sinister figures. Hitchcock offers a modern version of a classic structure first articulated by Plato in *Gorgias*. Gorgias is a more or less likeable figure who doesn't want to recognize the potentially horrific consequences of his elevating rhetoric over philosophy. As is the case with Rupert in *Rope*, the teacher may have students who are less polite but more consequential.

Hitchcock is very much aware, here as with the subconscious impulse, of a theoretical gesture toward evil, unspoken or spoken, that can in the end be realized. In *Strangers on a Train* Babs says that it is good that Miriam is dead. Further, Babs romanticizes murder: "it would be wonderful to have a man love you so much he'd kill for you." Babs's comments do not lead to any obvious consequences, but they do advance an ugly attitude toward human life. Guy is tempted to kill out of his love for Babs's sister, Ann, and himself says on the phone after a frustrating meeting with his estranged wife: "I'd like to break her foul, useless little neck . . . I could strangle her," after which we cut to a shot of Bruno's hands.

In *Rope* Brandon and Phillip have learned from their prep school housemaster, Rupert, the idea that for superior human beings murder can be both just and artistic. The film opens with their killing a classmate, David. According to Rupert's view of justified murder, the "privilege of committing it should be reserved for those few who are really superior individuals." Brandon shamelessly continues his teacher's thought: "And the victims—inferior beings whose lives are unimportant anyway." Inferior persons do not deserve to live. Brandon continues: "The few are those men of such intellectual and cultural superiority that they're above the traditional moral concepts. Good and evil, right and wrong were invented for the ordinary average man, the inferior man, because he needs them." The natural state of affairs justifies the advantage of the stronger; conventional morality elevates the weak. This is essentially Nietzsche's position in *The Genealogy of Morals, Beyond Good and Evil*, and *The Antichrist*, where he develops his theory of master morality and chastises Christianity, which protects the weak against the naturally strong.

Just as an ordinary person can become extraordinary in a positive way, rising to undertake heroic acts, so do we encounter here a more sinister version of the relationship: in *Rope*, as in *Strangers on a Train* and *Shadow of a Doubt*, the extraordinary declare their right to take life away from those who are simply ordinary. Hitchcock was familiar with the idea from Nazi Germany, whose diabolic regime had been conquered just three years before *Rope* was released. David's father, who resists the ideology as immoral and horrific, notes as its source Nietzsche and Hitler. But for Brandon inferior human beings have no spark of transcendence. They are mere flesh and blood: "the Davids of the world merely occupy space." Good and evil are inventions of the inferior, designed to protect them, the very position Nietzsche adopts in his critique of Christianity. In the end Brandon acts like God, not only killing David but also rearranging the pair of lovers by trying to connect Janet with Ken instead of David. In a further perversion of Christianity, the food is placed above the dead body, with six candles atop the old chest. Not only is the Eucharist reversed; in Christianity the number six signifies evil.

The model for such a teacher-student relationship is Plato's *Gorgias*, which introduces by way of Callicles an early version of Nietzsche's idea that justice is the advantage of the stronger.[7] Plato's dialogue has implicitly four acts, each centered on a central figure, Gorgias, Polus, Callicles, and Socrates. Unlike other Platonic dialogues, here the main interlocutors proceed one after the other. The ordering explicates what is implicit in the previous position. In the end, Socrates uncovers the hidden truth of Gorgias's elevation of rhetoric, with its implicit equation of power and justice. The dialogue's first word is *polémou*, war or battle, a major category for Callicles, who implies that Socrates is a weakling because he arrives too late to hear Gorgias's speech. But Socrates does not like long speeches, so he did not miss much. Moreover, the real battle is the dialogue, not the preceding speech. Callicles does not understand that Socrates cannot be late for the fight because only with the arrival of Socrates does the real battle begin.

The dialogue commences with Socrates asking Gorgias what his profession is. Socrates enacts the basic philosophical pursuit of clarifying concepts. Gorgias's field is rhetoric, but Gorgias has trouble defining it. He eventually admits that rhetoric teaches conviction, not knowledge, and that it can be used for immoral purposes, but the teacher, he thinks, should not be held responsible for such consequences. Still, to his own surprise Gorgias concedes that good rhetoric presupposes knowledge of good and evil (460a). At the outset Gorgias states that he can answer any question and has not heard a new question for some time (448a). The passage is ironic, for Socrates' questions and ideas are, as Polus later elaborates, "shocking and fantastic" (467b). Still, despite Gorgias's vanity and poor philosophizing, including his lack of existential curiosity (esp. 458b, and with the sole exception of 506a–b), the philosopher is portrayed as polite and respectful. For Gorgias, power is not an end in itself (457a), even if his students will use it that way. Gorgias does not personally elevate power above all else, but the philosophy he represents, if thought through to its conclusion, passes over into power positivism, the idea that might makes right. Because his philosophy is not rooted in knowledge of good and evil and because he has no arguments as to why people should not abuse rhetoric, his position inevitably leads to the stances of Polus and Callicles. Gorgias wants to believe that rhetoric is not bad; it depends on how you use it. But without ethical constraints, rhetoric becomes autonomous, divorced from good and evil.

Polus takes over for Gorgias, arguing that the goal of action is pleasure (461b). Socrates counters that the immoral person is unhappy and the immoral person who is not punished the unhappiest of all. For Socrates causing misfortune is worse than suffering misfortune, and punishment is a kind of cure. The worst misfortune is to act unjustly and not be punished (478e). Polus and Callicles think Socrates must be kidding (481b). Polus does not offer an immanent critique. Instead, he approaches Socrates with different presuppositions and with laughter, what Socrates calls an odd kind of refutation (473e). The virtue of Polus is his curiosity. As a result, he changes roles: Polus, not Socrates, begins asking the questions, for Polus genuinely wants to understand what Socrates is saying (462b; 474c).

When Polus reaches a dead end, Callicles counters that Socrates has simply tricked his interlocutors. They have been refuted only because they are not shameless: they are unwilling to pursue their positions to their logical conclusions (482c–483a; cf. 461b). The others do not say what they believe. As Callicles takes center stage, he drops the mask of social convention and openly argues that wrongdoing is only considered shameful; it is not by nature wrong. He speaks with contempt of all who are "weak" (483b). Callicles unveils himself as an unrepentant power positivist.

The refutation of Callicles has at least three moments. First, Callicles has trouble defining the stronger. This is in effect also one of the strategies employed by David's father in *Rope*. Who is to say who the superior person is? Socrates observes that if it is a matter of pure power, then as long as the weaklings cling together and have collective power, they are right (488d). If power decides, then the power of the majority, which may consist of weaklings, justifies itself. This obviously disturbs Callicles, who then alters his position. Callicles eventually says that the superior are those who are wise and courageous, but temperance or self-control is missing from his list of virtues. Within the Platonic universe and indeed from any rational perspective you must exert power over yourself before you can exert power over others.

The debate turns to whether the more reasonable and courageous person should also be more temperate. We return thereby to the elevation of pleasure that began with Polus. Here, too, we see a parallel to *Rope*. The murder is linked with fun and artistry, with pleasure, danger, and intemperate drinking. The murderers think they are happy;

they indulge in pleasure to the point of intemperance, but they are revealed to be completely distraught. Philip is unable to control his emotions; his non-verbal gestures give him away. If you assume a hedonistic philosophy and believe that pleasure is the ultimate pursuit, then it is difficult to argue that some pleasures are bad. There must be some qualifying restrictions; otherwise, all pleasures are good. The pleasure of drinking is increased through the pain of thirst, but one cannot make the same argument with regard to the good. Goodness is not a comparative measure; it is a measure in itself. Because pleasure is dependent on pain, it is ontologically deficient. Absent danger and external approbation, the murderers remain unfulfilled; their action has no intrinsic value. If you assume that pleasure is the only good, then a person who has pleasure cannot be bad, and no pleasures can ever be bad. By conceding, however, that good and bad pleasures exist, Callicles relinquishes his hedonism. For Socrates you do the pleasurable for the sake of the good and not vice versa (500a). To counter this, you would need to argue that virtues have no intrinsic value and can be reduced to pleasure, but that position had already been refuted.

Second, as part of his defense, Callicles contends that what most people call justice is injustice and that true justice is the advantage of the superior. However, Callicles cannot consistently adhere to this position. He falls back on traditional categories. When he empathizes with Socrates, who might be put on trial, gaping "openmouthed, without anything to say," perhaps even put to death (486a), Callicles claims that others would have committed an injustice (486a). This inconsistency becomes a fascinating emotional refutation of his own intellectual position. If the others are in power, then their taking Socrates by force could not be an injustice. Callicles' humanity shines through to undermine his own power positivism. His position is further undercut insofar as Socrates, as we know from *The Apology*, was hardly speechless before his accusers.

The final refutation functions self-reflexively. Plato was both artist and philosopher. He had a profound sense for the unity of topic and performance. *Euthyphro*, a dialogue about piety, exemplifies that very virtue: it enacts the idea of piety by reflecting on the forms as a guide to pious action. In *Laches* we see courage enacted in the pursuit of a cogent definition of courage. The *Gorgias*, in turn, is an instance of good rhetoric, the turns of phrases being subordinate to the arguments and the final myth a means of conveying to a wider audience the dialogue's philosophical truth. *Gorgias* is about the conditions of dialogue, which Socrates adduces as "knowledge, goodwill, and frankness" (487a), including a willingness to be punished by accepting better arguments (505c). As soon as one engages in dialogue, one accepts certain basic principles. If Callicles were a complete power positivist, he would not even enter the dialogue. As soon as the power positivist communicates his theory, he contradicts himself. Callicles also undermines himself when he criticizes philosophy (485a–e). When we discuss whether we should philosophize, we are already philosophizing. The person who argues against reason is lost. Eventually Callicles gives up dialogue altogether (499b). Like Polus earlier (468c, 468d, 470a), Callicles slowly becomes silent (509e; 515c; 519d). He withdraws from the dialogue and relinquishes the search for truth. Callicles not only deceives Socrates, he deludes himself. He is not willing to be punished, which is for Plato the condition of moving toward truth, that is, allowing oneself to be refuted, to undergo the pain of relinquishing a cherished but false position. Callicles even shifts to the third person (489b), that is, he avoids addressing Socrates directly. Callicles appeals to the audience, for he cannot face Socrates' arguments. Then he appeals to shame, which he had earlier claimed to abandon (494e). Callicles is the truth of Gorgias, but Socrates, by way of his refutation, is the truth of Callicles.

Similarly, Brandon is the truth of Rupert. Rupert is at some level a good person who does not intend to realize the concept he articulates. He advances his views for shock and effect. He performs for his audience; he is not interested in truth. In short, he is a rhetorician. Others, however, are more consistent and follow his ideas — to his horror. Spoken evil, like subconscious evil, can lead to dreadful consequences. Rupert advocates for his ideas but does not mean to enact them. After uncovering the murder, he defends himself with a long address:

> But you've given my words a meaning that I never dreamed of! And you've tried to twist them into a cold, logical excuse for your ugly murder! Well, they never were that, Brandon, and you can't make them that. There must have been something deep inside you from the very start that let you do this thing, but there's always been something deep inside me that would never let me do it, and would never let me be a party to it … You've made me ashamed of every

concept I ever had of superior or inferior beings. But I thank you for that shame, because now I know that we are each of us a separate human being, Brandon, with the right to live and work and think as individuals, but with an obligation to the society we live in. By what right do you dare say that there's a superior few to which you belong? By what right did you dare decide that that boy in there was inferior and therefore could be killed? . . . You've strangled the life out of a fellow human being who could live and love as you never could.

Rupert is the better person, but Brandon is the better philosopher. Brandon draws the consequences of Rupert's position, which, once visible to Rupert, suddenly become shameful and abhorrent. Rupert, who joins Phillip in getting blood on his hands, is clearly criticized. His modest limp suggests associations with the devil, even if it is presented as the result of the war, and is as such ambiguous. The books, a symbol of learning, are tied together by the rope used to strangle David. The trunk in which David lies dead also housed the books, which are then placed on the top and lay scattered on the floor after the trunk is opened. An unleashed idea can be enacted by others. We are not far from *Strangers on a Train*, where a thought and a desire can lead to horrific, unintended consequences.

A third model we can bring into conversation with Gorgias-Callicles and Rupert-Brandon is Nietzsche-Hitler, to which *Rope* explicitly alludes. Unlike his sister, Elisabeth Förster-Nietzsche, who edited Nietzsche's manuscripts and advanced anti-Semitic and nationalist ideas, eventually supporting national socialism, Nietzsche himself would likely have found the Nazis abhorrent. But his personal views matter less than the logical consequences of his philosophical positions. Nietzsche has no argument against those, including the Nazis, who draw the consequences of his having abandoned any concept of objective reality or universalist ethics. One can be a Nietzschean and a good person, but the Nietzschean has no argument against the power positivist. One reason Hitchcock links truth and goodness is that he is aware that to relinquish the one is to endanger the other.

Nietzsche's ultimate view is that all positions are illusory, untenable, and ungrounded. The philosopher insists on the impossibility of first principles. All truth is perspectival, all knowledge hypothetical, and all categories historically conditioned. For Nietzsche there are no transcendent norms, "no eternal horizons and perspectives" (2.135). He writes: "there is no 'truth'" (3.497). The philosopher in fact recasts truth as a form of error that serves life (3.844). Values are measured by the strength and richness they give a particular valuing will (3.441). The falseness of a judgment is no argument against it; indeed, false judgments that promote a particular life or species are to be privileged (2.569). Contradictions are to be endured or embraced, not overcome (2.175).

Such perspectivism may at first glance appear liberating: because one's truth is not final, one is free to listen to other positions, to develop "antennae" for other perspectives (3.441). This is a possible consequence, and it is surely the position of the mild Nietzsche and that of many attracted to the Nietzschean worldview. One must ask, however, not what may be a contingent response to Nietzsche's worldview, but instead what is its logical consequence. A tolerance for other positions—without a first-world measure by which to judge them—means that one has no valid argument against the position that itself denies tolerance. If no perspective is grounded, then why should I take seriously any perspective other than my own? If there are no first-world norms, my own particular interests or those of another gain a stature they would not otherwise have. If all objective standards are abandoned and "nothing is true, everything is permitted" (2.889). If everything is permitted, then so, too, one individual's assertion of power over others. No compelling argument can be given against those who wish to decide what is valid and what is invalid life.

Drawing on Plato, I have argued elsewhere that both relativism and power positivism are self-canceling positions (*Benn* 58–9). Here I want to add a historical argument. The Nazis argued that if one accepts the position that there are no binding norms or values, then national socialism can be advanced without refutation. We see this connection in Alfred Rosenberg, a Nazi ideologue, who, following Nietzsche, advanced the claim that there are "no absolute values" (22). Moreover, if there were any such values or truths, it would be impossible for us to grasp them (681). Given the absence of any first-world values, the fourth world alone determines values: they are to be created, not discovered. The eventual war criminal Rosenberg elevated blood and race. He favors "an entirely different conception of 'truth'" and continues: "for us truth does not mean anything *logically* correct or false; instead an *organic* answer is demanded to the question: fruitful or unfruitful, autonomous or unfree" (690, emphasis in the original). Race usurps reason, history transcends philosophy; each culture, each race has its own "highest value" (116). But if the highest value of one race calls for the elimination of another race, any protest is conditioned by the inferiority of the race that is to be eradicated. The Germanic race has the right to assert its superior path over others. The highest values of other cultures restrict one's own and must, therefore, be eliminated (700). Rosenberg lays down the gauntlet against all who fail to recognize the supremacy of blood, specifically German blood: "the honor of the German name ... fights against all powers that do not want to accept it as the first and highest value" (701). Since reason is not supreme, no argument against the Germanic worldview is valid: "the new myth and the new creative power that today fight with us for expression simply cannot be 'refuted'" (700). *Rope* shows us, as do *Gorgias* and the Nietzsche-Hitler connection, that certain seemingly innocuous ideas when taken to their logical conclusion have horrific consequences. They are not, contra Nietzsche, liberating. In *Rope* liberation comes only at the end when Rupert casts open the window, fires three shots into the air, and implicitly invokes the mode of justice that Rupert, Brandon, and Phillip had previously scorned.

Resisting Evil

As with the power to enact evil, where Hitchcock reflects on both theory and practice, here, too, in the realm of resistance, the director engages ideas and strategies.

Defending Human Dignity

The first mode of resisting evil is the reverse of spoken evil: it involves a defense of human dignity, an appeal to the normative realm. More than once Hitchcock names evil as contrary to a higher concept of humanity. When in *Shadow of a Doubt* Uncle Charlie speaks of "horrible, faded, fat, greedy women," Charlie alludes to the dignity of human beings: "But they're alive! They're human beings." When Babs says in *Strangers on a Train* that the deceased Miriam was "a tramp," her father responds: "She was a human being." The spoken appeal to humanity can arise whenever a person is objectified or dehumanized. Alex says of the alleged murderer in *Spellbound*, "We are speaking of a schizophrenic," to which Constance responds, "We are speaking of a man." Because this appeal to the first world, to the idea of human dignity, tends to be more a matter of intuition than action, Hitchcock does not dwell on it. He does not want to portray people talking, but he does suggest that those who risk much to realize the good are driven by an intuitive vision of what is just.

In *Lifeboat* the Americans appeal to international law and to Christianity, even if they are unable to live up to those ideals. In fact, when it is time to avenge Willie for having betrayed them, the nurse, who could not understand "people hurting each other and killing each other," is the first to charge. It is telling that Joe, who is Black, is the only one who knows Christian prayers and the only one who does not attack the German. Someone who can identify with the victims of lynching will be less likely to join a mob. In *Rope* Mr. Kentley resists Nietzschean rhetoric concerning the superior and the inferior, stating that he cannot tell whether they are joking or whether they mean what they are saying. He recognizes that the difference is enormous. As the discussion takes place and he looks out the window, the camera dwells on him and his concern for his absent son. Here our identification shifts from Brandon to him. When the artist-murderers insist on their reckless views, Kentley objects to their "contempt for humanity and for the standards of a world I believe is civilized." He recognizes that such an abandonment of human dignity can have only horrendous consequences.

The embrace of human dignity arises most frequently in the films that are informed directly or indirectly by the threat of Nazism. In *Foreign Correspondent* Van Meer says to the Nazi spy Fischer that "beasts like you will devour each other," evoking an argument we see multiple times: evil destroys itself. In contrast, Van Meer elevates those who are the victims of the rush to war and who care about even more vulnerable creatures, "little people everywhere who give crumbs to birds." These little people, he argues, will not be conquered.

Understanding Evil

The next strategy involves not simply an abstract appeal to human dignity. It goes further, analyzing how evil functions. The desire to comprehend evil, to uncover the hidden logic of power, to name its various facets is a deeply philosophical task. Hitchcock's films carry within them the implicit idea that we must understand evil. How do we recognize it? What are the best strategies for gaining and holding power? What methods are necessary to overcome evil? Precisely his dispassionate desire to understand power, to integrate it into a broader concept of enacting goodness (for power is necessary to fight evil) allows the director to identify with murderers, to see the world through their eyes.

In Hitchcock's fallen world many persons are capable of evil. Recognizing who is and is not evil is a difficult task. Mistaken clues are often applied in both directions. Characters suspect that an innocent person is a criminal, and criminals hide in accepted circles. Both moments are visible in *Secret Agent*, where the spies kill the wrong man, and Marvin, who seems both charming and comical, turns out to be the real spy. In *The Lodger* we suspect, with the parents and even Joe, that the Lodger may be the murderer: Hitchcock's cinematic clues point us toward this false conclusion. In *The 39 Steps* Hannay is mistakenly thought to be a murderer, while the mastermind of the spies is a powerful societal figure. The double agent working for the British has a German accent, while the foreign spy is a British gentleman. A similar structure exists in *Saboteur*, where the pro-Nazis are prominent members of the Manhattan social class. Doubles are another way of expressing this combination of deception and vulnerability, as we see in *Strangers on a Train* and *Frenzy*. Criminals are difficult to recognize, and normal people are in principle capable of darkness. Both moments are prominent in *Shadow of a Doubt*.

Knowledge is related to evil partly by way of incongruities, most prominently appearance versus reality. Elster in *Vertigo* uses an elaborate ruse to enact his scheme of getting rid of his wife. As the bookshop owner Pop Leibl notes, in earlier eras men had the power simply to dispose of a wife or lover, to throw the woman away. With advances in our understanding of justice, power turns to more deceptive strategies. In playing with appearance and reality, Hitchcock identifies a theme that is both suspenseful and comic. The uncertainty of intersubjective relations, not knowing who is a killer or when a killer might act, can be deeply suspenseful, but the appearance-reality dichotomy is also a prominent dimension of comedy. Comic figures, especially evil figures who ultimately fail, deceive others in order to pursue illicit goals. Molière's Tartuffe comes to mind. The duped, such as Orgon, see only appearances. The appearance-reality chasm can also be tragic, as with *King Lear*, where both Lear and Gloucester are deceived by their children. In Hitchcock we see both comic and tragic dimensions. In *The Lady Vanishes* Iris scorns, then loves, the musicologist. The Lady seems innocuous but is an impressive British spy. The brain surgeon is in truth a murderer. The nun turns out to be his accomplice. Sifting appearance from reality, for example, batting away convention before arriving at a more rational definition of a concept, is also one of the first tasks of philosophy.

Hitchcock understands that knowledge is deeply related to the battle of good and evil and the enactment of power, one facet of which is the battle of information. Information itself becomes a weapon in *Foreign Correspondent* and *The Man Who Knew Too Much* (1956). Both films, along with several others, including *The 39 Steps, Notorious,* and *Topaz*, are driven by espionage. Disinformation becomes a strategy. In *Foreign Correspondent*, the Van Meer who appears on the steps of the government building in Amsterdam is an imposter. The real Van Meer has been taken prisoner by spies. International organizations and political conferences, with their open discussions, are not the locus of power, an insight that is extended to *North by Northwest*, where the real action is not in the United Nations General Assembly but behind the scenes. The uncertainty in intersubjective relations that animates some of Hitchcock's love stories has its parallel in the world of espionage, where one does not know whom one can trust. *Topaz* interlaces both motifs and shows, furthermore, as did *Sabotage*, how involvement in espionage can destroy a family.

To have knowledge and be forced into silence, as with Fr. Logan in *I Confess* or Barry in *Saboteur*, neither of whom for different reasons can open up to or go to the police, who are already on the wrong track and suspect the hero, is to draw a weaker hand. To withhold knowledge, as Willie does in *Lifeboat*, is to gain power. In *The Paradine Case*, Keane has enough knowledge that he could successfully defend a murderer, but not enough (not knowledge of Mrs. Paradine's love for André Latour) that he could avoid what he most feared: that she would confess her crime and express her hatred for the attorney. In short, Hitchcock interweaves knowledge and power. The more information we have—knowledge of motives, conditions, and strategies—the more refined our calculus will be for making moral decisions. To realize the good, we must understand evil in its details and not simply as an abstraction.

Part of Hitchcock's analysis is that evil persons can be ambiguous, evil but still holding on to a moment of dignity. Some turn away from evil. The woman in high heels dressed as a nun in *The Lady Vanishes* decides no longer to support the enemy. In *Jamaica Inn* Joss risks his life by saving Mary and thereby turning on his gang. In *Foreign Correspondent* Fisher, the spy who has not hesitated to torture and kill, sacrifices himself when the floating wing of the downed aircraft cannot support all persons clinging to it. The female kidnapper in the second *Man Who Knew Too Much* does not want to see the boy hurt and so defies her husband. Then we can consider evil persons who have a moment of goodness. In the first *Man Who Knew Too Much* Abbott suffers genuine grief at the death of Nurse Agnes, even holding her in a pieta pose. In *Notorious* Sebastian, who is charming, seems genuinely to love Alicia; it is difficult to hate him. The Nazi scientist Dr. Anderson is endearing and caring toward Alicia, and we cannot help but recognize his gentleness. Even Tony in *Dial M for Murder* is forced to realize at least momentarily the horror of what he is hearing on the phone. Hitchcock plays here with several different ideas: the evil person may appear appealing or charismatic, the evil person might be won over to the side of goodness, and the evil person is a human being with a moment of dignity. Recognizing humanity in even the worst criminals, Hitchcock attacks the vices, not the person. He achieves these ends partly by manipulating audiences to identify, at least for stretches, with criminals, even in brutal films such as *Rope*, where early on we are encouraged to laugh at the macabre jokes and worry that the chest will be prematurely opened.

In Hitchcock evil tends to destroy itself. This follows an ancient wisdom, evident already in *The Republic*, where Plato makes clear that one cannot argue for injustice without presupposing the just rules of dialogue; that even a robber band must work together within basic rules of justice if they do not want to destroy themselves from within; and that a person must have order in the soul even to achieve unjust ends. In short, justice is primary to injustice, and injustice, because it depends on justice, is self-cancelling. In *Spellbound* the doctor whom Constance uncovers as the murderer of Dr. Edwardes takes his own life. The killer cannot sustain his position. In *Notorious* the Nazis are as ruthless with each other as they are with their enemies. In *Family Plot* Shoebridge cannot avoid conflicts with his partners, Maloney and Fran. Moreover, his criminality ensures that he will not inherit what would otherwise have been his. Philip in *Rope* is fearful and upset, unlike Brandon, who is cavalier and exhilarated. When Philip resists, Brandon insists that "being weak is a mistake," to which Philip responds, "Because it's being human?" The two murderers are at each other's throats, out of fear of being caught and out of disrespect for one another. After his conscience unnerves him the entire evening, Phillip eventually regrets his actions, exhibiting thereby a glimmer of goodness. The seed of goodness that Alma displays in *I Confess* ensures that Logan's suffering will not endure. In response Keller kills Alma and thereby also his own soul. Thus, at the end, when Keller asks, "Where is my Alma?" Hitchcock reveals him to be saying, "Where is my soul?" (In Spanish "alma" means "soul.") Essentially: Have I killed it? Have I, in destroying love, destroyed myself?

Combating Evil

Beyond embracing goodness and understanding evil is a third mode of resisting evil, actively combating it. This can be done effectively or ineffectively. The latter is frequent in Hitchcock. Consider the invariably clueless police or the mobs that do not know the truth and are driven by simple answers. Force without knowledge is either useless or counterproductive. Effective models of combating evil combine a moral compass with theoretical or intuitive knowledge of evil and some combination of ingenuity, courage, and grace.

The motivation for combating evil often comes from an inspiring vision. Barry in *Saboteur* speaks of "people that are helpful and eager to do the right thing; people that get a kick out of helping each other fight the bad guys." In *Foreign Correspondent* Jones is driven by his profession, a calling to uncover a story and unveil the truth. Not surprisingly, the good heroes are willing to risk their lives to help not only good persons but even criminals. If internal combat and self-destruction are features of evil, goodness is characterized by consistency. In *Saboteur* Barry risk his life trying to save Fry as the criminal dangles from the Statue of Liberty.

In Hitchcock knowledge, as in the case of Young Charlie and Alma, wins out over physical power, even if it comes at a cost. Knowledge is a weapon in both directions. One way to combat evil is to adopt its deceptive techniques without, however, causing harm, so, for example, Hannay in *The 39 Steps* must lie in order to get people to believe him. In *Lifeboat*, Connie is quick enough to yell out, "Herr Kapitän," and so to catch from Willie's response that he was in fact the captain of his submarine. In *Stage Fright* Eve, who had gotten in trouble by playing so many roles, potentially destroying a developing love relationship with Ordinary Smith, must return to play acting in order to deceive Jonathan and save her life. At times to capture a criminal, one must adopt the criminal's methods. Deception is a power strategy by those enacting evil as well as by good persons seeking to expose them. Hitchcock suggests that we can discover evil only by thinking our way into the mind of the deceiver and ourselves becoming deceivers. In *Dial M for Murder* Chief Inspector Hubbard develops an elaborate double ruse to confirm Margot's innocence and uncover enough details to ensure that he can prove Tony's guilt.

The situation, however, can easily exceed bounds. Just as evil can reveal its hidden dignity, so can goodness comprise itself. Not only must Michael Armstrong, a double agent in *Torn Curtain*, lie to authorities, he must deceive his fiancé, and when he is uncovered, he must kill a man in order to preserve his clandestine identity. Combating evil is not a pure activity; here we see one of Hitchcock's many forays into ambiguity. The good hero, the American, ends up acting very much like the communists he seeks to infiltrate.

Power is not only physical; power can derive from the perception of power. If someone seems to have power (but does not), that is itself a form of power (Hösle, *Morals and Politics* 312–13). The ruse of the non-existent spy George Kaplan in *North by Northwest* is a good example. Roger Thornhill, a perfectly innocent person who cannot fathom what is at play, is seen by enemy spies as a great threat. That gives him inordinate power, and in the end he becomes a genuine threat. The symbolic idea behind this misunderstanding is that an individual has more capacities than he thinks he does—if he can rise to the occasion.

Another strategy is use of a third entity, which renders dual relations more complex (Hösle, *Morals and Politics* 337). In *Notorious*, Devlin is able to escape with Alicia only because he knows that Sebastian and his mother do not want him to reveal to a third party, the other spies, the truth about Sebastian having been betrayed. In *North by Northwest* Roger attracts attention at the auction. Why? Because he can evade his kidnappers and would-be assassins by causing such a ruckus that he is "rescued" by the police. In a dual struggle Roger would have lost. By attracting the attention of a third party, he limits his opponent's power. The third party becomes an unwitting weapon in pursuit of his goals. Those Hitchcock characters who turn to the good, such as the female kidnapper in the second *Man Who Knew Too Much,* also function as third parties who aid the hero. An appeal to common values can be a source of power, but the strategy does not always work: Barry's attire in *Saboteur* and the standing of the hostess make it impossible for him to win over the guests.

In public settings, such as the party in *Saboteur*, Hitchcock reveals the diverse ways in which evil is realized or thwarted (Smith 76–8). By rendering the consequences communal, he increases the drama. Hitchcock shows how individuals seek power by manipulating others. Think of Mrs. Danvers, who in *Rebecca* encourages the second Mrs. DeWinter to wear the first wife's dress for the costume party, which leads to an explosion from the husband, which the wife does not at first comprehend, or of Lil in *Marnie*, who invites Strutt to the party. His presence and recognition of the heroine adds another layer to the power dynamic. In *Notorious* multiple gatherings reveal the ways in which persons create diversions, act out betrayals, or survey the field. Evil plays out in public settings, but not all can recognize what is at play. The same is true with counter-actions.

The ways in which evil is fought can only be fully addressed in our next section, which explores evil's two strongest counter-forces, courage and love. The courageous hero gains inspiration from the first world but risks much in the three other worlds, including life, to realize goodness. Love is the opposite of employing power to enact evil. It reaches its pinnacle in symmetry, whereas power presupposes asymmetry, such that the will to power and love are mutually exclusive (Hösle, *Morals and Politics* 367). In love we see a different intersubjective relationship, not organized around conflict, not driven by means-end thinking, and not essentially a contract. Love is not simply a means to an end, for example, generating sexual pleasure or producing a child, but also an end in itself, which lifts the values of both partners and gives them dignity (Scheler 118–23).

Embodied Virtue

Hitchcock emphasizes, along with the temptation of evil, the human capacity to meet an extraordinary challenge. The typical Hitchcock hero is an ordinary person who is placed in extraordinary circumstances, confronting events that are beyond their control. They are thrown into their situations not unlike our being thrown into life, an idea Martin Heidegger analyzed in §38 of *Being and Time*. Hitchcock heroes fall into existential predicaments. The question is not, how did they get there, but how will they respond? Who will they become in these unexpected circumstances? Their first reaction may be frustration or alienation, but the deeper question becomes, what do they make of their thrownness. In Hitchcock's universe it is important to find the capacities to survive and succeed. Not only to recognize what should be done, but to realize the good in the face of despair and threats requires courage. Whereas courage is often an individual act, a second answer to evil is love. Both are more than ideas: they are embodied, and so these philosophical virtues lend themselves to artistic exploration. Courage is a vital virtue, a virtue of action, and thus of all the cardinal virtues the easiest to elevate on the screen. Just as suspense operates at the dialectic of fear and hope, so, too, does courage. Hitchcock brilliantly interweaves stories of developing courage and embodied love.

Courage

Plato's early dialogue *Laches* is the greatest and most nuanced work ever written on courage. One must struggle to decipher Plato's argument, but one can do so with courage. The comment is counter-intuitive, but Plato associates courage not only with military action on the battlefield but also with knowledgeable perseverance in seeking the truth. Hitchcock's heroes often engage in physical courage, but at the core they seek knowledge.

Plato explores also the emotional dimensions of courage, including how we cope with challenges such as poverty, illness, or despair. Courage on the battlefield means clashing with enemies, but there exists also an inner courage: combating base instincts and resisting momentary temptations in order to achieve what is worthier and more enduring. Holding oneself together in the face of an entirely arbitrary and inexplicable attack, as we see in several Hitchcock films, is a form of courage. There is no reason for the heroes of works as diverse as *The Wrong Man*, *North by Northwest*, or *The Birds* to land in their predicaments. The heroes' lives turn out to be unpredictable, precarious, and at some level absurd. They must respond to this adversity not with despair but with courage.

For Plato ideas relate to what we value and how we live, which helps explain the philosophical fascination of art. Plato does not simply evaluate propositions. For Socrates philosophy is about how we relate our lives to those ideas. This is clear from his pre-trial discussions of piety and justice. Plato interweaves the criticism of ideas with the evaluation of persons. Individuals who are full of themselves, dogmatic and self-assured, will not uncover truth, nor will those insufficiently self-confident to encounter the views of the opposition. Someone who is willing to weigh new options is on the right path, and a person who is prepared to risk their identity, reputation, and life in the search for, or defense of, truth is likely to be on a meaningful, if potentially tragic, journey. Are we up to the challenge? Does the challenge form us? We see that philosophy is not unrelated to drama.

Plato elevates speaking one's mind even if one's views are unconventional and unpopular. Socrates asks, what do you yourself think, and can you defend your views? For Plato discovering truth requires opening up to the world of ideas, the first world, even if this means a radical departure from all social norms, that is, a break with the fourth world. To hold on to a view even against consensus when you are convinced of its validity is to experience social isolation for your allegiance to truth and is thus an act of courage. Often the Hitchcock hero knows the truth or gradually uncovers the truth but is unable to reveal it or to win over the views of others. The existential significance of combating a consensus theory of truth is prominent in Hitchcock's works from *The Lodger*, with its mob scenes and crucifixion imagery, to *Frenzy*. The untenability of a consensus theory of truth is prominent in at least another dozen films, among them *Murder!*, *Young and Innocent*, *The Lady Vanishes*, *Foreign Correspondent*, *Saboteur*, *Spellbound*, *I Confess*, *To Catch a Thief*, and *The Wrong Man*. In each of these, the majority is wrong.

Moreover, in each film either the wronged man or someone who believes in him must rise to ensure the *realization* of truth, in both senses of the word: others need to acknowledge it, and the hero needs to make it a reality. In *Saboteur* Barry is suspected of a crime he did not commit. He quickly learns that he will not be believed, such that he must ferret out the spies himself. He is willing to take great risks, including jumping off a bridge; winding his way into the inner circle of spies; and cleverly enacting a bold escape, after which he risks his life trying to stop the sabotage. Hitchcock infuses the American tradition that elevates the individual hero with a veneration of esoteric knowledge. And yet, among those who are in the know, who believe the good hero, are outcasts, such as the circus performers in *Saboteur*, so Hitchcock paradoxically democratizes the concept or, one could say, offers a counter-intuitive aristocracy of knowledge and goodness. Those who are not part of the power structure may see and recognize more. In contrast, the established figures tend to fail: the police are inept, and the wealthy often corrupt. Evil cloaks itself in goodness. In *I Confess* the murderer, Keller, dons the robe of a priest to escape detection.

Hitchcock is aware that democracy is complex. By strict definition democracy means majority rule, as in the vote-taking scene in *Saboteur*. But the limits of democracy are evident insofar as Hitchcock challenges the consensus. Consider the many cases of authorities and citizens accusing and chasing the wrong man. The mob scene in *Lifeboat*, another wartime film that thematizes democratic vote taking, shows that majority rule can lead to the erasure of minority rights and with that human dignity. Democracy has implicitly a second element, a meta-level dimension, the idea that everyone's vote counts because each person has dignity, but this involves more than what we understand by democracy as process. Today political philosophers would call the recognition of human rights liberalism and the process by which the majority rules democracy, such that one can speak of a liberal democracy and an illiberal democracy, but when Hitchcock was active, democracy was a richer term. In *The Coming Victory of Democracy*, a widely read book that was partially excerpted in *Reader's Digest* and which was based on lectures given across America during 1938, Hitchcock's contemporary Thomas Mann defines democracy in this more expansive way, suggesting that democracy presupposes "the inalienable dignity of mankind, which no force, however humiliating, can destroy" (20). In contrast, Mann equates "mob rule" with "fascism" (21). In other words, democracy refers, on the one hand, to the concept of human dignity that is anchored in the first world, and, on the other hand, to majority rule, whereby a process in the fourth world can obliterate first-world norms. Like Hitchcock, Mann recognizes the "depravity" of humankind but cautions that we cannot "despise humanity" (24). Both figures endorse tempering human wickedness with education, faith, optimism, and respect for human dignity. The ideas sound modestly foreign today, where widespread distrust feeds cynicism, but they were central to the anti-fascist mentality of America's European immigrants. These thinkers, Hitchcock among them, answer human depravity with an appeal to the first world, with its concepts of dignity and justice. Hitchcock does not give us easy answers, but he does present *ex negativo* two illicit positions, mob rule and appeasement or pacifism. In *Lifeboat* Joe's attitude, while noble, could not be universalized against a threat like Nazi Germany.

A challenge for many Hitchcock heroes is to retain identity and values even when isolated or under attack. Despite the world's resistance the hero forges ahead out of allegiance to a higher ideal. To pursue the ideal with self-discipline and a willingness to risk one's life is to exhibit courage. It is not surprising that Hitchcock would elevate courage, for fear is his dominant cinematic emotion, and the virtue that surmounts fear is courage. Courage involves overcoming fear by a vision of (or hope for) a better future and by knowledgeable endurance in battling challenges. This is essentially the definition to which Plato's *Laches* indirectly alludes, though Hitchcock would implicitly add the Christian element of trusting in ultimate goodness.

The Hitchcock hero tends to be unfazed by public opinion. An ordinary person, an otherwise normal character, is thrust into a difficult predicament and rises to the challenge, embracing a new role and becoming extraordinary. Hitchcock's heroes assume a sovereign attitude and adjust to unforeseen circumstances. In *Young and Innocent* a simple screenwriter, after being accused of murder, resolves to solve the puzzle himself, acting as a sleuth while he evades the police. In *The Man Who Knew Too Much* (1956) the hero is a surgeon from Indianapolis who appears to have no strong political views and looks to be everything but a hero. His lack of heroism is ironically underscored when his son overinflates his role during the Second World War: "Daddy liberated Africa." That McKenna is not exactly fit for the spy role is further evident when he has trouble managing the odd cushions at a

Moroccan restaurant and eating his food according to local custom. When McKenna is indeed challenged by adversity and rises to the occasion, the minister, who is a criminal, preaches that adversity makes us better persons. The line is both true and funny, such that Hitchcock plays even when he is serious.

It is typical Hitchcock that the individual must rise to the occasion and solve things themselves. In *The 39 Steps* Hannay is thrust into a comic predicament where he must give a speech to an assembly without having any knowledge of the context—and he succeeds wildly. The hero adapts to new roles and navigates obstacles in his path. There seems to be a sovereign and continuous joy in playing the various roles. In *Foreign Correspondent* John Jones, whose name is adjusted to the pen name Huntley Haverstock, is a crime reporter who is pulled aside from his ordinary beat to become a foreign correspondent: the newspaper's editor wants a real reporter. Symbolically significant, the ordinary American at first knows nothing of Europe or the impending war, yet Jones ends up unearthing a major spy plot: he chases an assassin, diagnoses a secret code (based on the movement of a windmill) that escapes all others, is not afraid to pursue the matter alone (after the police have departed the scene), escapes the assassins who uncover him, evades another assassin, eventually uncovering the plot with the help of another reporter. For comic relief a third reporter is oblivious and spends his time drinking, carousing with women, and gambling, even if he, too, provides some help. *North by Northwest* may be the most vivid illustration of the ordinary person rising to the occasion. Roger Thornhill is the target of multiple assassination attempts, but he survives and willingly risks his life further. He is both a modern everyman and a Christ figure who gains his identity by risking his life to save another; the connection is evident in his name, Thornhill, an allusion to Golgotha; in the multiple crosses at the Prairie Stop, the cross road visible from the aerial shot and two sign posts; and in the blood on his injured hand.

Courage is not only a virtue, it is strategically advantageous. In terms of power dynamics, revealing one's fear is counter-productive. Hitchcock tends to admire, and exhibit on behalf of his characters, a kind of fearlessness. Hitchcock loved Cary Grant's seemingly effortless confidence. Fr. Logan expresses fear only when he walks the streets alone. When he turns himself in to the police, he is again sovereign. Keller says that he and Logan are alike, both isolated and alone. Keller has lost his wife and turned away from God. It is true that Logan is alone in an earthly sense, having become marked as a likely murderer, but he has not abandoned God. His strength comes from his religious vows. They give him the courage to adhere to his ideal and endure earthly isolation. Logan's lack of power in this world is compensated for by his allegiance to the first world: his moral vision gives him courage. In his portraits of courage, Hitchcock interweaves two elements: the sovereign individual and identification with a higher purpose or goal. While *I Confess* portrays at its two poles Logan and Keller, the middle is occupied by the mediocrity of the crowd. Its combination of obliviousness and callousness is evident in the shot of the woman onlooker who eats an apple as she watches Logan being abused (Figure 3).

Not only the police but the larger governmental institutions are incapable. During the trial, the Crown Prosecutor accuses Logan of being unable to control his passions (and thus capable of murder), but

Figure 3 The mediocrity of the crowd, both oblivious and callous, is evident in the shot of the (uncredited) woman onlooker in *I Confess,* who eats an apple as she watches Fr. Logan being abused. Alma, played by Dolly Haas, recognizes the injustice. *I Confess* directed by Alfred Hitchcock. © Warner Bros. 1953. All rights reserved.

the film audience, unlike the courtroom audience, knows that Logan's reticence derives precisely from his controlled passions and thus his ability to preserve the sanctity of confession.

The police incompetence rampant in Hitchcock triggers a need for individuals to fill the vacuum—and that demands courage. Philosophers of history recognize that as principles of justice become institutionalized, law is no longer embedded in the strong individual. Instead, institutions guarantee justice. With Vittorio Hösle I have analyzed this transition in John Ford's *The Man Who Shot Liberty Valance*. Vico is the great theoretician of this development. In his account of the evolution of culture, Vico distinguishes three phases: the age of gods, the age of heroes, and the age of men. The age of gods is characterized by a theocratic government: it is anterior to any differentiation of the various aspects of culture, such as religion, politics, or art. The age of heroes is dominated by the conflict between classes, the heroes and the plebeians. This age does not yet have a state; therefore, force and violence reign. The right of the stronger is the main ground of legitimacy. The central characteristic of the third stage, the age of men, is the rule of law based no longer on force but on reason. A monarchical or democratic state replaces the aristocracy of the heroes, whose distinguishing event was the duel, one-on-one with both lives at stake. In the age of men the principal equality of all human beings is recognized. Not only within the state, but also within the family, relations tend to become more symmetric. With the process of rationalization also a de-personalization takes place: the great individual is no longer necessary; the due procedure of the institutions characteristic of the age of men now guarantees the order without which societies cannot survive. Vico recognizes progress in this development, but he also acknowledges loss. The necessity to risk and to sacrifice one's life, which was so characteristic of the age of heroes, disappears, and with it a great source of morality vanishes. By fighting for his life, the hero acquired a depth that is missed in representatives of the age of men. A century later Hegel argued that tragedy is much more difficult in an era where the strength of any one individual is limited by ties to the existing order. After discussing justice and law, Hegel comments: "The individual is now no longer the vehicle and exclusive actualization of these powers as in the heroic age" (13:255). Universal ends, he argues, are not accomplished by singular individuals: "on the contrary, such ends prevail by their own force, partially with the will of the many, partially against it and without their knowledge" (15:558). In *Problems of the Theatre*, the Swiss dramatist Friedrich Dürrenmatt extends this tradition of thought into the present, arguing that the individual in today's complex, bureaucratic, and decentralized society has even less chance to assert power and assume responsibility. As a result, tragedy, with a singular hero changing the course of events, must give way to comedy.

The development that Vico, Hegel, and Dürrenmatt analyze makes responsibility more complex, power more difficult to wield; it does not, however, eliminate them. In our analysis of Clint Eastwood's *Gran Torino*, Hösle and I argued that situations arise when the institutions of justice do not suffice. Modernity sees increasing moments of isolated violence, which the police cannot always address. Moreover, modernity develops a lethargy or complacency that lacks a moral vision. The resurgence of violence and a contemporary emptiness of higher meaning result in a renewed need for heroes. As Dürrenmatt expressed his resigned insights in a Europe turned inward toward self-reflection, America rejoiced in Westerns, where power is in the hands of individual villains and heroes, and in the works of Frank Capra, the focus of which is the power of the individual to shape history. Although Hitchcock never directed a Western, he comes close to two of its conceptual elements. First, he celebrates the singular individual. His interest was not for the most part in organizational systems, but in the responsibility of the individual and the individual's relation to others. Second, he elevated the individual in a world in which the police and other authority figures are inconsequential, not because they do not yet exist, as in the Western, but because they are characterized by incompetence, inertia, and even corruption. Threats continue to exist—and indeed surface almost everywhere and must be countered. Hitchcock responded to this world of depersonalization by elevating the ordinary person turned hero. When the police, the guardians of security, cannot respond or react wrongly, then the world suddenly becomes even more precarious and fragile than in an earlier age. The Hitchcock hero is thrust out of an ordinary existence, at times filled with lethargy, complacency, or boredom, and must respond. We are as inspired by the ordinary person's potential for courage as we are horrified whenever those whom we trust or invest with authority are not as they should be.

The motif of incompetent police, and with it the need for a hero to step in to replace the floundering institutions of justice, arises already in the British films. In *Blackmail* the police as a whole are oblivious, and Frank is corrupt. In the first *The Man Who Knew Too Much* the police are counter-productive, as they take away the very person who could lead them to the kidnappers. At the end Betty's mother, a sharpshooter, not the police, shoots the criminal on the roof as he approaches Betty. When in *The 39 Steps* the hero turns to the police, the authorities believe the enemy spy, not the hero. In *Young and Innocent* Tisdall must find the criminal because the police and the lawyer have settled on the most obvious but wrong subject. In *Saboteur* the police move too slowly. When Uncle Charlie escapes the police at the beginning of *Shadow of a Doubt*, we rejoice with him, as we hear the joyful clarinet. In *Strangers on a Train* the police cannot uncover Bruno. They even shoot an innocent person. They are not only unable to uncover evil, they wield their power indiscriminately. Similarly, the police shoot recklessly at the end of *To Catch a Thief,* though here the comic tone, reinforced by the incongruity of the policemen wearing period costumes, signals ridiculous incompetence, not danger. In *The Birds* the sheriff is comically oblivious to the real horror. In some cases the police must be sidelined, as in *The Man Who Knew Too Much* (1956), and when they are eventually called, they are either unable to help or an active hindrance. In *North by Northwest* the police fail to uncover that spies have overtaken the home of an important UN figure. The detectives are unable to capture Thornhill on the train or at the station, and the Chicago police are used as a means of escape, unwittingly playing taxi service. The state has more power in modernity, but in Hitchcock's universe it is incompetent, lacking flexibility, instincts, and initiative, at times even morality, all of which are more visible in the isolated hero.

Problems arise not only with the police. In *Secret Agent* government spies take out an innocent man, whose dog howls movingly at his death. In *Notorious* the U.S. exploits Alicia. She is vulnerable, and the government, whose mission leader, Prescott, is egotistical, cynical, and complacent, does not hesitate to instrumentalize her. He rents her, much as he does the necklace he places on her neck. He endorses her marriage to a spy and elevates the mission over her safety, as he munches crackers from his bed. When a government agency acts in violation of moral norms, it loses its dignity and legitimacy—and

Hitchcock shows this, thus revealing both the power that evil wields and the compromises governments undertake to combat it. At times tragic choices arise, the conflict of one value versus another, such that even in choosing a higher value, we violate a lesser good, which is unavoidable but regrettable. However, in *Notorious*, the government officials do not express regret. Only Devlin is uneasy, but he does not convey his sentiments to Alicia, and he acts very late. In *North by Northwest* the CIA is implicated: the organization gathers knowledge and ignores negative externalities.[8] When the professor is confronted by the horrendous situation of Thornhill, who is mistaken for the CIA's non-existent spy and is charged with multiple crimes, the professor's initial response is: "We do nothing." The officials relinquish the very ends, the higher values, for which the country claims to be fighting. Here Hitchcock rebukes the American government, just as in *Shadow of a Doubt* he mocks oblivious Americans. Hitchcock is no less critical of the British. In *The Lady Vanishes*, which was released in 1938, he criticized the British who reacted to German ascendance by acquiescing and negotiating, as with the barrister. Hitchcock responds with a gracious smile toward the originally indifferent cricket players who join the fight before it is too late. In *Notorious* Devlin risks the mission to save Alicia, and in *North by Northwest* the rescue of the undercover agent comes mainly from Thornhill, who finds his identity in resisting the government and risking his life for someone he loves.[9] The only legitimate responses to such endangerment and callousness are courage and love (Figure 4).

Love

Enacting evil is the opposite of falling in love. An evil person imposes power on others for their own gain, whereas love involves selflessly sacrificing oneself for a higher value, a higher good, or another person. Courageous self-sacrifice, which is a privileged form of love, can result in tragedy. In *The Birds* Annie gives her life in order to protect young Cathy, an act of self-sacrifice prefigured by the red of her mailbox and her sweater. Self-sacrifice is a complex philosophical concept insofar as it involves a dialectic of individualism and collectivism. Self-sacrifice presupposes courage and so individual strength. But the act of self-sacrifice consists in obliterating the individual. The meaning or truth

Figure 4 After Thornhill, played by Cary Grant, learns that Eve is an endangered double agent, he resolves to become steadfast and a hero, overcoming his earlier inconsistency and self-obsession. The dissolve, which is both comic and serious, symbolically captures the next chapter in his journey. *North by Northwest* directed by Alfred Hitchcock. © Turner Entertainment Co. and Warner Bros. 1959. All rights reserved.

of the individual, however, finds its fulfillment in the other, for whom the sacrifice was enacted. Self-sacrifice recognizes that a deeper fulfillment lies in recognizing the value of what transcends the self, not simply another individual, but what that individual represents—a family, a nation, an idea, humanity as a whole. The dialectic is complex, for, as Hösle has argued, self-sacrifice for another person who embodies higher values is at a paradoxical level and on a meta-scale also a form of selfishness (*Morals and Politics* 197–210). To sacrifice oneself for values that transcend oneself is to merge one's own self with those higher values and so embodies (an admirable) self-interestedness, which contributes to the evolutionary stability of one's own position. But it is more than that: self-sacrifice is also an act of love.

In *Spellbound* Constance risks her life to help a seemingly dangerous murder suspect who suffers from amnesia. She, who is otherwise always focused on reason, in particular the rational analysis of emotions, gives way to her intuition, to her trust in the other person. She, who had mocked the poets' "delusions about love," herself falls in love. The stress on intuition is modestly analogous to Rupert's argument in *Rope* that a healthy instinct prevents some persons from harming others. Hitchcock has a layered sense of emotions and recognizes their value as a catalyst for insight, empathy, and love. This is appropriate for a filmmaker, for the sensuous dimension is one way in which art distinguishes itself from philosophy. Thomas Hyde's comments on *Spellbound* could be said to apply to *Rope* as well: In *Spellbound* Hitchcock portrays "the inadequacy of intellectual analysis when it is divorced from compassionate, understanding involvement" (157).

The 39 Steps brings forward a combination of courage and love. Four different motivations exist in the film for spying: the leaders of the 39 Steps want to exert their power; the apolitical Mr. Memory is unwittingly used by these spies; Annabella Smith, who is shot early in the film and had sought to stop such persons, works not for love of country (she has no country) but "for money"; and Hannay willingly risks his life for a good cause but is quickly forced into a second rationale: to escape the police and save his good name. The hidden logic of this structure is that Hannay can reach his own goal only by sacrificing himself for a higher good. Autonomy is gained through action for others. The broader structure of the spy and wrong man narrative is interwoven with the love story. That Hannay wins his freedom only after being handcuffed to Pamela is comic for the audience but horrific for her. She fully embraces him only after she is free. Their love is a synthesis of union and autonomy.

Hitchcock plays at times with religious motifs, partly seriously, partly tongue-in-cheek. We see a resurrection—and so an avoidance of tragedy—when Hannay, who is shot in the chest, is saved because a generous, self-sacrificing woman had given him her husband's coat, and the bullet stops not in his chest but outside, in the hymnal, which is in the breast pocket. Hitchcock intertwines love with what transcends human willing, for love, like grace, is not something we simply will. Mark says to Marnie, "It seems to be my misfortune to have fallen in love with a thief and a liar." We do not fully control love. Instead, love involves the manifestation of something higher than the self and so represents the opposite of imposing one's will on others. In *Vertigo* Judy relates a similar concept: "I fell in love. That wasn't part of the plan." In acrophobia we simultaneously desire and fear falling; the condition is in this way an apt, if unorthodox, metaphor for love, which involves submerging oneself in another at the risk of losing one's previous self. This transcendence of the third world entails a relation to the three other worlds: an ideal of selflessness, physical attraction, and a deep connection to another person.

Love is related not only to courage and the confrontation with evil. It is central to the puzzle of uncertainty in intersubjective relations. We love what transcends us, but to which we are drawn, and that often involves a moment of mystery. Almost all Hitchcock love relationships involve seeking to understand the hidden depths of the other, what has not yet been revealed. The desire to know is very close to the desire to love, a connection that reaches back to Plato. Consider Scottie's fascination with Madeline in *Vertigo*. Scottie senses that there is depth to who she is, something enchanting. This mystery can of course be a ruse or in the end revelatory of something unappealing, but the idea of hidden depth seems universal in Hitchcock's concept of love. That is one reason why Midge cannot attract him. The irony of Judy's situation is that she plays the role of Scottie's lover only to fall in love with him, but Scottie's love is not to Judy but to the mysterious role she was playing. The dialectic of appearance and reality in this case makes love impossible. Love cannot be based on the love of someone else. Cloning, be it metaphorical or literal, is at odds with the distinctive identity of a human being.

The narrative of human relationships in *The Birds* is driven by a dialectic of independence and dependence. Melanie Daniels and Mitch Brenner are strong, independent spirits, yet both experience a longing. Still, they express their love, especially early on, in ways that can be said to alienate the other. In any love relationship one wants to hold something back and be seen as not fully dependent on the other. This can lead to a game of one-upping the other. When Mitch enters the bird shop and sees Melanie, whom he recognizes from an earlier court case, he decides to play a prank: he pretends that he has mistaken Melanie for an employee and asks her to help him. Melanie, unaware of the charade, in turn plays with Mitch, posing as the salesperson for whom he seemingly mistakes her. When Melanie finds herself attracted to Mitch, she continues playing games, secretly leaving the sought-after love birds in Mitch's home while trying, only half-heartedly, to escape unnoticed. Further, she lies to Mitch about why she visited. And when after dinner Melanie is ready to leave, Mitch mocks her for her shallowness, as he did in the pet store. To his "You really like me, huh?" she responds, "I loathe you." Both characters hover between wanting to express their love, which is implicitly evident, and wanting to remain independent and keep their distance. Only when they face a collective challenge from outside do they truly come together. Also Mitch and his mother, Lydia, tussle with one another, as Mitch seeks independence from her, and Lydia fears being abandoned. Lydia thus keeps her distance from Melanie. The encounters between Melanie and Lydia oscillate between generous hospitality and subtle sparring. Melanie and Lydia, too, come together only in the wake of an external attack. In contrast, the young, less complicated, less self-conscious Cathy loves without inhibitions. An outside challenge can strengthen bonds and solidify community, but this common bond can also be driven by a scapegoat mentality, as when the mother at the diner falsely blames Melanie for the birds attacking everyone. Even one of the most effective solutions to cultivating positive human relations can be fraught with error and horror.

Although Hitchcock makes a great deal of the hero's capacity to rise to the occasion and battle evil, he also recognizes that the hero needs help along the way and has a telos that is more than simply individualistic. Hitchcock parades before us a series of characters who generously help the hero. That they are often not of the upper echelon of society is one way in which the director embraces a democratic impulse. Consider two helpful figures, the wife of the suspicious and abusive crofter in *The 39 Steps* and the destitute china-mender Will in *Young and Innocent*. In *Saboteur* Barry receives assistance from a truck driver, a blind man at a cottage, and the circus performers, who endorse central tenets of American patriotism—that they should make a complex decision democratically, that a person is innocent until proven guilty, and that it is right to help another human being ("The normal are normally cold-hearted," we hear from one of the seemingly abnormal performers). Eventually Barry wins over the woman, Pat, who at first scorns him. We see in Barry's fate a combination of autonomy and providence. Independence and action are wedded with the values of being helped by, and embedded within, a larger community. In order to clear his name, John Robbie in *To Catch a Thief* finds that he must first work with an insurance agent who wants to recover lost jewels and then with Jessie and Francie Stevens, who take part in a charade that deceives the police into thinking that John is with them and not on the roof trying to catch the real cat burglar. Even the hero cannot succeed alone.

Figure 5 Fr. Logan, played by Montgomery Clift, is portrayed multiple times as a Christ figure. Here the shadow of a cross adorns his forehead, as he hears the confession of Keller, played by O. E. Hasse. Keller, who is not truly repentant, is not consoled but spiritually imprisoned. *I Confess* directed by Alfred Hitchcock. © Warner Bros. 1953. All rights reserved.

Love is interwoven with knowledge. As characters slowly unveil themselves, an often initial coldness melts away. Moreover, one can love not simply another person but an idea. In *I Confess* Logan willingly agrees to suffer in order to pay for the sins of another, and he is taunted by a crowd unaware of his holiness. The mocking line, "Preach us a sermon, Logan!" echoes the heckling of Christ: "Prophesy to us, you Messiah!" (Mt. 26:68).

A series of shots present Logan as Christ's deputy: the early portrait of Logan in the Church looking for Keller, in which Logan emerges from an image of the crucified Christ; the light from the candle, which Logan carries with him as he approaches Keller; the shadow on Logan's forehead, which during Keller's confession takes the shape of a cross (Figure 5); the powerful shot of Logan down below on the street and behind a silhouette of Christ carrying the cross; and finally, the close-up of Logan as he is testifying, which includes a symbolic icon of Christ.

As much as Hitchcock associates Logan with Christ, the film also shows Logan's deficiencies. Logan is so one-sidedly oriented toward the first-world ideal that he neglects the fourth world: he exhibits no empathy for Keller. Logan's coldness is a weakness, yet it can be further understood, and rendered complex, as God's withdrawal from Keller, insofar as Keller is not truly remorseful.

Together knowledge and love help to form a stable identity. Eros drives both knowledge and love, and in eros one finds one's higher purpose. Precisely its trans-rational dimensions make love an effective subject for emotion-laden cinema, for love is the emotional experience of a value (Hösle, *Morals and Politics* 240). A person truly in love thinks not about one's own being in love but about the beloved. This is certainly the case with Hitchcock's irreflexive characters who are oriented toward higher values and other persons. As a result, their identity is formed through their action on behalf of and with others.

An emotion, an action, an institution is moral when it is as it should be (Hösle, *Morals and Politics* 70). That correspondence motivates love. In contrast, we hate something and recognize it as evil or ugly when it is not as it should be. Hitchcock recognizes that we may hate those who know of our faults because they remind us of our not being who we should be. We hate the pain that comes with coming closer to a truth that is difficult to endure. In *Spellbound* Constance says, "That's what happens in analysis. As the doctor begins to uncover the truth for the patient, said patient develops a fine, hearty hatred of said doctor. You're going to hate me a great deal before we're through." Yet that hate is a kind of suffering that leads to healing.

Hitchcock is a fascinating analyst of contemporary culture because he offers in a sense a dialectical analysis of what fails us. On the one hand, he is critical of certain aspects of modern existence, including the complacent, indistinguishable, humdrum existence many of his characters experience before some great event pushes them beyond their "complacency" (*Alfred* 44). Consider Roger Thornhill in *North by Northwest* and Melanie Daniels in *The Birds*. In response to this superficial immersion in non-identity, Hitchcock elevates the individual who steps into the void, addressing challenges to self and others. Hitchcock affirms individualism, but his embrace of ordinary individuals who find themselves in unexpected and dangerous situations plays out before a cinematic audience. When Hitchcock speaks of his work as a director, four concepts surface again and again. Three are related to style. The first two are universal elements of film, the visual image and montage. The third is his signature capacity to awaken suspense and to modify it with comic relief. The final element involves his eliciting emotions, above all fear—and with that our vicarious caring about the fate of the characters. We identify with figures who have otherwise no connection to us, we develop a sensibility for, and sympathetic understanding of, the challenges of others, which is essential for any relationship that is more than transactional and any society that is not reducible to a social contract. Cinematic empathy awakens in us a sense of human dignity. We identify emotionally with the values the person embodies and feel the threats they encounter. That is, Hitchcock cultivates in viewers an attitude that recognizes the value of the individual and the indistinguishable worth of empathy. We share in the characters' suffering and joy, which has, on a formal level, something loosely analogous to, and preparatory for, the highest value Hitchcock recognizes, love. Indeed, many of Hitchcock's lovers, such as Erica in *Young and Innocent*, begin by experiencing empathy toward the hero, and the audience is encouraged to share in that experience.

Moreover, when Hitchcock manipulates us into identifying with an evil act, he sobers us up to our weaknesses and vulnerability, our sense of how evil we ourselves could become. Hitchcock's villains are more like us than we might otherwise be tempted to think. The director thereby humbles his audience. In any battle no side represents pure evil, and even in the criminal we recognize human dignity. Moreover, a certain logic lies hidden in the encounter with evil, a sense that while the hero should fight it, the contest also forms them, and out of this battle goodness emerges.

Humor as a Worldview

Hitchcock not only thematizes love, he integrates it into his form. The comic, like the horrific, performs, as we saw, a violation of categories. The comic is the incongruous insofar as it is harmless. Clowns are notoriously too fat or too thin, too short or too tall, or in some other playful way distorted; when hit by clubs, they are unfazed, inhumanly resilient. Whereas the threat of violence arouses fear and horror, clowns trigger amusement and mirth. We recall the Platonic-Aristotelian insight that the comic is an ugliness or deficiency that is neither threatening nor painful. A particular form of the comic that has received extensive philosophical analysis is humor, which the neo-Kantian Hermann Cohen associates with love.

Cohen argues in his two-volume aesthetics that mature art deals not only with beauty but also with ugliness (1.58). Cohen relates the ugly to the material dimensions of our being, suggesting that we should not despise it but instead accept it as part of our humanity (1.304). He writes: "Love would become insincere if it did not want to embrace also the ugly. Love embraces and transforms ugliness, making it a moment of beauty" (1.289). Cohen rejects Kant's linking only the sublime to the ethical and finds also in humor, the opposite of the sublime, an aesthetic connection to ethics. Whereas the sublime distances itself from finitude, humor embraces it. Via loving critique, humor diffuses finitude: "Thus the great art of humor seeks out the ugly in human beings in order to portray it as worthy of love" (1.304). Compassion with the insufficient is "like a vindication of God's goodness and justice in the face of the existence of evil . . . Ugly people have a share in systematic beauty, and it is the artist's highest calling to reveal this" (2.386–7).

Something akin to Cohen's concept of humor is visible in Hitchcock, whose characters are neither idealized nor so harshly criticized that we hate them. In *Shadow of a Doubt* Hitchcock mocks the family for its ignorance, but he does so gently and humorously. Young Charlie distances herself from the family, for she sees reality more clearly than they do, but she still loves them. Hitchcock's critique of the family along with the neighbor Herb, while clear, is hardly bitter or ruthless— it is layered with humor and respect. Cohen's concept of addressing ugliness mildly, with critique, but loving critique, is a fascinating aesthetic option to which Hitchcock seems drawn.

Audiences tend to have some level of sympathy even for Hitchcock's criminals, including both Marion and Norman in *Psycho*, a film that draws us in to identify with the characters (Wood 142–51). Though a murderer, Mrs. Paradine is able to overwhelm and attract her attorney. Hitchcock's villains are often charismatic. Their attraction has partly to do with the deception of evil. Hitchcock draws attention to the ease with which we place ourselves into the mind of a criminal or even a murderer, especially if they have some admirable characteristics. The attraction also comes from the idea that one should resist but not hate the criminal. Our reconciliation with evil is also related to the ideas that the audience requires it for drama and the characters need it for the development of virtues. Both Scottie and Judy, the two main characters in *Vertigo*, are deeply flawed. Scottie exhibits an obsessiveness with death and a manipulation of another person that are perverse, and Judy is an accessory to murder, yet with Judy regretting her earlier action and risking exposure because of her love for Scottie and Scottie being so vulnerable and so driven to recreate a moment of seeming love now lost to him, we cannot help but sympathize with them. The critique of reality is filled not with hate but with love. Hitchcock pushes back on the desire simply to eradicate what one hates.

In other films as well, we see a kind of loving critique. Human beings are deeply sinful but not without dignity. Ample human limitations are manifest in *The Birds*. Melanie is superficial, Mitch is difficult, Annie is jealous, and Lydia is cold, but the bird attacks are hardly justified by any actions they or the children undertake, and in these difficult circumstances each person exhibits some level of valor or kindness. Even in a world where much that is painful and inexplicable befalls human beings, we are able to recognize human dignity. The long shots and aerial shots that present human beings as vulnerable, for example, the long shot of Melanie isolated in the water, are coupled with close-ups that show active resistance to external threats, as when Mitch seeks to keep the birds out of the home. The characters' flaws arise from fear, such as fear of isolation or ridicule, and these subjective and intersubjective trepidations are layered with dread of nature, which enhances our sense of human fragility. But this very vulnerability— perhaps best expressed by Lydia's lament, in her first intimate scene with Melanie, that she does not want to be left alone—conveys *ex negativo* the value of human relationships and of love (Wood 165).

Hitchcock is a sober analyst of evil and so lets us know that we are often deceived, that the criminal can be charming, and that we must be on guard. But he also recognizes that not everyone has the capacity to see through the villain, and he is forgiving of those who do not have these unusual capacities. At the same time Hitchcock presents ordinary people as heroes, thereby suggesting that we are at times surprisingly capable of that level of insight and courage. And in portraying evil figures as alluring, he not only warns us, but also suggests that even as we reject them for not being what they should be, we should seek to understand them. Hitchcock elevates the heroic individual, but he also embeds that individual within a larger whole. Grace and providence play roles in guiding heroes to the good; the corresponding concept is that even as villains are responsible for who they are, they are also ambiguous, the result of larger forces, such that we can empathize with them and their fate. Hitchcock awakens such empathy with both distinctly cinematic and broadly artistic strategies.

Chapter 2
Hitchcock as a Master of Form

Film as a Distinctive Art

Only with the eighteenth-century advent of aesthetics does reflection on distinctions among the arts emerge. Lessing's *Laocoön: Or, On the Limits of Painting and Poetry*, published in 1766, is the first work to analyze the diverse arts systematically and includes a major distinction between the spatial and temporal arts. Lessing's pivotal standing is evident in *Film as Art*, written by the early film theorist Rudolf Arnheim, who entitles one of his chapters "A New Laocoön: Artistic Composites and the Talking Film." The last philosopher still widely read on the systematic relation of the arts is Hegel, who places literature, and specifically drama or theater, at the top of his scale, but Hösle makes the intriguing claim that film must today occupy that slot (*Hegels System* 638).

Why would film be the most synthetic art form? Film offers a distinctive combination of the arts, as it is both spatial and temporal. Film is visual, like architecture, sculpture, painting, and photography. But film also belongs to the temporal arts, which places it together with dance, music, and literature. Unique to dance, theater, and film is the blending of the spatial and the temporal. Film includes, as do dance and theater, staging, lighting, actors, gestures, movement, and music. Theater and film differentiate themselves from dance by employing language, which adds another layer of meaning and complexity. By its integration of language and a narrative arc, film, like literature, has the capacity to introduce the greatest level of intellectual complexity among the traditional arts, but only theater and film are embodied.

Moreover, film not only integrates the diverse arts, but three additional dimensions allow it to transcend even theater.[1] First is the camera, which frames our sight in ways that theater does not. Prominent here are distance, angle, movement, focus, and point of view. The camera conveys meaning in ways that do not apply in theater, offering angles that render figures prominent or diminished, that allow for a sense of loneliness, that express agitation, and so forth. The frequent long shots in *Rebecca*, for example, emphasize the titular figure's diminution and disorientation.

Second, is editing or montage, which involves the length of the shots as well as the sequence of cuts. Vsevolod Pudovkin identified editing as "the creative force of filmic reality" (26). The Soviet director and film theorist analyzed five possible hidden meanings of montage: contrast, parallelism, symbolism, simultaneity (which can drive suspense), and leitmotif (75–8). Whereas Pudovkin underscored connections, his contemporary Sergei Eisenstein stressed collisions. At times both moments are at play: in *The Manxman* the overlap dissolve from Kate's attempted suicide, as the water overtakes her, to Philip's dipping his pen in ink reinforces their connection and separation. *The Wrong Man* has an unusually high number of lap dissolves, including one of Manny's rosary and the courtroom (Figure 6), which stresses the discord between first-world and fourth-world justice and which anticipates one of the longest dissolves in Hitchcock: the revelation of Manny's double, which affirms his innocence.

Camera and editing combine to give us settings that have far greater range than in theater, such that one could speak of mis-en-scène (the totality of expressive content in the filmed image, from setting, props, and costumes to gestures, facial expressions, and lighting) as a third distinctive category.[2] Film's capacity for realism exceeds all other art forms, even photography, which lacks temporality. Film can visualize reality in ways that are ontologically richer than the other arts, even theater, as the setting of a film can draw on possibilities that exceed what is available on the limited and artificial horizon of a stage. Film is more capacious and discontinuous in terms of space and time than theater (Sontag 108). As a result, film audiences are better able to envisage an alternate reality.

Figure 6 This lap dissolve in *The Wrong Man* unites an establishing shot of the courtroom with a close-up of the rosary that Manny holds as he faces an unjust trial. A longer lap dissolve later in the film will eventually resolve the conflict of divine and secular justice. *The Wrong Man* directed by Alfred Hitchcock. © Warner Bros. 1956. All rights reserved.

Classic film criticism has traditionally fallen into two camps, a formalist and a realist model. In the history of film criticism, formalists, such as Pudovkin, have stressed montage, with its manipulation of images, whereas realists, such as André Bazin, have elevated mis-en-scène and privileged the realism of deep focus, medium shots, and fewer cuts. The distinction is not easy to maintain. For example, Robert Wiene's early Weimar film *The Cabinet of Dr. Caligari*, which is hardly realist, placed arguably greater emphasis on mis-en-scène than on editing. Any endeavor to think about film holistically must seek to integrate the best from both traditions. Modern film criticism has in most cases sought to integrate both elements, montage and mis-en-scène, though it has also, and to an equal degree, been deeply influenced by a variety of theoretical perspectives, many of which emerged independently of film and not all of which, I have argued elsewhere, are equally compelling (*Why Literature Matters* 87–115). At times the importing of non-film-specific theories has moved film criticism away from interpretation and certainly away from the distinction of film.

Film, like all the arts, offers a window onto a reality that is not exhausted by the empirical world. Consider the improbable plot of *Vertigo*, which nonetheless illuminates the longing for an ideal, the eroticism of love and knowledge, and the human tendency to fall victim to deception and self-deception. Here an unrealistic film opens a window onto hidden aspects of reality. In *Marnie* the confining, painted set of the mother's street, with the imposing ship at the end, is not realistic if we define realism as correspondence to physical reality, the second world, but the painted set does illuminate the deeper psychological and social realities that have formed Marnie. It sheds light on the third and fourth worlds.

We do not need to make the bold claim that film is uniquely capable of introducing certain philosophical ideas, but we can easily defend the more modest claim that cinema raises philosophical questions, explores philosophical puzzles, and makes implicit philosophical arguments (implicit because art conveys meaning indirectly) and does so via strategies that are, first, partly common to art in general and, second, partly unique to cinema. The capacity of art to unveil a higher reality is why philosophers as diverse as Aristotle, Hegel, Nietzsche, and Scheler have addressed the concept of tragedy and why thinkers have turned to a wide range of the arts to muse on philosophical concepts. But film does not simply engage philosophical questions, as the other arts do. In some cases, it draws on the distinctive capacities of the medium to elicit insights in unique ways. Still, even if certain philosophical ideas and analogous emotions may be uniquely advanced via film, these are not reducible to the medium or untranslatable, even if other media, as well as interpretive efforts, lack the aesthetic richness of the original. Although I can analyze what a film conveys, I cannot exhaust its embedded meaning.

Turning to the ontology of film, we can say, aided by Roman Ingarden, that film has three ontological levels, three modes of existence. First is the screen itself, a two-dimensional form with moving images and sound, which can come from within the action or outside the action. Here we see also the expression of various dimensions of the form, such as camera angles and editing. A second level of reality consists of the actors who are both on the screen and in our reality. Hitchcock recognizes that when a star plays a role, we are more likely to identify with that character's predicament, to be concerned about their fate— that is, extra-diegetic elements shape the spectator's perception (*Alfred* 36, 92, and 137; Bogdanovich 476; *Hitchcock on Hitchcock* 1.272 and 2.223; Truffaut 145). Here we can also place Hitchcock's cameo appearances. The third ontological realm is the reality depicted in the cinematic narrative itself, that is, the possible world that is created by the actors' appearances on the screen and their interactions. As a result of the camera work, editing, and mis-en-scène, this world has in principle a greater proximity to portraying reality than any other art form: the distinction of film allows viewers to see objects on the screen as if they were part of the spectator's reality even when they transcend what is possible in empirical reality.[3]

How is film positioned to convey ideas distinctively and, even in some ways better than the other arts? Obviously, suspense is enhanced when we have not simply a frozen frame but a temporal sequence. Moreover, the temporal arts are better positioned to portray resolutions that emerge from the threat of evil. As in literature, so in film, language externalizes ideas in discernible ways, making possible greater complexity. Sound adds an emotional dimension, but can also be intriguing cognitively, when, for example, it conflicts with the words or images. Sound includes dialogue, music, both diegetic and non-diegetic, and sound effects, all of which can be woven in various ways with the image, in terms of harmony or tension. Although many of these dimensions can be expressed in theater, for example, the incongruity between lyrics and music in Bertolt Brecht's *The Three Penny Opera*, the settings of film differ from theater, being more vivid and diverse as well as more realistic. Moreover, camera angles and montage in their combination make possible a range of meaning not available in any other art.

Film-Specific Formal Features

Hitchcock is rare in having entered the profession during the silent era and having continued well into the period of color films with sound. All along he was an innovator, introducing new concepts and innovative shots and executing them with technical mastery. Moreover, he carried forward from his silent films a sensibility for telling a story with images. Hitchcock speaks frequently of "true cinema" or "pure cinema," by which he means a focus on the visual dynamic, ensuring that the visual is more prominent than dialogue (*Hitchcock on Hitchcock* 1.214; 1.288; 1.290; 2.96). He adds: "To put things together visually, to tell the story visually; to embody the action in the juxtaposition of images that have their own specific language and emotional impact—that is cinema" (*Hitchcock on Hitchcock* 1.214). Hitchcock viewed silent cinema not as a deficient mode but as in some ways a purer cinematic form. He repeatedly criticizes films that are simply "photographs of people talking" (*Alfred* 90, 91, 158, 183, 184; *Hitchcock on Hitchcock* 1.290, 2.52, 2.95; Truffaut 61). His cinematic techniques evoke the "emotional power" that Spoto has rightly called "the mark of Hitchcock's creative genius" (*Art* 354). Having begun already as a production designer, Hitchcock had a vision for his films, to convey meaning via framing, editing, and sound.

Anyone who has seen Hitchcock's silent films, including works such as *Easy Virtue, The Farmer's Wife,* and *The Manxman*, understands his capacity to express meaning without words. Consider, for example, the scene in *Easy Virtue* where the switchboard operator listens to John and Larita as they discuss a possible marriage: the operator's expressions take us through the conversation, to which we are not privy: interest, pleasure, warmth, unease, promise, doubt, promise, uncertainty, and relief. Even some of Hitchcock's sound films are beautifully effective in their silence. Very little dialogue takes place when Hannay in *The 39 Steps* is with the crofter and his wife in the Scottish Highlands; the gestures and expressions convey the interpersonal dynamics. When Lisa enters Thorwald's apartment in *Rear Window*, we not only observe her as if she were on the screen, the entire encounter with Thorwald and then the police, which takes place across the courtyard, plays out for us like a silent movie. Toward the end Hitchcock even offers a self-conscious nod to silent cinema: not only is Jeff long silent when Thorwald enters the apartment and asks a series of questions, the circles that follow Jeff's light bulb flashes recall the iris of silent cinema (Figure 7).

Silence can shift our focus. When in *The Birds* Lydia uncovers the body of her neighbor Dan Fawcett, we see a succession of quick shots—broken teacups, a shattered window, dead birds, and then the body, clothed in pajamas, dead, the eyes pecked out. We move from more distant shots to an eventual close-up of Fawcett's head and vacant eye sockets (Figure 8).

There is no dialogue here or afterward, only the haunting jump cuts and Lydia's nonverbals, her inarticulate rushing to the truck and her racing home on the dirt road, dust in her wake. As Hitchcock comments, "the

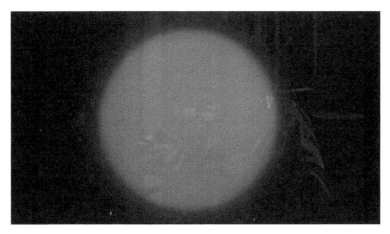

Figure 7 In *Rear Window* multiple scenes play out as if we were watching a silent film. Here Jeff, played by James Stewart, has finally broken his long silence, and the effect of the flashes, by which he seeks to blind Thorwald, offers a self-conscious nod to the iris of silent cinema. *Rear Window* directed by Alfred Hitchcock. © Samuel Taylor and Patricia Hitchcock O'Connell as Co-Trustees. 1954. All rights reserved.

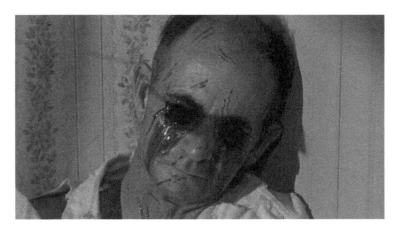

Figure 8 When in *The Birds* Lydia uncovers the body of her neighbor, we see a series of jump cuts, with four quick shots of the dead body, culminating in the pecked-out eyes. The shots emphasize not only the objective horror but also the subjective shock of recognition. *The Birds* directed by Alfred Hitchcock. © Universal Studios 1963. All rights reserved.

speed of that truck expresses the anguish of the woman" (*Hitchcock on Hitchcock* 1.301).

Silence is haunting in the long scene in which Michael and a farmer's wife kill the Stasi agent Gromek in *Torn Curtain*. Various attempts are made to kill Gromek, all undertaken quietly, so as not to arouse the attention of the taxi driver waiting outside. The lack of sound and music underscores several ideas. Michael is in completely foreign territory, not only spatially but also psychologically (indeed, he becomes almost indistinguishable from the enemy). The audience recognizes that Michael must eliminate Gromek, and so we are implicated in the killing. The scene underscores the horror and messiness of murder. Moreover, the silence contributes to a certain level of sobriety, while the multiple attempts become hauntingly grotesque (which is partly reinforced by Gromek's having previously been portrayed as a comic character, a Stasi figure who constantly espouses fond memories of America). Thus, there is no triumph, only a haunting bracketing of an explicitly moral frame, which is all the more brutal, as the use of a gas oven links the American agent with the Nazis.

Silence can be interwoven with uncertainty and suspense, and the absence of sound can have symbolic meaning. In two scenes in *Topaz*, first at the florist and then at the hotel, two characters speak with one another, but we cannot hear their dialogue. We experience as viewers some of what the characters themselves undergo in their suspense-laden cinematic world. In *Frenzy* silence is powerfully combined with a retreating camera: the soundtrack vanishes, and the camera tracks backward down the winding stairs and along the deserted corridor to signal the death of Babs, while those carrying out their daily routines are completely unaware. Sound commences when we return outside. Death is close but hidden.

Sound, too, conveys unease and suspense. In Hitchcock's first sound film, *Blackmail*, a woman gossips unceasingly about the previous night's "murder." Alice, who is implicated in the homicide, hears her drone on, with only one word recognizable—"knife"—again and again and again, the last time as a shout, and we take part in this distortion of reality, a continuation of her subjectively oriented nighttime wandering, both of which underscore her emotional and moral despair. When in *The 39 Steps* the woman who discovers the dead body screams, the train whistle blows, resulting in a creative sound match. The story has made it to the newspapers on the train, where the hero will soon be falsely accused. In both versions of *The Man Who Knew Too Much* Hitchcock winds diegetic sound into the plot. The assassin is prepared to shoot just as the cymbals clash, and in anticipation of that moment the mother of the kidnaped child screams, thwarting the attempt but endangering her child.[4]

Also fascinating are scenes where sound and image are at odds with one another, where, for example, the discussion is about one topic, but the real energy lies elsewhere. The theater-like innovation of *Rope* does not prevent effective framing or tension between image and sound. The camera lingers on the trunk, which contains the dead body, as Mrs. Wilson proceeds to clean it off, removing the dishes, candles, and tablecloth. She is basically preparing to open it and put away the books while the voices are off camera and seemingly oblivious to her inadvertent movement toward uncovering the body, even if she is effectively thwarted at the end. The long takes in this film represent more than an experiment. They constrict our space, forcing us to be in the same room with the dead body. The film's claustrophobic feel underscores the isolation of Brandon and Phillip, whose ideas are divorced from any kind of ordinary or commonsense morality. The outside world does not count. Only their own subjectivities matter and with them the guests whom they seek to impress as they risk exposure.

Introductory and overhead shots convey atmosphere and meaning that is simply not possible on the stage. Consider the opening shot in *Rebecca*. Its moving camera and voice-over capture the mood in seconds. Overhead shots can emphasize anguish. Consider the crane shot of the mother and father in the second *Man Who Knew Too Much* as they listen to their captive son's voice (Figure 9).

The couple is diminished, but brought together after the everyday bickering we saw earlier. The shot evokes a combination of human isolation and almost divine-like empathy. In *Notorious* a crane shot makes its way down the spiral staircase, canvassing the large party to identify in a close-up the hidden story, the key in Alicia's hand that is central to her dangerous mission. Keys are symbolic of love, and Alicia has stolen the key from Sebastian and given it to Devlin. The shot is partially mirrored later: when we see a diminutive Alex, after he realizes his stupidity; when Alicia realizes she has been poisoned; and finally when Devlin and Alicia make their difficult descent down the staircase

Figure 9 In the second *Man Who Knew Too Much,* the mother, played by Doris Day, and the father, played by James Stewart, listen to their captive son's voice. The couple is diminished, but brought together after the everyday bickering we saw earlier. The aerial shot evokes a combination of human isolation and almost divine-like empathy. *The Man Who Knew Too Much* directed by Alfred Hitchcock. © Samuel Taylor and Patricia Hitchcock O'Connell as Co-Trustees. 1955. All rights reserved.

after having confessed their love. An extended overhead shot in *Dial M for Murder* as the murder plot is laid out gives us the sense that God is watching in judgment, and the characters are hardly in control. *Topaz* gives us a beautiful overhead shot of Juanita, with the camera winding around her and slowly moving upward, as she is shot. The camera stops at the moment she collapses, her purple robe spread across the marble floor, like a flower opening. She dies in a moment of self-sacrifice, and the purple, which combines the red of blood and the blue of the heavens, links her to Christ, much as the tortured couple who helped Juanita and the Americans in their espionage had earlier been portrayed in a pieta image.

The subjective camera brings us into the film world, evoking empathy, enhancing suspense, or accentuating horror. Toward the end of *Downhill,* shots taken from the character's point of view lead the audience to identify with the hero's despair and disorientation: objective reality recedes for the character and for us, whereas earlier in the film we had looked down on him from higher angles. Hitchcock uses the subjective camera to enhance identification when in *Notorious* Alicia is introduced to the Nazi spies and when she realizes in a stupor that she is being poisoned. In some cases, the subjective camera implicates us in the actions of criminals. In *Frenzy* we search with Rusk through the potatoes looking for the tie pin that, if not retrieved, would implicate him.

In contrast to point of view shots are the many high and low angle shots that Hitchcock uses to communicate meaning. High angles often convey isolation or vulnerability, low angles tend to convey admiration or power. When Hannay gives his rousing speech in *The 39 Steps*, we see him via low camera angles. In the courtroom scenes in *I Confess* high angle, distanced shots of Logan, minimizing his power, contrast with low angle shots of Keller, as his face dominates the screen. An aerial shot of the first disinterment in *The Trouble with Harry* renders the characters small: they are less in charge of their fate than they imagine. In *North by Northwest* Thornhill is filmed via very high aerial shots as he runs from the United Nations and again at Prairie Stop, which underscore his vulnerability.

Relative distance can be used to draw out emotions and highlight objects. At the start of *Marnie*, the camera dwells on a close-up of Marnie's purse, which establishes her outer decorum, but the symbolism of yellow, suggesting caution, awakens suspicion. Her stolen money, we later discover, is hidden there. Close-ups frequently convey emotions, as with some of the close-ups of Mrs. Verloc in the second dinner scene in *Sabotage.* She silently wavers at the thought of killing her husband, and the camera dwells on her hands and the knife. Long shots can convey isolation and loneliness, as in the long shot of Mrs. Verloc after the death of her kid brother or in *Vertigo* the final shot of Midge in the psychiatric institute. Long shots can also be used to evoke mystery, as in the multiple long shots, often only in profile, of Madeleine in *Vertigo*. Above all in *Rope* we see how film differs from theater, with the camera offering us meaningful close-ups of Philip's broken glass, just after Mrs. Atwater mistakes Kenneth for David; of the initials in David's hat, which Rupert recognizes; and of Brandon's revolver as he awaits Rupert's return. *The Trouble with Harry* uses few close-ups; the film celebrates not individuality, but community, which is better captured with medium and long shots. Indeed, Hitchcock takes the point so far that in one beautiful long shot he captures five figures, simply in silhouette, their faces erased (Figure 10).

Figure 10 *The Trouble with Harry*, which uses few close-ups, celebrates not individuality, but community, which is better conveyed via medium and long shots. Indeed, Hitchcock takes the point so far that in this beautiful long shot he films five figures, simply in silhouette, their faces erased. *The Trouble with Harry* directed by Alfred Hitchcock. © Samuel Taylor and Patricia Hitchcock O'Connell as Co-Trustees 1955. All rights reserved.

Hitchcock is also a master of special effects. Consider the technical achievement of the ocean crash in *Foreign Correspondent*. A daredevil pilot pulled as close to the water as possible. The sequence was projected onto a screen made of rice paper, behind which was a large water tank. At the key moment, the water was released, demolishing the screen as the water burst into the cockpit and flooded the crew. The dramatic shot reinforces the severity of the German challenge and the pressing need for an American response. The glowing milk in *Suspicion* (via an inserted lightbulb) leads viewers to fear that the drink may contain poison; the clever and imaginative shot, with shadows casting a spider web on the wall behind Johnnie as he ascends the stairs with the milk, adds to the drama. In *Vertigo* Hitchcock portrays Scottie's disorientation by dollying the camera away from the subject of the shot as he zooms toward it with the lens. Among Hitchcock's most famous concluding shots is the match cut in *North by Northwest*: Thornhill lifts Eve up from the precipice at Mt. Rushmore, which suddenly becomes the top bunk in their train cabin. "Mrs. Thornhill," he calls out, after which the train enters a tunnel. Beyond the obvious sexual symbolism, the cut emphasizes the ways in which Roger's risking his life for Eve culminates in their marriage.

Other signature shots include, for example, the murder in *Strangers on a Train*. Bruno's strangling Miriam is refracted through her glasses, which in the scuffle had fallen to the ground. Symbolically, we see the murder through her perspective, and the physical object becomes a kind of silent witness. The famous crop-duster scene in *North by Northwest*, reinforced by the long silence, underscores that threats are unpredictable and come out of nowhere. One of Hitchcock's most magnificent scenes occurs in *Vertigo* when Judy as Madeleine emerges from the bathroom, and we, with Scottie, view her via a ghostly and mysterious green fog lens. This is followed by a kiss with an emotional 360° camera movement, during which the background shifts three times. In *Torn Curtain* Michael and Sarah go up a hill for a private conversation. She thinks he has betrayed his country, and as he speaks, she turns away, her hands on her ears, but soon she relaxes and faces him. The camera takes us from the back of her head to the front. The truth has been silently revealed by way of what Hitchcock calls "the language of the camera" (Bogdonavich 544).

Hitchcock uses editing for various purposes, including establishing hidden connections and intensifying suspense. Consider in *Blackmail* the subtle parallels evoked by the chief inspector wringing his hands, which is immediately followed by the blackmailer making the exact same motion. Not only is the inspector implicitly associated with a criminal, the inspector rubs his hands in confidence that he has found the murderer, but unbeknownst to him he has the wrong man. After Bruno in *Strangers on a Train* has murdered Miriam and is leaving the amusement park, he checks his watch. The film then cuts to Guy on the train also checking his watch. Guy identifies his alibi and is implicated at one and the same time. When Guy is suspected of murder, under surveillance, and playing a tennis match, he must finish quickly because Bruno, the murderer, is preparing to incriminate Guy by planting his lighter at the crime scene. Bruno accidentally drops the lighter down a drain, and we watch him seek to retrieve it, as Guy tries to close out his match. As the crosscutting continues, the scenes become shorter, which increases the tension. Crosscutting likewise enhances an already suspenseful situation in *Notorious*, as Hitchcock cuts between Devlin and Alicia in the basement and Joseph (and eventually Sebastian) above. Here the spatial proximity adds to the angst, and our heart races at the tension. In the famous shower scene in *Psycho* the rapid cutting intensifies the horror. In contrast, the slower but equally unmistakable montage in *The Birds* awakens suspense: shots of Melanie smoking a cigarette are followed by a few crows on the jungle gym, then back to Melanie, who is turned away from the birds, then back to the jungle gym, and so forth, until the danger is apparent to viewers, but not to Melanie.

Among the various developments in film studies over the past few decades has been increasing interest in reception aesthetics, including the embodied experience of spectators.[5] This turn to the affective realm has brought to the fore such topics as: what assumptions and categories viewers bring to the film experience; how active they are when engaging cinematic images and sounds, not only intellectually but also emotionally; how elements of sympathy and empathy guide a viewer's engagement; how recipients simulate the experiences of cinematic characters and yet remain cognizant of the events as fiction; and how visceral reactions relate to more considered emotional evaluations as well as eventual interpretations.

The analysis of viewers' emotions is primarily a form of reception aesthetics, but it can also attend to those features of cinematic form that give rise to emotional responses. Ideally, then, it, too, partakes of the study of form, including exploring such questions as: how characters' facial expressions, posture, eye movements, and tone of voice influence our emotions; how camera position, editing, lighting, and music affect viewers; how genre categories and overall pacing and rhythm guide our reception; how film situations weigh on viewers' emotions; and even how the overarching style of work or director affects our film experience.

Although the intense critical emphasis on cinematic emotions emerged after Hitchcock's career had ended, few directors were better able to foster in audiences a range of emotional experiences, above all, as we have discussed, fear, suspense, despair, ambivalence, laughter, hope, and love. To be fully immersed in the viewing of a Hitchcock film is to be attuned not only to ideas but also to a range of affects, emotions, and moods. How Hitchcock achieves these cinematic emotions differs from my focus on how he orchestrates ideas, but the two intersect insofar as distinctly cinematic features—from settings, staging, gestures, and acting to camera position, editing, colors, and music—influence both our emotional responses and our interpretations.

Among the many moments in Hitchcock that stimulate strong emotions, one could consider examples from virtually every film, given how much emphasis Hitchcock places on crafting works that trigger a strong audience response. We experience a range of emotions across his works, for example, a mixture of excitement and delight in *The 39 Steps*; desperation and relief in both versions of *The Man Who Knew Too Much*; confusion, dread, and unfulfilled longing in *Vertigo*; and a sense of joyous adventure, peppered with moments of fear, laughter, and hope, in *North by Northwest*.

Let's consider a few examples to underscore how a focus on embodied emotional responses can draw renewed attention to form. Consider two sequences in *Blackmail.* Alice demurs several times before agreeing to visit the artist's studio. Her professed lack of fear, as she hesitates and naively agrees, conflicts with the audience's unease at what might happen there, especially as the unknown and suspicious Tracy looks on from afar. Moreover, we get a prominent shot of the artist's phallic cane, which he holds prominently and horizontally to his body. When Alice and the artist walk up the long flight of stairs, the balusters give the impression of being prison bars, and the two figures cast their shadows onto the wall. Our foreboding continues, as Alice, who is increasingly sexualized, remains not fully aware. After her self-defense and the artist's death, we empathize with her nighttime wanderings through the streets of London. The close-ups, the subjective camera, the distorted and unresolved rendition of Miss Up-to-Date, and the early morning fog, a landscape of her soul, all reinforce her and our sense of disorder and despair.

In *Notorious* frequent close-ups and point-of-view shots, coupled with a sympathetic and vulnerable character, encourage audiences to empathize with Alicia. We enjoy the close-ups of Devlin and Alicia kissing on the balcony and in the apartment but are frustrated by their eventual alienation, expressed in insults and lies as well as body language and tone of voice. Despite the tension, we watch closely for signs of genuine love, which are visible on Devlin's part only in comments that Alicia does not hear and on her part via facial expressions that Devlin refuses to acknowledge. Sebastian, too, watches the pair closely, though his attentiveness is layered not with frustrated desire, as with the audience, but with suspicion and fear. We also long to see Alicia safe and her sacrifice both recognized and halted. Her bodily sacrifice separates her from Devlin; this is foreshadowed in an early shot in Miami (Figure 11), where two crosses, one more dramatic than the other, divide Alicia and Devlin, as they listen to a recording where she criticizes her treasonous father and expresses her love for America.

Her eventual sacrifice is reinforced by three subsequent crosses, one as we look at her through the window just after she has received her assignment; the second above the race track before a difficult meeting between Alicia and Devlin; and the third a very large cross above her bed just before the poisoning begins. When Devlin finds Alicia bedridden and embraces her, we see backlighting, which gives Alicia a halo effect. Not long thereafter the tense and dramatic rescue on the stairwell ends in relief.

Since Hitchcock excelled at creating coherent artworks, where the parts gain their full meaning only in the whole, one could also seek to

Figure 11 In Alicia's apartment in Miami two crosses, one more dramatic than the other, divide Alicia, played by Ingrid Bergman, and Devlin, played by Cary Grant, as they listen to a recording where she criticizes her treasonous father and expresses her love for America. The crosses prefigure Alicia's sacrifice, which will dramatically separate the two of them. *Notorious* directed by Alfred Hitchcock. © ABC, Inc. 1946. All rights reserved.

identify in each of his films as well as across his oeuvre something like an overarching set of interrelated emotions, what Daniel Yacavone calls a "cineaesthetic world-feeling" (200). With this term, Yacavone seeks to capture the immersive experience and emotional atmosphere of a film or a director, which, however, could only be fully articulated with attention also to the artworks themselves.

German Cinema

Hitchcock first experienced how films can convey an overwhelming emotional experience from the masters of German expressionism and New Objectivity. During the Weimar Republic, Hitchcock worked in Germany as a writer, art director, and eventually director. He was on the UFA lot, watching F. W. Murnau, as the German director filmed arguably the greatest silent film of all time, *The Last Laugh*, which had award-winning acting, an impressive moving camera, and only one intertitle (*Hitchcock on Hitchcock* 2.249). The German influence was formative for Hitchcock, who occasionally cited Wiene's *The Cabinet of Dr. Caligari*, with its visionary expressionist sets, along with the directors Murnau, Fritz Lang, and Ernst Lubitsch (McGilligan 64). From them, Hitchcock understood the value of atmosphere, stark camera angles, extreme close-ups, and the moving camera. Above all, he learned to tell a story visually instead of simply with words (*Alfred* 58). Hitchcock's capacity to imagine the finished product and to film with that vision in mind was a technique he absorbed from Murnau, who told him: "What you see on the set does not matter. All that matters is what you see on the screen" (McGilligan 63).

Hitchcock directed his first two films in Germany, and his third and fourth films, *The Lodger* and *Downhill*, are visibly influenced by the Germans, but the legacy endured beyond these early years. Via the Schüfftan process, which was invented in Germany, Hitchcock integrated live actors with photographically reproduced sets. We see this technique in the chase scene in *Blackmail* and the Royal Albert Hall scenes in *The Ring* and the first *Man Who Knew Too Much*. His third sound film, *Murder!*, was filmed also in German and released in Germany as *Mary*. *Strangers on a Train* presents the amusement park as chaos, a theme Wiene had introduced in *Caligari*. Distorted camera shots, which were part of the German expressionist repertoire, continue at least to *The Wrong Man*.

We see a canted shot right after the unusual Hitchcock cameo, a backlit silhouette in extreme long shot. Later *The Wrong Man* uses dizzying camera movement to capture disorientation and desperation as the innocent everyman, Manny, faces a night in prison. At the end of *Stage Fright* Hitchcock presents haunting close-ups of the vulnerable murderer in a crowded prop room, a clear echo of Peter Lorre's face in the cluttered attic room, on which Lang's camera dwells in *M*, as we watch the child murderer and listen to the approaching gangsters. Gottlieb, who traces the German influence, cleverly calls Hitchcock "one of the great German directors" (56). German expressionism was deeply philosophical, beginning already with *Caligari*, and it was richly interwoven with politics, including issues of power and morality, most effectively perhaps in *M*, whose portrayal of police activity and integration of New Objectivity are echoed in *The Wrong Man*. Asked who his mentors were, Hitchcock replied, "The Germans! The Germans!" (Ackroyd 23).

Artistic Strategies

Hitchcock also employs artistic strategies that are not per se cinematic. Mirrors, both real and metaphorical, including reversals, combine similarity and difference. In *Rear Window* the tables are eventually turned: Thorwald stares back at Jeff and invades his privacy. Mirroring often implies that the distinction between a criminal and a more or less likable character can be modest. Scottie's making Judy into Madeleine mirrors the earlier staging undertaken by Elster, who blatantly seeks the "power and freedom" of the past, even as he depends on his wife's money. But Scottie, too, harks back to an earlier era: he cannot love a modern and independent woman, such as Midge, and is drawn instead to women who satisfy his asymmetrical desires, either a vulnerable woman who must be saved (Madeleine) or a woman who can be dominated (Judy). Mirrors are not only metaphorical; the cracked mirror in *The Wrong Man* effectively externalizes Manny's split identity and distorted existence (Miller 126–30).

Doubling is a metaphorical mirror that accentuates similarities and differences. The technique can reveal a split identity and be quite serious, as in *Spellbound*, but it can also be playful, as when in the same film the house detective says to the psychoanalyst who pretends to be a regretful wife that he is "a kind of psychologist." The detective is confident that he sizes people up accurately precisely when he is wrong. In *Vertigo* Judy when dressed as Madeleine becomes a double for Madeleine, the true wife. When after the real Madeleine is dead, and Scottie discovers Judy, he dresses her as Madeleine. She thus becomes the double of a double, twice removed from reality, an allusion to Plato, which is reinforced by Scottie's idealizing his beloved. Some of Hitchcock's doubling is quite subtle: in *The Lodger* Daisy screams when Joe confronts her with handcuffs, which leads to their separation; later she screams when she sees a mouse, which propels her into the Lodger's arms. There may be no Hitchcock film in which doubling does not occur. Even in the one film where the antagonist could not possibly be a double, Hitchcock's cameo signals that doubling is still present. In *The Birds* Hitchcock walks out of the pet store with two dogs on a fork leash, a signal to look even in this film for doubles: Mitch and Melanie, Annie and Melanie, and Lydia and Melanie.

Hitchcock often invokes shapes that unite artistic and cinematic dimensions: consider the prominent triangles in *The Lodger*, which underscore character constellations and have religious significance. Hitchcock was also attracted to circular structures. The first *The Man Who Knew Too Much* begins at an alpine resort, with a ski jump and with the mother missing a shot and losing a skeet shooting competition to a stranger; it ends on a steep-sloped roof in London, where the mother makes the shot, kills the assassin, who is also the man who beat her in the competition, and so saves her daughter. The dancers in *Shadow of a Doubt*, who embrace each other almost like a circle, also move in circles, both as couples and among each other, which anticipates the ring symbolism. A circle can symbolize perfection, but it can also suggest stasis. Uncle Charlie is driven by a perverse nostalgia, which leads him to hate the present. The circular symbolism in *Strangers on a Train*, associated with the record store and the carousel, represents a closed and stagnant world from which the characters cannot easily break free.

Self-reflexive Art

Hegel argues that each art has distinctive capacities that make it an ideal form for certain kinds of content, so, for example, sculpture is the appropriate art for a classical mode in which the representation and depicted object mirror one another, whereas literature, which, points beyond itself, is a fitting art for Christianity, whose meaning is not exhausted by what is visibly present. As a modern art, film is often immersed in what I have suggested elsewhere are the three most distinctive characteristics of aesthetic modernity: ugliness, including physical, emotional, intellectual, and moral ugliness; technology (indeed film itself was made possible by way of technological advances); and self-reflection, that is, art that reflects on art itself ("Idealistische Ästhetik"). Hitchcock is immersed in all three elements. His self-reflection lifts his films into the realm of philosophy: they reflect on art and on the relation of art and world.[6] He employs self-reflection and the breaking of the plane of verisimilitude to elicit comedy, to contemplate role-playing as a mode of understanding social interaction, to analyze the appearance—reality divide in the world, to shed light on the power and limits of film making and film viewing, and to weigh the relationships of art and life, of reflection and art, and of reflection and life. Not by chance the first scene in the first Hitchcock film, *The Pleasure Garden*, takes place on stage. *Rear Window,* Hitchcock's most obviously self-reflexive film, contains abundant references to sight, to objects of viewing, to cameras, lenses, binoculars, and the like. The film opens with bamboo shades being drawn upward, like a curtain upon a stage, and the entire work reflects on similarities and differences between theatrical and cinematic space (Belton). We see artistic roles throughout: dancer, sculptor, composer, and photographer. Jeff, the photographer immobile with a broken leg, and the viewer are fixed in position and sometimes misled. Like Jeff, we watch uneasily. We don't merely observe Jeff, we become his double. "Tell me everything you've seen and what you think it means," Lisa says to Jeff and implicitly the audience.

At times ruptures in the cinematic narrative are comic, which tends to elicit reflection. Brecht after all built his theory of epic theater on comedy, not tragedy. Whenever Hitchcock makes his cameo appearances, we are reminded that we are watching a production, not real life, and we step back from the action. Often the director's appearances offer hermeneutic clues. In *Strangers on a Train* Hitchcock carries a double bass onto the train, which itself seems like a physical double to the large Hitchcock. He signals thereby the doubling that drives the film. Though Hitchcock's appearance here is comic, the low and dark instrument is foreboding. Usually, he appears early (so that we are not overly distracted looking for him), but occasionally we must wait, as in *Notorious*. His consuming a glass of champagne signals the importance of drinking and underscores his identification with Alicia, whose drinking is prominent and whose subjective camera has led the audience to identify with her. But, most importantly, the unusual speed with which Hitchcock downs his liquor helps push the plot forward: the bottles will run out, and Sebastian will need to get more from the basement, where Alicia and Devlin are hunting for secrets.

Self-reflection allows Hitchcock to play with the appearance-reality dichotomy. Indirect (or hidden) meaning makes art possible but is also prominent in the world. Play-acting is a form of deception and a means of wielding power. In *The 39 Steps,* the hero not only combats a spy who is taken to be an upstanding member of British society, he must also play various parts in order to escape the role (of murderer) that the world has assigned to him. He writes and directs his own salvation, but others contribute as well: the crofter's wife is self-sacrificing, and eventually Pamela helps as well. His counterpart, Professor Jordan, is always acting, but he does so without others knowing, and so it is fitting that, when finally exposed, Jordan ends up on stage (Drumin 38). In *Foreign Correspondent* evil lurks within the family, such that seeming and being conflict. In *Notorious* the levels of play-acting, even before the heroine adopts her assigned role, are great, as neither Devlin nor Alicia wants to admit having feelings for the other. On the park bench when they speak of spying, the subtext is scorned love. When finally, they pretend to engage in a kiss, the charade becomes truth: appearance is reality, whereas the marriage is a facade. In *Dial M for Murder*, not only does Tony, who is seeking to murder his wife, play various roles, the police must enter into an extensive charade in order to gather all the evidence that leads to the husband's justified arrest. Hitchcock's fascination with the deception of everyday reality and the idea of hidden meaning is captured in the tropical flower that Mark describes to Marnie: it is exquisitely beautiful, but as you approach it, you recognize that it consists of thousands of tiny insects that have formed themselves as camouflage against birds.

Deception can become a way of expanding one's identity. One rises to meet the role and become more than one was previously. So, for example, when Pamela in *The 39 Steps* is forced to play the wife of Hannay or when Eve in *Stage Fright* assumes the role of Ordinary

Smith's lover, they eventually find that their roles have become reality. In *North by Northwest* Roger Thornhill is not only viewed as an agent; in saving Eve, he acts like an agent. Moreover, Eve realizes that her seducing him (as part of her role as a double agent) is her destiny. In a sense role-playing, a mere means, becomes in these cases its own end. And that is analogous to our identifying with the roles on the screen; even if art elicits new ideas, it is also its own end.

Hitchcock employs self-reflection to elicit viewer reflection on art and reality. In *Murder!* we encounter within the cinematic universe two different plays and a circus performance. According to Sir John, artists normally "use life to create art," but he wants also to "use art to criticize life." The film mocks the all-too-easily-swayed jurors and elevates artists for their capacities to think themselves into the positions of others, an aesthetic capability that helps Sir John uncover the truth. In *Sabotage* viewers watch and enjoy violent films even as they are oblivious to the crimes being plotted in the same building. They are attracted to violence, and we find in them mirrors of ourselves. In this film, Hitchcock douses our vicarious enthusiasm for suspense and violence with a brutal event, the explosion of a bomb that kills a little boy whom we have gotten to know and like, whom we last see playing with a puppy, and who is innocently carrying the explosive. While in mourning for her little brother, Mrs. Verloc briefly enjoys a cartoon (cinema as relief), but the film's self-reflection also suggests that cinema is a window onto evil. We can watch violence with amusement and occasional horror, or we can learn from its subtle insights. In *Saboteur* a chase scene moves into Radio City Music Hall. Viewers within the cinematic universe experience a reality that mirrors what they see on the screen, and we as viewers see beyond our own reality to two levels of fiction. The viewers in the theater, however, cannot distinguish artifice from life, so they initially laugh when real bullets are fired and a man is shot. In *Dial M for Murder* Mark invents an elaborate story to help free Margot. Ironically, his story corresponds point by point to what happened, a reference to the idea that art can grasp reality in ways that shed new light on reality. Ideally, good ideas transform reality in a positive way, but other options are possible. In *Rope* Rupert is appalled that his ideas have been realized. His students turn murder into an art form.

Hitchcock's immanent reflection on filmmaking and on art includes also self-criticism. In his cameo in *Blackmail* a little child torments him;

we identify not only with Hitchcock being disturbed but also with the child mocking the director (Wood 273). This film, like *Frenzy* at the end of his career, mocks public obsession with morbid curiosity. Consider also *Lifeboat*, where Connie is more concerned with her filming and writing than with saving others. Her long speech on wonderful shots of the disaster is effectively countered by Kovac, who criticizes her self-obsession. When Connie sees a baby's bottle floating in the water and gets ready to film, Kovac bats it away. "What did you do that for?" she asks. He responds by drawing attention to her heartlessness: "Why don't you wait for the baby to float by and photograph that?" Hitchcock thereby mocks both himself and his audience.

In a few cases, multiple elements overlap. *Stage Fright* opens with a self-reflexive curtain on the film itself. The title is clever, for the literary meaning of the term "stage fright" is displaced by a deeper resonance: fear for one's life as one plays various roles in seeking to ferret out criminals and evade the police, at times directly on stage. Eve wrongly believes that Jonathan is innocent; she plays disparate roles in order to gather information to solve the crime. Role-playing can lead to a strengthening of identity (against wrong opinion), but it can also trigger identity confusion as one slowly transitions to a new identity. Eve pretends to fill in as a dresser for Charlotte in order to get close to the woman who allegedly framed Johnny. Later Eve doubles as a surrogate detective. She believes that Charlotte set Jonathan up for a murder charge and risks her life to clear his name. Charlotte is not only an actress on stage; she plays the role of the mourning wife, asking in confidence whether her black dress might not have some color or a bit of a plunging neckline.

The film offers constant banter about role-playing,[7] and we experience a combination of suspense and comedy when Eve's roles collide, and she just misses being discovered by Smith and others. In the relatively safe setting of Eve's home, we laugh when Eve's mother is told the truth—Jonathan is a fugitive wanted for murder and Mr. Smith is a detective—to which the mother responds that she doesn't believe either story. These truths are told by Eve's father, who otherwise likes to deceive, which only adds to the amusement. The one person who is consistently honest (with the exception of when he lures Jonathan out of Eve's home) is Smith, whose truthfulness with Eve when he leaves her the evening he met her, contrasts deeply with her deception. Again, comic contrast can have a darker side.

Figure 12 In *Stage Fright* the reaction shots of Eve, played by Jane Wyman, reveal her horror as she listens to Jonathan's confession. The shadows on her face draw us to her eyes and add to the sense of claustrophobia. *Stage Fright* directed by Alfred Hitchcock. © Warner Bros. 1950. All rights reserved.

The father-daughter relationship has a certain level of playfulness and beauty, but both family members are in fact endangered by aiding a fugitive. As with many Hitchcock heroes, however, Eve, who is animated by the idea of protecting a wrongly accused man, expresses more courage than fear in relentlessly pursuing the knowledge she believes will exonerate Jonathan. The film ends with a twist: not only does Eve fall for the detective, also Jonathan turns out to be the killer, and he threatens Eve's life. Reaction shots disclose her horror as she listens to Jonathan confess his murder (Figure 12), but she wills herself to play still one more role: she pretends that she will help him escape.

Eve leads Jonathan out, locks the entrance, and screams for the police. Just as Eve was duped by Jonathan, so was the audience misled: the film opens with Jonathan's long flashback to Eve that is later unveiled as a lie. Hitchcock shows how easily we can be deceived.

Not only can the murderer and his accomplice be charming and deceptive. Via close-ups, Hitchcock also exposes the criminal's vulnerability. In the prop room below the stage, Jonathan is disheveled and frightened. In her final scene, Charlotte is in soft focus: she becomes the lost soul who was willing and able to move another person to murder her husband when her love for her husband was met with rejection, even hate. Moreover, just before Charlotte is uncovered, she exhibits a certain kindness and warmth. In other words, Hitchcock gives even cold, calculating villains moments of humanity.

In *North by Northwest* the widespread role-playing encompasses self-reflexivity, power relations, and the comic. At the auction Vandamm says to Thornhill: "Has anyone ever told you that you overplay your various roles rather severely, Mr. Kaplan?" The line is amusing, for Thornhill is trying to be himself, but Vandamm sees him as pretending to be someone other than Kaplan. The dialogue continues, as Thornhill says: "Apparently the only performance that's going to satisfy you is when I play dead." Vandamm responds; "Your very next role. You will be quite convincing, I assure you." Though Vandamm refers to his desire to kill the person he thinks is Kaplan, the truth is that Cary Grant playing Thornhill playing Kaplan does in fact play dead, as Eve shoots him with blanks, and the role-playing is good enough to convince Vandamm, so the criminal ends up saying a truth he never intended.

Vandamm and the Professor act as surrogate directors for Thornhill, orchestrating scenarios for him, instrumentalizing him, or both. Indeed, one way in which Hitchcock integrates self-reflection with analyses of power relations is by using directorial moments in his works, some of which could be called director's films, that is, films in which the action is directed by one of the characters or in which we see a conflict of two or more competing directors.[8] In Hitchcock's director's films we see a fascinating combination of self-reflection and power struggles. In *Murder!* Sir John directs Fane in a partially written screenplay, but Fane refuses to play his assigned role; Fane writes his own ending, which costs him his life but allows him to retain control, with Sir John relegated to the audience. In *Stage Fright* Eve's father takes action into his own hands, directing the little boy to bring the blood-stained doll to Charlotte and later proposing the charade with the hidden microphone, which is designed to get Charlotte to confess. *Strangers on a Train* has one primary director, Bruno, and one recalcitrant player, Guy. In *Shadow of a Doubt* two competing directors emerge, Charlie and Uncle Charlie. Transitions between surrogate directors often reflect power shifts. In *Rope* Brandon stages the action within the film world until Rupert usurps him. In *Dial M for Murder* the husband directs the action, and when the script is rewritten, he adjusts, but in the end, the detective has the final word: he recreates what happened on the day of the murder and narrates the action as Tony incriminates himself. Often an evil figure directs the action, as in *Lifeboat*, where Willie reigns until the mob kills him. In some cases, the director within the film world has benevolent intentions and seeks to help another. This is clearly the case in *Spellbound* and *Marnie*; in both cases a love interest overlaps with the effort to heal the other. Even in seemingly less self-reflexive works, directorial moments occur. Once Manny is arrested, the police in *The Wrong Man* direct his every movement, asking him to repeat multiple actions, such as having him writing out a dictation and humiliating him before shop owners. Manny even appears on a sound stage with a microphone that blocks his body and symbolically his identity. *Vertigo* has two competing surrogate directors. Elster dominates the first part, Scottie the second. Not by chance, Hitchcock arranges his cameo in the shipyard (and so on Elster's terrain) just before Scottie appears. Together Elster and Scottie seem to constitute Hitchcock: one manipulates the audience for suspense and intrigue, the other awakens a sense of longing for higher meaning. Fascinating are the films where no one is in charge or where at some point forces beyond the characters take over, as at the end of *Vertigo* or in *The Trouble with Harry* and *The Birds*. Here the absence of a surrogate director exposes not power relations but forces at play beyond our will, which can be horrific and so test human capacities or providential and so guide human beings who might otherwise be lost.

A long debate asks whether knowledge aids or hinders the artist. Vico was the first modern thinker to bring the issue into sharp focus. He developed an analysis of art as in a privileged sense pre-reflexive, which gave him new insight into the oral tradition, as he articulated how poetry could develop over time without its aesthetic unity being destroyed. We find in the Homeric epics not the calculated creation of one person but a national poetry that evolved over centuries. Despite living in an age that felt repelled by the Middle Ages, Vico recognized the greatness of Dante. In Vico's analysis, Dante matched Homer in imagination and in the range and sublimity of his language, and was found wanting only in his learnedness, which for a poet can be but a burden. Vico's position, advanced in analogous ways by Hegel, argues that art and philosophy are distinct spheres and that as soon as an artwork becomes philosophical, it becomes less artistic. A competing tradition, represented by Aristotle and Horace, among others, views philosophical reflection as healthy for art insofar as it educates artists, offering them moral and formal guidance, including helping them understand the distinction of genres. In elevating reflection, modern art is aligned with the second tradition, but it differs to the extent that it integrates reflection into the artwork itself, thus representing an implicit challenge to both traditions.

Modern art has received some of its strongest impulses and most distinguishing characteristics by integrating the very self-reflexive tendencies that Vico and Hegel lament. Reflection on art has become for modern artists a central element of the artwork itself. Reflection need not be outside the artwork, functioning as a guide to the artist, nor does reflection necessarily harm the artwork. Instead, reflection within the artwork becomes a means of making art more fascinating—and, one can add, more philosophical. But too much self-reflection awakens the challenge that the sensuous moment, the indirection of art, can be diminished, the aesthetic moment weakened or even destroyed. Vico recognized the limits of too much self-reflection, as did those modernists who turned to primitive art. A further danger is that self-reflection about art within an artwork can render art solipsistic, such that art turns inward, becoming only about itself and not also about the world.

Hitchcock integrates self-reflection into his films without making them about self-reflection as an end in itself and without excluding the world. He has achieved an attractive and modestly uncommon synthesis: self-reflexive cinema that does not interrupt the audience's viewing pleasure and that integrates into its self-reflection new windows onto reality. Moreover, in an age in which self-reflection is a dominant characteristic of culture and includes no small amount of tortured circling around one's own private subjectivity, Hitchcock's characters tend to be refreshingly intuitive. When they are not, as with Jeff in *Rear Window*, they are mocked, in this case by the blunt and perceptive nurse Stella. It is charming that many of Hitchcock's heroes, as in *The 39 Steps* and *North by Northwest,* act with powers they themselves do not grasp, including information whose meaning they do not understand.

These characters move through a complex world with an unassuming ease. Recurring integration of the comic further removes Hitchcock from tortured self-reflection. *The Farmer's Wife* mocks misdirected introspection and deliberation, and *The Trouble with Harry* pokes fun at all forms of self-obsession. *Family Plot* is a self-reflexive homage to common Hitchcock motifs, including role-playing and doubling. Virtually every character plays multiple roles, and the piling on of role-playing is richly comic.

Genre and Mode

Hitchcock is most frequently associated with the suspense film. How the action will unfold is uncertain, and the audience is invested in the fate of one or more characters. We hope for the heroes against difficult odds but also fear for them. Uncertainty and concern are the two elements that Carroll elevates in his analysis of suspense ("Paradox"). Carroll makes the cogent argument that we enjoy watching a film for a second or third time (and even experience suspense although the outcome is known to us) because we can in the course of the unfolding drama "entertain the thought that the relevant outcome is uncertain or improbable" ("Paradox" 87). We know the truth but suspend that knowledge as we delight in the unfolding drama and wrap ourselves in it. The experience of suspense arises because we suspend disbelief for the sake of imagination, much as we know that the reality of the film is not the same reality as our own reality—and yet we immerse ourselves in that fictive world as if it were real and feel genuine fear and longing on behalf of the characters.

Hitchcock himself emphasizes that we must be able to empathize at some level with the hero, that is, we must care about them. This identification can arise from formal strategies: the camera work and editing may encourage us to see the world from the hero's perspective. It can arise from our own conflation of the reality beyond and within the film, that is, our concern for the actors whom we know and admire who are playing the characters with whom we identify. It can also arise from a common sense of humanity or a common set of values; we may share the values of the hero and know the hero to be in the right. When we empathize with the hero also in terms of values, we experience the two dominant emotions of suspense—fear and hope—and these are not by chance the two sentiments that since Plato have been associated with courage. Courageous heroes overcome their fears with the hope of realizing a vision of what is good.

Hitchcock was not drawn to other film genres of his day, such as the Western, the gangster film, science fiction, or animation, though some of Hitchcock's films, while remaining suspense films, overlap with other genres or styles: *Shadow of a Doubt*, *Notorious*, *Strangers on a Train*, *The Wrong Man, Rear Window*, and *Vertigo* all include elements of film noir, and *The Birds* and *Psycho* are also horror films. Hitchcock can perhaps best be understood if we consider those genres, such as tragedy and comedy, that situate his works in a larger aesthetic tradition and give them a bit more nuance than the simple concept suspense film (or thriller), which as a genre designation tends to capture action but not characters and ideas.

Tragedy

Hitchcock often integrates the possibility of tragedy and has even directed a few tragedies. His earliest tragedy is his last silent film, *The Manxman*. In this love triangle, there is no possible resolution without suffering or disaster. Because of delays, arising from the good intentions of trying to circumvent suffering, the tragedy intensifies. Pete, a poor fisherman on the Isle of Man, and his dear friend Philip, a successful lawyer, both love Kate. When Kate's father rejects Pete, the young man resolves to return wealthy. Kate will wait, and Philip promises to watch over her. But when news reaches the island that Pete has died, Philip and Kate indulge the love for one another that had blossomed during Pete's absence. But Pete unexpectedly returns. Philip insists that Kate honor her promise. Pete and Kate marry, but Kate is miserable and leaves Pete after a child is born. In her absence Pete shows himself to be a loving father. When Philip elevates career and friendship over Kate, she attempts suicide. Kate is brought before Philip on his first day as judge, and he is eventually exposed as Kate's previous lover and the father of her child. Philip resigns his position, and the community mocks him and Kate. Pete is left alone.

The hero of *I Confess*, Father Logan, enacts for the greatest part of the film a tragedy. Logan suffers two kinds of tragedy, most prominently, a tragedy of self-sacrifice: he does the good knowing

Figure 13 In the courtroom of *I Confess*, Father Logan, portrayed by Montgomery Clift, faces off against the crown prosecutor, played by Brian Aherne. Divine and secular justice stand in opposition to one another. *I Confess* directed by Alfred Hitchcock. © Warner Bros. 1953. All rights reserved.

that he will suffer for it, that is, he preserves the sanctity of confession, even when he himself is tried for the murder to which Keller confessed. Logan perseveres, adhering to the confidentiality of confession, and the greatness of his act leads to his suffering. The film also displays a more complex tragic structure, a collision between the divine justice of preserving the inviolability of confession and the earthly justice of apprehending and sentencing a self-confessed murderer (Figure 13). In conflict throughout the film are the demands of religious confidentiality and the claims of secular justice.

Eventually, not only Logan's life but also the lives of others are endangered. Keller murders his wife and then in flight kills a hotel worker, yet the priest still refuses to betray the sacrament of confession. The one-sidedness of Logan's position is reinforced when it is necessary for earthly justice (the police) to shoot Keller and so save the priest's life. The higher principle may be divine justice, but the divine needs the assistance of the earthly powers.

Logan's one-sidedness has two facets. First, he adopts a religious perspective that denies the claims of secular justice, thereby allowing Keller to kill two additional persons and endanger even more. It is almost as if Logan lives in a transcendent sphere, beyond the concerns of other humans. If one lives in the first world and ignores the fourth, the fourth world will go its own way. Second, even as Logan adheres to a religious and moral code, he finds it difficult to adapt to the needs of others, primarily Keller and Ruth, and so convince them of his position without first causing more suffering than seems necessary. Both Keller and Ruth confess to Logan in various ways (Perkins). Logan, with his eyes transfixed on the divine, has difficulties approaching other human beings as individuals. His imperative to Keller is clear: Keller must turn himself in, but when Keller desires to speak with Logan again, to be counseled in his fear and to experience Logan's empathy, the priest curtly asserts that he has nothing more to add. Logan does not seek out ways to assist Keller and can't fully adapt to his weaknesses. We admire Logan for his moral steadfastness, yet this very greatness is also a weakness: he cannot empathize with the weaknesses of others. An excess of one virtue can mean the neglect of another, and such one-sidedness has negative repercussions. In his unwavering insistence on truth and morality, Father Logan bears a certain similarity to the tragic hero of stubbornness who abstractly pursues a moral ideal, leaving victims in his wake.

When Logan meets with Ruth on the ferry, he denies the existence of any love between them and abruptly counsels her to stop hurting herself. He speaks openly and directly, but also tactlessly. His condescension offends her, and the scene concludes with Ruth and Logan turning away from one another. Logan has trouble dealing with others in intimate settings. His isolation gives him strength for his moral code but takes him away from others. Not only would a less tragic character be right, but he would also attempt to work with Keller to turn him toward God. And he would know how to encourage Ruth's acceptance of his calling. Logan eventually obtains both goals, but only after Ruth is disoriented and humiliated and Keller has suffered alone and hurt others. The black and white of the film formally underscores the black-and-white morality of Logan, who cannot easily deal with shades in between (which is, ironically, precisely where the law places him—not guilty but only because of insufficient evidence).[9]

As we know already from Sophocles' *Antigone*, the structure of tragedy often involves a conflict between protecting a more private sphere, be it family or the divine, and a more public sphere, including the interests of the state. In both versions of *The Man Who Knew Too Much* the parents elevate the safety of their child even if it means possibly allowing a political assassination. Their conflict has dimensions of a Hegelian tragedy insofar as they are culpable however they act. In *Shadow of a Doubt* Charlie protects the family's idyllic atmosphere and her mother's love of her brother, thereby risking that her uncle will take another victim. All of these conflicts, including the private-public antagonism in *I Confess*, are in the end favorably resolved. Indeed, distinctive about Hitchcock is his consistent movement beyond tragedy.

In the second *Man Who Knew Too Much* Dr. McKenna wants to protect his child and so is willing to be silent about an assassination, but he recognizes: "I don't know what's the right thing to do." He chooses at first not to involve the police, which means that he must act as a hero himself, and he rises to the occasion, escaping captivity, struggling with the assassin until he falls to his death, and saving his son by eluding his kidnapper. The film is a serious and substantial conflict that could end in tragedy but does not: the assassination attempt is thwarted, the evil figures weaken (Mrs. Drayton does not want to kill the boy) or are overcome, the boy is saved, and the family is reunited. Despite the deaths, including the early death of Bernard, the film moves beyond tragedy.

Hitchcock is not only aware of the often-inevitable conflict of goods, he seeks to recognize which good is higher, and for Hitchcock that higher good is rarely represented by the state. In *Notorious* and *North by Northwest*, we see a conflict of goods, involving the state and the individual, but the institutions instrumentalize the individuals. Obsession with knowledge can lead to immoral acts. Larrue's primary duty in *I Confess* is to protect the citizens, but in seeking the truth, he violates this ethical demand. His desire to know, which is good and is part of his profession, is coupled with a willingness to risk innocent lives, as when he says that Keller must be taken alive. To serve the people, he must find out the truth about the murders, but to do this he endangers the people he serves.

Vertigo likewise has dimensions of a tragedy, less in the form of a Hegelian conflict of two goods and more in the sense of a Hegelian collision that is impossible to resolve.[10] At the end, Judy, who pretended to play Madeline and in that role betrayed Scottie, genuinely loves Scottie. She had played the roles of being Madeleine and falling in love with Scottie but then became one of the roles she was playing, but she had already deceived Scottie and could not go back. It is, as she says to him, "too late." When Scottie rediscovers her, she risks her freedom to enter back into a relationship with him, but the effort cannot be realized. Scottie loves not Judy, but the Madeleine she played. No resolution is possible, for Scottie loves the ideal in his imagination, and insofar as reality differs from that illusion, that ideal, he cannot accept it, let alone love it; he must hate it. At the end of the film, he, too, recognizes that it is "too late" to turn back.

Time is an essential element of tragedy. *Vertigo* is very much about the effect of the past on the present, which is an element not only of necrophilia but also of tragedy, for some misdeeds seem too great to be forgiven. When Scottie comes desperately close, a higher force enters the scene, not chance, but fate. Neither person is able to realize their ideal, and the appearance of the nun, with her "God have mercy," seals the tragedy. In reality, the ideal is not fully possible, and that, so Hegel, is how tragedy emerges. The ideal is split into two, and the doubling prominent in the film, not only the doubling of Judy and Madeleine, but the contrast between the real but less erotic Midge and the unreal but alluring Madeleine, underscores the tragic dualism. Yet what makes this film a tragedy loosely compatible with Cohen's concept of humor is our sympathy for these troubled characters. Judy is dead, and we lament that. Scottie is entirely broken, and we bemoan that. We sympathize with the characters, both of whom acted out of an idealism of love. Our focus is less on their faults, Judy's contribution to the real Madeleine's death and Scottie's apparent adultery, his perverse relation with death, or his manipulation of Judy, than on their desperate and human longing for an ideal in reality.

Comedy

Not only *The Farmer's Wife, Waltzes from Vienna*, *Mr. and Mrs. Smith,* and *The Trouble with Harry* are comedies,[11] scarcely a Hitchcock film is without comedy, humor, or irony. Even one of his non-pure comedies, *To Catch a Thief*, has been aptly likened to the style and atmosphere of Lubitsch, a master of comedy (Durgnat 268). Throughout his oeuvre, Hitchcock does a remarkable job interweaving suspense and comedy. Into that mix, he also integrates power relations and love.

Take as an example the comic thriller *The Lady Vanishes*. Iris knows that she is being duped, and no one believes her until finally the musicologist Gilbert, with whom she had a difficult encounter the previous evening, placates her and later, when he uncovers a clue, becomes fully convinced. Iris is certain of the truth and fights to reveal it against those who are willing to be bribed (an ironic echo, for Iris had bribed the innkeeper to kick out the noisy musicologist the night before). She also battles those who don't want to become involved, either because they want to pursue other interests (in this case cricket) or stay out of the papers (because of already illicit actions). The name of the lady who vanishes, Froy, rhymes with joy: the plot is in some ways a comic series of events designed to restore merriment, which Iris, it is clear, would not have found in her impending marriage. So, at the train station she, too, vanishes, and her fiancé searches in vain. As in traditional comedy, Iris at first thinks she loves someone else, but the events reveal her to be wrong. However, about the vanishing lady, she is right. The film effectively interweaves power relations, suspense, comedy, and romance. Among those who are killed in this film are a barrister who is out for himself and who abandons the woman with whom he is having an affair and some of those fighting the evil characters. Iris exhibits courage, as does Gilbert, who risks his life. Even the Brits whose main interest had been crickets become fully engaged in the mission. Amusingly, at the end, Gilbert cannot remember the secret tune because he keeps humming "The Wedding March." Love displaces power relations.

A recurring element in the comic tradition is a focus on subjectivity, including the protagonist's self-obsession, which is mocked, because they do not know what they think they know, because broader forces delimit their subjectivity, or in the case of evil characters, such as the comic Tartuffe, because their devious plans fail. In the overwhelmingly comic *Family Plot*, the frequent high angle shots underscore the idea that the individuals do not control their own fates. The unraveling of the protagonist's conscious intentions can come from a variety of factors, including chance and fortune. Hitchcock's affinity for comedy reinforces his occasional elevation of nature. In *The Lady Vanishes* we see an abundance of animals—a reference to the realm of nature over that of consciousness. The integration of love and nature harks back to the comic tradition and allows Hitchcock to link his private stories with a larger, symbolic narrative. Consider the walk in *Spellbound* or the forest reunion in *North by Northwest*. By integrating the larger, natural world, such works delimit individual subjects. Comedies end with the transcendence of pure subjectivity, with love, even at times multiple marriages or unions, as in *The Trouble with Harry*. Comic works mock otherworldliness and absent-mindedness. Consider the reader who is so absorbed in his intellectual world, as with the doctor in *The Trouble with Harry*, that he is oblivious to the body over which he stumbles. It is appropriate that the artist in this comic film, Sam, receive not a cash payment, but a gift for each of his friends and for himself a double bed. Earlier he seems to lose his chance at a sale because he is so absorbed in helping Miss Gravely get ready for her date; in true comic fashion, however, his selflessness is in the end rewarded.

The Trouble with Harry engages the comic mode partly by its natural setting, which suggests that the subjects are hardly as important as they think they are; partly by the double-courtship, which affirms the collective (including the old and the young); and partly by its mockery of agency (in the end no one killed Harry, for he died of natural causes). Here, as in other comedies, chance and providence reign, and self-obsession and self-importance are ridiculed. Even the metaphysical reflection early on—that it was perhaps Harry's destiny to die at that point—delimits individual agency. The chance events that bring the couples together and which are tied up with death, are part of a larger pattern that can be reinterpreted as a cosmic force, as divine grace.[12] Brill notes that the film offers a "profound confidence that death lacks the power to destroy and that hope can scarcely help but prosper" (284). Hitchcock's embrace of a divine and beneficent providence that transcends subjectivity is not unrelated to his Catholicism.[13] In *The Trouble with Harry* the iteration central to the comic mode is interwoven with religion. Whereas dualism represents collision and thus tragedy, three is the number of synthesis and of course Christian transcendence: three people mistakenly confess they committed the crime, three times the body is buried and disinterred, three bullets are fired (and accounted for), three times the doctor appears at the scene, and three times the door opens on its own.

Both *Rich and Strange* and *Mr. and Mrs. Smith*, have aspects of what Stanley Cavell calls the comedy of remarriage,[14] even if the latter, with its high-key lighting, is much more joyous and optimistic. In each film, the couples become disengaged but then rediscover one another and return. Affirmation of what we have is greater once we have contemplated alternatives. The structure of affirming what is present after weighing alternatives is also evident in *The Farmer's Wife,* which Maurice Yacowar justly calls one of Hitchcock's most underrated works (47). The film reinforces the comic theme of the heroes not quite knowing themselves and needing to be led by others to their own subconscious goals.

Beyond Tragedy and Comedy

Hitchcock once called his works melodramas (*Hitchcock on Hitchcock* 2.76–77). If by melodrama, one means a series of seemingly improbable, strange, and bizarre events, with "lots of ups and downs," that elicit in the audience strong emotions, then the designation makes sense (*Alfred* 42). In traditional melodrama, however, characters tend to be black and white, and obstacles are rarely taken seriously (Brooks). Hitchcock's fascination with suspense and ambiguity works against any but an idiosyncratic concept of melodrama.[15] Traditional melodrama does not give us what Hitchcock favors, "sympathetic and intelligent criminals, attractive murderers" (*Hitchcock on Hitchcock* 2.82). Moreover, his interest in understatement and realism is removed from traditional melodrama, with its psychological simplicity, its unchanging characters, and its moral archetypes (Roche, *Tragedy* 250–5).

Indeed, if we were to think of a serious genre beyond tragedy that fits Hitchcock, not melodrama, but the problem play and, even more so, the drama of reconciliation would rise as worthy candidates. The three genres—melodrama, problem play, and drama of reconciliation—can be understood dialectically as three variations of drama beyond tragedy and comedy (Roche, *Tragedy* 250–5). Melodrama is by far the simplest. The antithetical genre in the sequence is the problem play. Here the moment of reconciliation is bitter, coming at an extreme price that mitigates the extent of reconciliation; partial, lacking either fullness or stability; or suspect, not fully earned, but artificial and so undeserved. The resolution, being partial or arbitrary, is called into question, as are the characters and institutions that appear to guarantee harmony. *Blackmail* fits the concept of a problem play more or less perfectly. The most famous creator of problem plays is Shakespeare, who is partially echoed in the laughing jester with which this film concludes (Figure 1). *Sabotage* is another example: the seemingly positive future of the detective and the widow will always be marked by guilt: Mrs. Verloc killed her husband, and though we understand that she had a rationale and the husband seemed to co-will it as a kind of atonement, she and the detective are silent about the crime.

The majority of Hitchcock's works fit a different genre, one that is modestly unusual in modernity, the drama of reconciliation.[16] The concept is briefly introduced by Hegel, who elaborates three dramatic genres, tragedy, comedy, and a third form ("the deeper mediation of tragic and comic conception"), in which resolution is achieved on stage: "Instead of acting with comical perverseness, subjectivity is filled with the seriousness of dignified relations and substantial characters, while the tragic firmness of will and the depth of the collisions are so far mollified and smoothed out, that there can emerge a reconciliation of interests and a harmonious unification of individuals and their aims" (15:532). Hegel mentions in this context Aeschylus' *Eumenides*, Sophocles' *Philoctetes*, and Goethe's *Iphigenia in Tauris*. One could add as further examples from ancient Greece Sophocles' *Oedipus at Colonus* and from Hegel's era Lessing's *Nathan the Wise*. We see in the drama of reconciliation a collision with potentially tragic results that nonetheless is averted, and so the work ends like a comedy, with a positive resolution; the conflict, however, is not insignificant, but substantial and moves along the border of tragedy. The drama of reconciliation can be defined either as an initially tragic conflict that culminates in reconciliation or as a comedy whose conflict is substantial, instead of superficial, and in the end resolved. Because film is a temporal art, like literature, it lends itself to dwelling on negativity that is eventually overcome. Moreover, whereas literature has moved away from the drama of reconciliation, film has not. As a newer art, film is less burdened by the tradition of modernity, which shies away from reconciliation. Hitchcock himself noted that he wanted his films to relieve tension and ensure some element of poetic justice (*Alfred* 171).

Most of Hitchcock's films end with a gesture beyond tragedy. Hitchcock's Catholicism reinforces this tendency, for Catholicism has a strong undercurrent of hope for universal salvation and while acknowledging original sin, it emphasizes it less than do many strands of Protestantism. Not surprisingly, then, we see profound gestures of hope in Hitchcock's most visibly Catholic film. As Logan leaves the court building in *I Confess*, he is at a low point: intellectual ridicule shifts to physical abuse. Alma can no longer hold back: she rushes through the crowd. As she approaches Logan, her husband takes out his pistol and shoots toward them, killing his wife. Alma immediately asks for forgiveness ("Vergib es mir!" in German or "Forgive me!"), and Logan absolves her of her sins. That she returns to her original tongue just before she dies suggests that the confession reveals her inner core.

During the ensuing chase, Larrue pushes Logan, asking him why he is trying to protect Keller. When Keller is finally cornered, the murderer hollers, "So, the priest talked. How kindly he hears my confession. And then, a little shame, a little violence, that's all it takes to make him talk. It was too much for you. You are a coward like all other people, aren't you? A hypocrite." Logan walks toward Keller, and as Keller raises his gun, one of the policemen shoots and kills Keller. Logan rushes to him as he falls. As his wife did earlier, Keller asks for the priest's forgiveness: "Oh, Father, help me. Forgive." Where at the film's opening Keller asserts, "No one can help me," the film closes with Keller's genuine plea for help. Confession had earlier been a means of escape for Keller, an unrepentant act as well as the catalyst for Logan's suffering; this institution, whose sacredness Logan preserves, becomes at the film's conclusion a tool of salvation. Keller's confession both opens and closes the film, but the symmetry is representative less of a static circle than a progressive spiral, a movement from darkness (the church, where the lattice of the confessional had metaphorically imprisoned Keller) (Figure 5) to light (the hotel room where Keller movingly asks for forgiveness).[17] In the film's last words Logan absolves Keller: "Te absolvo in nomine Patris et Filii et Spiritus Sancti." Keller's underlying love for Logan, the devil's recognition of God, is here stressed. Keller's turn is late, but he is like the repentant criminal whom Jesus forgave even as he was dying on the cross (Lk. 23:43). Christ identified with the lowliest of the low, and in this final scene, the priest and murderer adopt a pieta-like pose. The priest's deed is recognized, and Logan redeems Keller. The reconciliation Hitchcock portrays is a consummation not only of Keller's hidden longing but also of the priest's holiness and forgiveness. Logan's self-sacrifice and collision are not final. The devil recognizes God and is thereby reintegrated. The depth of Keller's malice, the substance of the idea of reconciliation, and the modesty of the gesture guard against the film falling into sentimentality.

Ruth's self-centeredness persists until she finally recognizes in the nobility of Logan's act—the priest's self-denial and non-betrayal of the sacrament—that his vocation is indeed sacred. Her simple and subtle departure with Pierre ("Pierre, take me home.") represents recognition of Logan even as she now binds herself in a new way to her loving husband.[18] Ruth is ennobled by Logan, just as Alma was earlier. Likewise, Larrue is affected. His first gaze at Logan is directed downward from Villette's window, and, as the camera suggests, the vision is of one eye only, a merely partial perspective.[19] Larrue's final gaze is upward and full of admiration.

We see gestures toward reconciliation in many other Hitchcock films, indeed all but a half dozen of his fifty-three feature films. This is partly what leads a critic such as Brill to speak of Hitchcock's films as comedies when, however, the potential of tragedy is very much present (32).[20] *Downhill* is a tragedy of self-sacrifice, layered with a portrayal of the hero's weaknesses, that could have ended in death but offers the audience late moments of recognition and forgiveness. *Young and Innocent* is comic insofar as it is a love story in which hurdles must be overcome to reach a happy end, and it contains ample moments of slapstick and of the appearance-reality dichotomy common in comedies, but the hero, Tisdall, is charged with murder, and the circumstantial evidence is strong. Erica must essentially betray her father, the constable, in order to aid Tisdall, thus evoking a tragic conflict. That the work ends harmoniously, though it could in principle have ended otherwise, is the basic structure of most of Hitchcock's works. We see here an eventual folding of the loving couple into the wider social fabric and even recognition of the validity of the police and of law and order. The individuals find their fulfillment in the wider whole. Suspense works best when the potential consequences are dire. Hitchcock interlaces suspense, including the hero's potential for conviction or death, with comedy, including bizarre incongruities, moments of relief, and a positive resolution.

Hitchcock notes that the triumph of goodness is not always possible, but he does acknowledge that his works are "fundamentally optimistic" (*Hitchcock on Hitchcock* 2.200). In *The 39 Steps, Saboteur*, and *Notorious*, each of which borders on potential tragedy, the hero and heroine survive and come together. Alicia and Devlin, for example, eventually learn to trust and confide in the other. Eve and Smith are reunited at the end of *Stage Fright*, Eve just having escaped death, but their bond of love, which had emerged earlier in the taxi, is now layered with a "slow, slightly discordant, minor-key variation on the piano theme which marked the beginning of their love" (Abel 12). The ending is harmonic, but muted, and that is the way in which Hitchcock prefers happy ends, with a touch of ambiguity. As a result, his dramas of reconciliation are never far from problem plays. Similar is the ending of *Topaz*, in which there is a kind of remarriage and the aversion of an international crisis, but deaths and betrayals lie in their wake. Conflict in Hitchcock tends to be triggered by a malignant action or a difficult situation or crisis, which gives some evidence of original sin and a disharmonic world, but the conflict is almost always resolved, which reinforces the virtues of courage and love as well as the concept of providence. Hitchcock elevates the human capacity to see the positive in the negative. For Hitchcock evil is deeply present but it does not prevail in any ultimate sense. To see in Hitchcock simply "a universe governed by a 'malign spirit,'" as does Mladen Dolar (43), or similarly Slavoj Žižek (212), is to truncate the complexity of his worldview. Even films that stress depravity and brutality, such as *Frenzy*, tend to include some gesture to poetic justice.

Four early British films—*Easy Virtue, The Manxman, Juno and the Paycock* and *The Skin Game*—and two late classics—*Vertigo* and *Psycho*—have arguably Hitchcock's most negative endings. *Easy Virtue*, based on a play by Noël Coward, is a satire, which focuses on the deficiencies of reality, even if it contains modest moments of generosity, such as Larita's encouraging Sarah to marry John; on the whole, it is a negative work, but as a negation of negativity, it implies, without showing, the ideal it fails to reach. *The Manxman* remains a tragedy, but there is modest consolation insofar as Pete has once before exhibited resilience; Kate has been rescued from suicide and revealed the truth instead of continuing to live a lie; and Philip has in the end likewise taken off his mask, resigned his position, and been reunited with Kate. The negative ending of *Juno and the Paycock* is partly driven by Seán O'Casey's play, but even here we notice a modest change. Whereas the original play ends with Boyle lamenting the terrible state of the world and unaware of his son's murder, the film brings us a series of scenes with eyes turned upward, first, Johnny praying the rosary on his way to death; second, Mary questioning God's existence; and, third, Juno praying to the Virgin Mary and then asking Jesus to take away "this murderous hate" and give us "thine own eternal love." The film ends there and does not include O'Casey's bleak and ironic final scene. *The Skin Game* takes its structure and much of its dialogue from an earlier drama by John Galsworthy; conflict between two families, led by a waning landowner and a successful factory owner, drives the narrative. The film, like its source, has a negative ending, though Hitchcock softens it in two modest ways: first, when the crass industrialist Hornblower hears of his daughter-in-law's sordid past, he is far more conciliatory toward her than in the original; second, after the dialogue is over, the film shows the industrialist's youngest son and the landowner's daughter reach for each other's hand, an unassuming sign of potential future reconciliation.

Of the two later films that are especially negative even at their conclusion, *Vertigo* and *Psycho*, Brill rightly notes that these are "not particularly characteristic of Hitchcock's films in general" (200). *Vertigo* is overwhelmingly dark but not without positive moments. Even though the ideal and real can never be fully united, we sympathize with those who long for the impossible. The film's final line, "God have mercy," while accompanied by death, at least gestures toward a higher realm, and the film ends with a major chord. The plot of *Psycho* offers little consolation. Only in the realm of the idea do we understand that Sam has resolved to marry Marion and that Marion has decided to return the stolen money, but neither intention can be realized. Still, Norman's crimes will cease, and the final shot breaks with the film's dominant downward imagery; we see instead Marion's car rising out of the swamp. Even Hitchcock's negative works tend to be not only negative; they retain some element of ambiguity.

Other works with negative endings have at least a modest level of positive resonance or ambiguity. In *The Paradine Case,* the alluring Mrs. Paradine will be hanged, and the attorney is exhausted as well as humiliated, but his wife accepts him. The film ends with their reconciliation. Even in *The Birds*, which has been described as having the most radical and most unresolved ending of all Hitchcock films (Sterritt 121), serious recognition finally arrives between Lydia and Melanie. Throughout the film they wrestle with one another. Lydia, a widow, fears being abandoned if her adult son marries, whereas Melanie comments to Annie, Mitch's ex-girlfriend, who likewise experienced Lydia's coldness, that the mother should be thinking instead of gaining a daughter. In fact, Melanie herself, although she comes from privilege, clearly suffers from her mother having abandoned the family. In the end, the figures' emergence from the dark house, with blood wounds on Melanie's bandaged head, which almost resembles a religious coif, and blood on Mitch's white shirt, which has elements of a resurrection, especially when coupled with the earlier pieta pose when Mitch carried Melanie down the stairs. In the car Melanie rests her head on Lydia's shoulder; Lydia holds her close and fondly presses her wrist. The distinctive green that links Melanie's clothing and Lydia's truck prefigures their eventual union as well as the possibility of rebirth. The inclusion of the love birds adds a further "optimistic note" (Truffaut 288). As befits modernity, we see gestures, not a full reconciliation. Uncertainty remains as to why the birds are attacking. In the final shot, light shines through, but the birds and the dark clouds dominate the apocalyptic landscape.

Another apparent exception to the norm of reconciliation is *The Wrong Man*, where even though the husband, Manny, is freed, the stress breaks his wife, Rose. Manny is imprisoned, and Rose is locked into her own private world of depression. Still, there are two hints at reconciliation—one profound, the other perfunctory. Manny is animated by religion, as is evident from his having rosary beads with him at all times. We are given three shots of the rosary beads. After almost giving way to despair, Manny prays for strength before an image of the sacred heart. Notably, he exhibits courage in one of the ways in which Plato analyzed the virtue, not risking his life but overcoming adversity, enduring pain. Elevating hope over fear and despair is also of course a Christian virtue. Manny was arrested because of the chance occurrence that he, who looks like the criminal, was at the insurance agency on a given day. The two persons who could have provided an alibi turn out to be deceased. Normally, the Hitchcock hero reverses their fate by searching for knowledge and evidence and battling with evil. Here that effort is in vain, and the resolution arises instead from a stroke of unexpected good fortune. The true criminal is apprehended as he seeks to commit another robbery. The coincidence that brings Manny

Figure 14 In *The Wrong Man* when Manny, played by Henry Fonda, prays before the sacred heart of Jesus, we observe him in a close-up as he silently moves his lips. Another image is then superimposed on his face—the real culprit, played by Richard Robbins, who is on his way to another holdup. In a moment of grace, the double will be apprehended and Manny exonerated. *The Wrong Man* directed by Alfred Hitchcock.

into the clear is presented as a moment of grace. When Manny prays before the sacred heart, we observe him in a close-up as he silently moves his lips. Another image is then superimposed on his face—the real culprit, who is on his way to another holdup (Figure 14).

The double walks toward the camera, and his figure, now enlarged, overlaps with Manny's, such that the unity and diversity of their features emerge. Eventually, Manny's image fades away, leaving only the criminal. Jean-Luc Godard calls this a "miracle" (54).[21] It is certainly more than mere chance. We might call it grace. Although Manny is praying here for strength, not justice, he receives both. In other words, just as Manny could not solve the puzzle through a search for knowledge, so he could not do so by prayer; what occurs transcends his subjectivity. The second gesture to reconciliation comes in a postscript, which tells us that two years later Rose was fully cured. Although this final information reaffirms an idea of reconciliation, Hitchcock allegedly protested against the studio intervention.[22] Hitchcock would presumably have preferred greater uncertainty, more of an 'on-the-one-hand, on-the-other-hand' gesture, which would have been more in line with the ambiguity he elevates in his other works. Still, even without the epilogue, the film is more than simply dark.

A film that shows how long and difficult and painful reconciliation can be is *Marnie*. Marnie longs for love and recognition. As a child she was taken out of bed whenever a customer called on her prostitute mother. One night during a thunderstorm, a sailor kisses Marnie, seemingly to comfort her, but Marnie screams, the mother attacks the sailor, a fight ensues, the mother is hurt and calls on Marnie to wield the iron poker against the sailor, who is then killed. Marnie blacks out the incident, save for nightmares and waking disruptions. One legacy, reinforced by the mother's upbringing, is the view that men are vile and touching them is filthy and disgusting. Marnie desperately seeks approval from her mother, who, while loving Marnie, nonetheless remains distant and fails to express love or approval. Marnie steals partly to buy her mother's affection, an act that in its own way mimics the payment for sex that is part of the mother's prehistory. After forced intercourse with Mark, Marnie tries to kill herself, and in free association with Mark, she responds to the word "death" with "me." What eventually opens her up to a potential cure, beyond a slow series of steps along the way, is her confronting the past: her being able to grasp the truth; her understanding that in some odd way her mother has always loved her; and her being willing to forgive herself. Mark says to her: "Marnie, it's time to have a little compassion for yourself."

Given that both Marnie and Mark are ambiguous characters, from whom we are driven away but to whom we are also attracted, we recognize to what extent Hitchcock's moral ambiguity and his loving critique are partners in his overall vision of hope. Although Marnie is a compulsive thief, we root for her not to be caught when we see her stealing money while the cleaner comes closer and closer. We anticipate that Marnie will after all get caught by the inadvertent sound of a shoe falling out of her coat pocket, but the cleaner is nearly deaf, as we later learn, so Marnie escapes. When Marnie returns to Mark's safe, we do not want her to steal, just as she does not and cannot, for she is slowly working her way through her neuroses. The zoom-in and track-out of her hand and the money visualize her indecision. Mark is a dominant and confident male, decisive and vital. He breaks all conventional morality, but letting Marnie go would be legally and morally irresponsible, while turning her over to the police would not lead to a cure. He tries to help her and satisfy his curiosity about her mysterious and alluring nature by taming her, as he puts it, or in essence blackmailing her into marriage. She tries to keep him at a distance, yet toward the end, she desperately wants help. "Help me. Oh, God, somebody help me!" she screams. Mark, indifferent to the views of others, tries to aid her: "I don't give one infinitesimal dime what Lil thought or thinks." Three times in the final scene, Mark tells Marnie's mother that she must help Marnie. Mark succeeds in bringing Marnie toward a cure, in helping her battle her past until it becomes a part of her.[23]

In other Hitchcock films that border on tragedy or integrate sadness and suffering, moments of reconciliation surface. *Under Capricorn* offers viewers a deep reconciliation after a series of three sacrifices. Despite not having murdered Hattie's brother, Sam makes a false confession and is imprisoned for seven years. Eventually, Hattie reveals the truth: she killed her brother, a confession that protects Sam from further harm even as it places her in danger; and Charles denies having had a confrontation with Sam, calling his gun wound an accident. He recognizes that despite his love for Hattie, she belongs with her husband. *Rear Window* ends not only with Jeff having endured Thorwald's attack, even if it did cost him another broken leg (a comic touch, given Jeff's itching to get moving again), we see reconciliation across most of the apartment complex: the struggling composer, with whom Miss Lonelyheart has developed a relationship, has finished his song; the couple whose dog was murdered has a new puppy; and Miss Torso has a mate (a comic touch is his smaller size and his appetite for food). Jeff is asleep at the beginning and end of the film, but now Lisa is with him, and we hear the beautiful song that in its troubled emergence mirrored the Jeff-Lisa conflict. The complexities of marriage are nonetheless given a nod, as with the bickering newlyweds and Lisa's reading charade. When Hitchcock gestures toward reconciliation, he often avoids sentimentality by interweaving ambiguity and humor. In *To Catch a Thief*, for example, Francie says to John Robbie after she chases him to his villa, "Mother will love it up here."

The fact that Hitchcock's films tend to end happily reaffirms an idea of providence, of hope in the order of the universe: in the end, despite horrors, threats, and evil, goodness prevails. Joe in *Lifeboat*, trusts God when all seems lost. When the survivors lament that "when we killed the German, we killed our motor," Joe looks up and says, "No. We still got a motor." Joe turns out to be right. The simple fact that Hitchcock portrays evil does not mean that he presupposes, as Leo Braudy would have it, "the malevolence of the natural order" (69). Hitchcock portrays evil *and* its overcoming and so brings us in the direction of a metaphysics that is not simply malevolent. Providence is a religious and philosophical concept. If objective evil makes possible heroic action and forgiveness, then we cannot only despise evil but must both hate it and accept it as part of a complex universe. This allows for an attitude of understanding and loving critique. Evil exists: it must be combated, but it can also be recognized as serving a hidden function, which triggers our understanding of complexity and brings forward unforeseen virtues. Drama unfolds in such a world, for even if evil is theoretically necessary, no necessity exists for any one particular evil, which we are obliged to fight. This insight helps to explain Hitchcock's complex acceptance of evil, even as it must be countered. It further reinforces his tendency to portray evil characters with a certain level of ambiguity. For Hitchcock true goodness emerges from conflict, and a higher power transcends both sides of any antagonism. Providence is reinforced not only by the fact that Hitchcock's plots gesture toward happy endings but also by his recurring suggestion that heroes invariably need the help of others. The phone booth scene in *The Birds*, which offers a mocking popular-culture allusion to the first superhero, Superman, symbolically suggests that as much as Hitchcock venerates the vital and clever individual, in the human world no savior will emerge to stem the attacks. These are calmed only when the characters come together in acts of love and mutual aid.

The theodicy asks two questions: why do good persons suffer and why do evil persons succeed? The discussion of grace and providence has focused on good persons moving beyond their suffering, but Hitchcock is also attentive to bringing evil persons to justice. At times a kind of chance or higher power is at play in ensuring that evil persons do not succeed; one could almost call it divine disfavor. For example, Rupert recognizes the initials of David Kentley in the hat that was mistakenly given to him. A seemingly chance event helps to uncover and bring down the murderers. In *Dial M for Murder* Tony makes two obvious lapses: he mistakes the murderer's latchkey for his own, and he spends too much money in cash too quickly, which results in his being uncovered. Moreover, the scissors, with which Margot saves herself, are on the desk because Tony encouraged Margot to work on his press clippings; symbolically, Tony's self-obsession leads to his self-destruction. One can plan the perfect murder, as Mark says, but in reality, things don't always work out.

In his essays, Hitchcock reflects on the conflict between despairing and hopeful worldviews. He embraces the idea that because the future is hidden, we are allowed to hope: "I've come to believe that a hidden future is one of God's most merciful and exciting gifts" (*Hitchcock on Hitchcock* 1.140). We can meet this puzzle with infinite anxiety and despair, or we can respond to it creatively, playing our part to help justice win, and believing that the story of humanity will end in some kind of higher fulfillment: "In other words, we can live in a state of chronic despair, or we can live with faith in the future, even though it is hidden from us" (*Hitchcock on Hitchcock* 1.141). Hitchcock's films provide suspense because neither we nor the characters know the outcome. That his works tend to end not with despair, but with gestures of hope suggests that his own tentative answer is optimistic. The negativity in his films does not have the final word. Nonetheless, Hitchcock is not blind to continuing challenges—and that is why he can leave unresolved ambiguities and make film after film after film. Though he is hopeful, challenges do not disappear. He seems to have not a simple linear concept of history but a more cyclical one. As Graham suggests at the end of the film to which we now turn, *Shadow of a Doubt*, we must always be vigilant, for the world "seems to go crazy every now and then."

Chapter 3
Ambiguities in *Shadow of a Doubt*

Hitchcock frequently described *Shadow of a Doubt* as his favorite film.[1] The work interweaves essentially all of Hitchcock's great themes and does so with both suspense and humor. *Shadow of a Doubt* addresses uncertainty in intersubjective relations, the burden of knowledge, the dialectic of love and hate, the relationship of the ordinary and extraordinary, and the dynamics of power. It embodies self-reflexive cinema and alludes to a range of genres and modes—the comic, the tragic, and humor. The film embodies two central dimensions of Hitchcock's worldview, the ways in which we can succumb to evil and must endeavor to fight it and the ways in which we can affirm humanity, even in its weakness. Moreover, the film has, as is so often the case with Hitchcock, both universal and historically specific resonance.

The basic plot is the following: Charles Oakley, initially presented as apathetic and tired of the world, visits Santa Rosa, the home of his sister, Emma, and her family, including young Charlie, who adores her charming uncle. Slowly, however, through a series of indirect clues, Charlie senses that her uncle may not be the ideal person she thought he was. Detective Jack Graham strengthens her suspicions, and Charlie discovers that her uncle is the "Merry Widow Murderer." The father, Joe, and the neighbor Herb follow the crimes from afar as they playfully imagine how best to murder each other. However, another suspect is accidentally killed, and the inquiry is closed. Aware that Charlie knows his secret, Uncle Charlie twice tries to kill her. Charlie does not turn him in to the police, as she fears that such a revelation would destroy her mother and her family, so she must challenge him herself. Finally, Charlie gains the upper hand, and Uncle Charlie is forced to leave town, but from the departing train he tries to kill her yet again. In the scuffle, however, he is the one who slips and falls before a coming train. Only Charlie and Graham know of Uncle Charlie's past; the family is spared this secret, and the community, which celebrates his life, is oblivious to his identity.

My analysis begins with Charlie's distance from, and discontent with, the ordinary world, which leads to her love for Uncle Charlie, who fascinates her with his secrets but who also threatens to destroy her. Their relationship exposes a complex dialectic of love and hate. I then turn to an analysis of the ordinary world, which is portrayed in its comic limitations but which is not without a certain dignity. I conclude by exploring the film's self-reflexive and historical resonance, which includes, on the one hand, a complex assessment of the special roles of the lover, guardian, and artist, including their awareness of depth and capacities for deception, and, on the other hand, the film's previously overlooked allusions to the Third Reich.

A Double Threat

The film opens with a warped version of "The Merry Widow's Waltz" from Franz Lehar's operetta (Schroeder 103–7). The Ukrainian composer Dimitri Tiomkin skews the music such that it is atonal and deviates from the original. Partly because of this distortion, the well-costumed dancing figures are not in harmony with the music. In fact, the distorted version of the waltz does not lend itself to dancing. The atonal sound and the conflict between sound and image are foreboding.

The film portrays a simple and naive world, which Charlie finds boring. Her family is in "a rut." She sees its problems—the inadequacies of the mundane, ordinary, and trivial—and the need for drama. She longs for someone to shake up their life. Unlike her mother, she is not happy to be typical. Her ability to see the inadequacies of everyday reality makes her exceptional; she is the "smartest girl in her class." This very capacity, however, alienates her from her environment. As Hegel notes, alienation, which is a necessary step in any meaningful education, involves distance from the present, a split from it, a kind of doubling, where reality and mind are at odds with one another (3.359–63). Charlie's knowledge of the inadequacies of her surrounding reality triggers a kind of alienation. She is no longer at home.

Having transcended this normal environment, Charlie lives in a split world, visually manifest in the film's central motif of doubling. The most obvious doubling is of Charlie and Uncle Charlie, with which the film opens. In sequential scenes each figure lies on a bed in an upper-story room. Each view is introduced by a canted or slightly canted shot of their respective windows. Each character is indifferent, discontent, and bored—unsatisfied with the world as it is. Each is uninterested in money, revealing a hunger for higher-order meaning. The theme of mental telepathy is underscored as each sends a related telegram to the other. Telepathy also emerges when Charlie can't get the Merry Widow Waltz out of her head. Charlie and Uncle Charlie are like one in the arrival scene at the train station, as alternating shots seem to blend one person into the other (Rothman, *Hitchcock* 188). Not only is there a dimension of unity between the two, but the way the shots are intercut is reminiscent of separated lovers reuniting (French 43). The doubling is underscored by Charlie's comment after her uncle's arrival: "We're sort of like twins." More subtle identification with Uncle Charlie arises when Charlie sleeps too long, which parallels her uncle's statement that he is tired, and when she is almost run over by a car, which foreshadows his falling victim to an oncoming train.

Doubling occurs elsewhere, for example, two detectives in the East and two in the West; two suspects being pursued, one eventually cut down by a propeller, another run over by a train; two amateur sleuths; two police visits to the Newton home; two stairwells; two dinners; two church scenes; two garage scenes; and two scenes at the train station.[2] The widespread doubling reinforces the complex relations between Charlie and Uncle Charlie. They are different, but similar, as their common name and deep affinity imply. Early in the narrative their bonds are strong, and they share a discontent with the present, but over time their differences sharpen. On a deeper level, doubling underscores not only the split in Charlie's consciousness but the dualistic nature of the world itself. As Charlie gains maturity, she rejects what is and longs for what should or could be. Underscoring the complexity of the moral vision once the simple and naive view has been relinquished, doubling also reinforces the film's overarching ambiguity.

Charlie's fall from grace does not begin with Uncle Charlie, though Uncle Charlie becomes central to her advancing beyond innocence. Charlie longs for someone who can confirm her reading of the world, and she is fascinated with the uncle who appears to have a secret. He represents something beyond banality (though what is beyond the banal can obviously take on various guises). Indeed, distancing can involve either progress, which involves a transcendence of present inadequacies, as we recognize that the world is not yet what it should be, or evil, a relinquishing of the just moral ethos of an age. Both Charlie and Uncle Charlie, having gained distance from the present, want more, and this desire for transcendence gives them a certain sparkle. Charlie seeks wonder and adventure. She tells Graham she doesn't want to be "an average girl in an average family." Uncle Charlie has insight and charisma as well as a carefree and cavalier attitude toward contemporary clichés. However, awareness of the banality of the world can, as we learn, also drive you crazy or get you killed.

Uncle Charlie's dark side is manifest immediately after the film's musical prelude. His inward emptiness is prefigured by an early shot of a junkyard. His feigned illness on the train suggests a sickness of the soul. Uncle Charlie and his surroundings are often filmed with canted shots—his apartment and window in the city, the outside of his room (as Charlie approaches with water), Uncle Charlie in the stairwell when the detectives are downstairs, and Uncle Charlie in Charlie's room (after the other suspect is caught)—all symbolic manifestations of his distorted mind.

Despite these associations, Uncle Charlie approaches us for the most part with wit and charm. His feigned illness gives way to a smile and a quick step. He seems beyond the ordinary. Charlie announces: "There's only one person who can save us." Uncle Charlie's miraculous escape from his pursuers gives him an "aura of the supernatural" (Hughes 111). Uncle Charlie embodies characteristics traditionally associated with Christ. He seems to represent the "miracle" that would save the family, he enters into their world almost magically, and he shakes it up, noting the world's deficiencies. Uncle Charlie is not himself religious, but he hosts the evening meal with wine and quotes St. Paul. In some ways he is the Antichrist: he appears to be the contemporary savior but is its opposite. Indeed, Hitchcock hints at this by associating Uncle Charlie with a distinctive inversion of Christ. When we first see Uncle Charlie, he lies still, as if in a coffin waiting for dark. The proprietor draws the blind, and a shadow crosses his face and body. On the train he lies in the dark, as he travels from the East. He refuses to be photographed, and Saunders, one of the detectives, asks Ann to tell him the story of Dracula. A vampire does not give innocent blood for the sake of the guilty but instead takes innocent blood for its own sake.

Uncle Charlie evokes this range of allusions partly because he has a conflicted identity. He is nowhere at home spatially, and in terms of time, he longs for the past. Distancing from the present can represent nostalgia for an era of simplicity; this is part of the meaning behind Uncle Charlie's elegiac invocations. Since the recurring, nondiegetic image of the dancers also evokes an earlier era and is associated with atonality and murder, we recognize this nostalgia as a perversion, a sign of Uncle Charlie's inability to accept the present. Uncle Charlie both envies and despises the world of "peaceful, stupid dreams," the world of sleepwalkers and blind people. His hatred stems from a recognition, in its structure not unlike Charlie's, that the world is not as it should be. But when Uncle Charlie is confronted with a jarring story from his past, he endorses instead the present ("Today's the thing. That's my philosophy."). He elevates the ephemeral and transitory over the eternal and transcendent. He connects with nothing beyond himself. He simply passes through: he flees one place and must seek another. Even his act of changing his name and the conflicting descriptions of his origins symbolize his lack of coherence. With no connection to the first world, he is spatially and temporally adrift.

Nonetheless, for a stretch of the film we root for Uncle Charlie. This places us in a parallel position to Charlie. He opens up new worlds for her. The waitress, Louise, observes that she never expected to see Charlie in the bar. In a sense Uncle Charlie is a metaphor for a part of Charlie that she discovers in herself and must eventually overcome; her discontent with the world borders on hatred and could have disastrous consequences. Early on we do sympathize with the killer: Charlie adores him, he comes from a loving family, and he is intriguing. We are at the table with him. We can be taken in, especially with the other characters being likewise oblivious. Yet Uncle Charlie places his identity above the family and endangers them. As Charlie loses her attachment to him, so do we. In the end of course we rejoice as Charlie frees herself from her uncle.

Though critics rightly stress the parallels in the opening scenes, differences exist. To the knocks on the door, Uncle Charlie responds with a feeble command, "Come in." Charlie answers with a query: "Who is it?" Where Charlie is curious, Uncle Charlie already knows what the world is like. His train arrives with black smoke. Shadows fall over him in the bedroom and again in the train. In contrast, Charlie is portrayed in light until the final scene (when she adopts the dress of a widow). A contrast between light and dark is evident when Charlie discovers the newspaper, and her uncle is shining his shoes. (Among the few scenes where Uncle Charlie is shown in light is at the bank, when he is dressed as a dandy, perhaps to underscore the difficulty of anyone deciphering his true identity.) Uncle Charlie seeks to return to the ordinary, to his earlier family life. Charlie, on the other hand, wants something extraordinary. She longs for enchantment, whereas Uncle Charlie has lost his sense of wonder. At the bank he comments: "The whole world's a joke to me!" At the bar he announces: "Do you know the world is a foul sty? Do you know if you rip the fronts off houses, you'd find swine? The world's a hell."

As the film develops, we begin to see reversals that render the doubling more complex. Uncle Charlie, as noted, has something of the dandy in him. Charlie, whose name is masculine, is described as the head of her family. She, not her father, drives the family car. The world beyond the ordinary is a topsy-turvy world, and it culminates in Charlie distancing herself from her uncle, surviving his early attacks, threatening him, and winning the battle in the train over the physically much stronger Uncle Charlie. The film is a director's film insofar as the two main protagonists battle for director status. Which of the two will truly determine the action? This plays out cinematically with a number of shot/reverse-shot sequences, highlighting the tension between the two characters; with diverse low-angle and high-angle shots, underscoring who has power at various stages; and with shots that capture both characters, but with one elevated above the other (Figure 15).

The battle is also portrayed thematically. For example, Charlie tries to uncover the truth via the newspaper hidden in Uncle Charlie's jacket, and Uncle Charlie tries to prevent her from seeing it. His decision to stay, which is accentuated by shots of him above her on the stairs, represents a partial victory for Uncle Charlie. However, our view of Uncle

Figure 15 *Shadow of a Doubt* is a director's film insofar as the two main protagonists battle for power. Here Uncle Charlie, played by Joseph Cotton, stands dominant over Charlie, played by Teresa Wright, as they hear the news that Uncle Charlie will no longer be suspected. *Shadow of a Doubt* directed by Alfred Hitchcock. © Universal Studios 1942. All rights reserved.

Charlie ascending the stairs is followed by another. He looks back at Charlie, and Charlie's unflinching gaze threatens him (Figure 16).[3]

Charlie's shadow reaches through the door and seems to approach Uncle Charlie. The high angle and cast shadow, along with the cross on the wall, might seem to echo the vulnerability she faced in the library, when she learned of her uncle's crimes, but here, as she faces the camera and her uncle, a second meaning surfaces: her knowledge, emerging from the light, unsettles Uncle Charlie. The bars of the stairwell and vertical shadows on the wall render him almost a prisoner. The entire sequence has moments of two figures about to enact a duel. He reacts by twice unsuccessfully trying to orchestrate her death. However, his eventual decision to leave after recognizing the ring on her hand and thus her preparedness to incriminate him, suggests that she is now directing the action. The uncertainty over who the surrogate director really is lasts until the end. Although the penultimate scene is a

Figure 16 Uncle Charlie looks back and sees Charlie, played by Teresa Wright, whose unflinching gaze unsettles him. Her shadow, which functions almost as her double, reaches through the door, as her knowledge, which emerges from the light, threatens her uncle. *Shadow of a Doubt* directed by Alfred Hitchcock. © Universal Studios 1942. All rights reserved.

battle, it also echoes and perverts elements of a dance and so alludes to the atonal opening. We see symmetry and mirroring, but the two figures compete, as each tries to take the lead. The dance is fraught with deadly conflict, a mix of the ordinary and the extraordinary, an intertwining of love and hate, a dance of death.

The Dialectic of Love and Hate

Charlie's desire for Uncle Charlie is a manifestation of her growing maturity, evident in her discontent with what is, and her sense of love, which gives her depth. A full love relationship involves giving oneself over to another and relinquishing thereby one's autonomy. One is no longer as one was before. In his classic commentary on love, Marsilio Ficino describes how love engenders dependence on the other and a loss of autonomy, which triggers internal unease, culminating in a dialectic of love and hate: we loathe the person who has stolen from us our independence (6.10). To love is to entrust yourself to another, to take risks, to let something new and unknown into your life. Love also makes us vulnerable. To reveal yourself, to be seen through, is unsettling. In love, we become aware of the world and of evil; love is a time of depth and danger.

Charlie is fascinated with what lies beyond the surface of Uncle Charlie, and she comments that she herself does not reveal all that she is to others. They love one another because each senses something deeper in the other. Charlie's love contrasts with Ann's unemotional matter-of-factness (with the one exception of her moving expression of love for Charlie when she comes out of the garage) and Roger's focus on facts and figures (e.g., how many steps from the house to the drugstore and back and how many minutes Charlie slept). Ann seeks to vacuum up knowledge. She has no existential connection to learning. Charlie seeks deeper meaning. To her father she responds: "How can you talk about money when I'm talking about souls?"

Love implies a particular kind of depth, which not only reveals and conceals, but also longs for more. Love implies the desire to become. In the Socratic tradition love is consciousness of an incompleteness; it represents an awareness of one's deficiencies, a desire to grow, a striving for more. For Socrates love is linked to education. We love those who can point out our weaknesses and help us become fuller persons. And yet, in a bizarre dialectic, we also hate the beloved for becoming aware of our weaknesses and objectifying them instead of our being able to hide them—even from ourselves.[4] In *The Apology* Socrates argues that you hate those who see through your weaknesses (21c–21e; 24a), and in the *Symposium* Alcibiades claims that those whom we love most, we also hate (216b–216c). We are most easily ashamed before persons we respect or admire, and an inner desire arises to remove the source of that shame. The devil hates God in part owing to his love for him. In this sense, the dialectic of love and hate is even more complex than Ficino suggests. It includes a dialectic not only of independence and dependence, but also of concealment and revelation. For this reason, Uncle Charlie will eventually not only love but also hate Charlie. Charlie's movement beyond love has a different catalyst: it relates not to a revelation of her weaknesses (though one could say that the relationship does bring out a new, combative side to her character), but to her discovery that Uncle Charlie is other than she thought he was and other than he should be. We are upset, then, not only with those who know that we are not as we should be but also with those who are not as they should be. The wound is greater still when we ourselves have misjudged them.

Love must be connected with a higher value, not simply the abstract idea of escaping from the present or the formal element of wit, charm, and allure, but some set of values with which we can identify and which give us dignity. Charlie does not find these in her search for love and identity through Uncle Charlie, which leaves her confused and endangered. Symbolic of Uncle Charlie's withdrawing his love is his manipulating the key when he tries to murder Charlie. The key is absent, which symbolically reinforces that the love is past, for the key is a traditional Christian symbol of love.[5] Uncle Charlie has the key and keeps it from Charlie: he loves only himself. Uncle Charlie has no desire to kill Emma or Joe. He wants to eliminate the person who knows of his weaknesses, who is aware that he is not as he claims to be or should be. In this sense knowledge and intimacy make one vulnerable. We recognize the vulnerability of love as well when Emma breaks down on hearing that Uncle Charlie will be leaving town. Most are embarrassed, but Charlie and Mrs. Potter look up; they have loved and know sorrow and depth. Love as the unity of unity and difference implies this very split and doubling, which Charlie, like her mother, endures.

Abundant sexual imagery underscores Charlie's awakening to adulthood and developing maturity as well as her longing and love for Uncle Charlie. The movie, as noted, opens with complementary scenes of, first, Uncle Charlie lying in bed fondling a phallic cigar and, then, Charlie lying in bed thinking. In his telegram Uncle Charlie sends "a kiss for little Charlie from her Uncle Charlie." He arrives at the station, hunched over, and when he sees her, he takes his coat off and stands erect. He wields a phallic cane. As he looks at Charlie, following her, he pulls out a cigar. In her room, he plucks a rose, a symbolic deflowering, and tosses his hat onto the bed, as if he were throwing himself onto precisely where she had previously lain. He takes her hand and places the emerald ring on her finger as if he were proposing marriage (Figure 17).

He sleeps in her bed, and in a second juxtaposition Charlie is passive in bed, followed by Uncle Charlie smoking a cigar and blowing circles of

Figure 17 The love between Uncle Charlie, played by Joseph Cotton, and Charlie, played by Teresa Wright, is manifest, almost perversely, in an early scene where he takes her hand, as she stands before a cross on the door, and places the emerald ring on her finger as if he were proposing marriage. *Shadow of a Doubt* directed by Alfred Hitchcock. © Universal Studios 1942. All rights reserved.

smoke; we hear the sound of a moving train in the background. Charlie says that they are not just an uncle and a niece. As they walk through town, the other girls become envious of what looks like Charlie's new boyfriend. He opens the phallic wine bottle. Several times he places his hand on Charlie's face. He intimates marriage when he refers to her maturity and his youth: "You're the head of your family, Charlie, everyone can see that. I'm not so old." She descends the stairs like a bride. Finally, in the train, their scuffle is almost like that of lovers. Ann, in contrast to Charlie, is completely asexual. She cannot find a pencil, and she does not get the telegram. She lacks the passion and sparkle associated with sexuality. In contrast, not only does Charlie get the telegram, she receives it while holding a pencil in her hand.

Some critics reduce the uncle-niece relationship to the sexual dimension and offer truncated Freudian readings of the film.[6] The sexual motif, however, cannot be viewed reductionistically. As with Plato, the desire for knowledge has erotic dimensions. Knowledge and love share elements of revealing and concealing, and we long for a sensuous realization of the spiritual ideal. However, the sexual dimension, in this case the incest motif, reveals the flesh-and-blood consequences of their relationship, including Charlie's vulnerability and Uncle Charlie's aggression, a sexuality free of love or higher purpose, which in its soullessness becomes baleful and ultimately self-destructive.

The desire to move beyond the ordinary is a common Hitchcock theme, one ripe with danger. Midge in *Vertigo* is sensible, practical, realistic, but she is not erotic or alluring like Madeleine. Scottie, like Charlie, is discontent with the ordinary and longs for something more, which, however, can be, as Hitchcock tells us, as dangerous as it is tempting. Whereas *Vertigo*, which seeks to emphasize the enchantment of the ideal, makes abundant use of soft focus, especially in the scenes with Madeleine, *Shadow of a Doubt* is soberer in assessing the dangers that lurk within everyday reality. As a result, there may be no other Hitchcock film shot so consistently in clear, deep focus.[7] Moreover, the film's concreteness, with references as specific as "46 Burnham Street," accentuates the idea that the diabolic inhabits the everyday (Kornhaber).

Charlie believes her uncle knows "something secret and wonderful," which she wishes to discover. Even with danger looming, she does not hold back. Charlie echoes Oedipus not only via the incest motif. Her unrelenting desire to know, even when her knowledge might turn horrific, makes her a partial successor to the Sophoclean hero. Both *Oedipus Rex* and *Shadow of a Doubt* are analytic works: we see a relentless search that culminates in discovery of past events. Charlie's first expression of unease is at the station. She can't quite grasp Uncle Charlie's quick transformation from old and disabled to tall and dashing. The initials in the ring do not at first make a strong impression. After she reveals that she knows her uncle is hiding something in the paper, she is victimized by his aggression. At the bank, she sees another side of Uncle Charlie, who embarrasses Charlie's father and spouts a kind of nihilism. Her face reveals unease when Uncle Charlie seeks to confiscate the film. As Graham intimates problems with Uncle Charlie, she grasps her hands, recalling Uncle Charlie's violence. In these cases, the out-of-the-ordinary is disorienting or unappealing. The more detailed conversation with Graham in the early evening adds to her unease.

Charlie wants to probe her uncertainty, so she rushes to the library, hoping to arrive before it closes. A sequence of longer takes is followed by more rapid cutting after she tries to cross the street. We experience a cinematic corollary to her unrest. In the library Charlie reads the headline and story, drawing the connection to the ring Uncle Charlie gave her. After this chilling recognition, the camera tracks backward from her hands over her shoulders and upward to a significant height (Figure 18). The shot, with her long, cast shadow, is then overtaken by the low-angle, recurring image of dancers and the warped version of the Merry Widow Waltz. This is one of the most dramatic scenes in the film, and yet it is one of knowledge, not action. Charlie obtains her information at night when the library is closed: her knowledge is exceptional, not the everyday knowledge that people garner during the day. (Interestingly, Charlie is also the only one in the family, besides Uncle Charlie, who exhibits suspicion toward the survey; she simply sees more than the others.) In the scene at the library we experience darkness, then light

Figure 18 In the dark library, Charlie, played by Teresa Wright, gains esoteric knowledge. The crane shot, which renders Charlie small and casts a long shadow, accentuates her isolation. *Shadow of a Doubt* directed by Alfred Hitchcock. © Universal Studios 1942. All rights reserved.

and knowledge, then shadows again. Silence confronts us after Charlie hears the chimes that may keep her from entering the library and again after she reads the headline. Knowledge leads to danger and emptiness. The crane shot, which renders Charlie small, accentuates the shadows and reinforces her isolation. Charlie's early recognition of the true story makes the plot even more engaging than a whodunit, for the film becomes a compelling story about the following puzzle: how in the face of danger does one deal with knowledge? How will she proceed, and will her knowledge lead to her death?

Charlie's emerging recognition triggers disorientation. On the one hand, we see her hurrying, hastening to the library to find information and running away from the dinner table conversation. On the other hand, she lies in bed all day long. The agitated and apathetic moments reflect her identity crisis. As her mother says, "She doesn't look quite herself." Charlie's crisis is accentuated by her having to bear everything herself. Charlie alone is aware of Uncle Charlie and suffers this knowledge by herself. The high angle, long shot of her behind and below the baluster, unable to reach Graham by phone, cinematically reinforces her isolation (Figure 19). The image suggests she is trapped—and not only by the danger of Uncle Charlie. She will no longer be fully at home in ordinary reality, even in her own house. The severing of the love relationship, which had been animated by trust and adoration, renders Charlie not only isolated but also vulnerable.

Loving Critique of the Ordinary

The film portrays the exceptional in the form of Uncle Charlie and Charlie but also the ordinary, which is exemplified by Charlie's family. Ann, Charlie's younger sister, lives a vicarious life through books. She frees herself of the distractions of reality, which seem not to matter to her. Though she is introduced to us eating an apple, it is not an apple of true knowledge. She reads fiction as truth. Joe and Herb play, but merely play, with serious issues such as murder. They are "literary critics," removed from reality, playing childish games, ignorant of the murderer at their table. Charlie, unlike Ann, has true knowledge and unlike her father and Herb confronts real danger. The film comically distances the audience from the world of ordinary Americans.

Figure 19 The high angle, long shot of Charlie, played by Teresa Wright, behind and below the baluster, unable to reach Graham by phone, cinematically reinforces her isolation. She is trapped by the danger of Uncle Charlie and no longer at home even in her own house. *Shadow of a Doubt* directed by Alfred Hitchcock. © Universal Studios 1942. All rights reserved.

Emma, the mother, takes the world as given and does not question it. Her simplicity is evident when she fails to recognize that she does not need to yell into the telephone. Yet the mother is not completely unaware. She struggles with some form of knowledge: "I just don't understand it; first the stairs, then ... [the garage]." Like Charlie, the mother has moments of mental telepathy; she, too, hums the Merry Widow Waltz. Love enables seeing, and the mother, who loves, almost gains insight. Moreover, her tears at Uncle Charlie's departure reveal a modest level of self-knowledge; she quietly laments that after leaving home and entering marriage, "You sort of forget you're you. You're your husband's wife." Emma has a partial recognition, but she lacks the richness of Charlie. She is witty, as when she suggests to Graham that Ann would be a better guide, but she does not have Charlie's acumen.

In the secondary literature, the mother is rightly lamented for lacking autonomy. Like Charlie, she is unfulfilled,[8] yet she has a generosity of spirit that cannot be reduced to her role. She does everything for others. Charlie reproaches her for taking care of everyone's whims, including Ann's calling her from downstairs. The mother responds: "I'm going downstairs anyway." She is not egotistical. One reason she is so accepting of her role is that, unlike Charlie, she has no distance from reality. She is not playful: she cannot pretend to break an egg or make a cake. She completely identifies with reality and the needs of others. She does not reflect on her role in the world. This is both endearing and limiting. Unlike Uncle Charlie, she would not instrumentalize a soul. She needs to be seen in her full complexity. She is both a problematic figure, in being held back, and positive in various traits that she embodies.

The family offers unconditional love and a sense of being completely at home. The feeling of being fully accepted, which children experience in nurturing families, is an irreplaceable value, toward which many long in their later lives. This unconditional love helps children develop moral sensibility and recognize the value of collective identity; the family offers a form of self-transcendence that overrides calculating self-interest. To be sure, family love can lead to elevating one's own relations and offspring over others, which counters principles of justice, but family love is also the seed of responsibility for others.

Charlie does not want Uncle Charlie captured within the family circle of Santa Rosa. When Uncle Charlie tries to keep Charlie from going to the law, he appeals to their kinship. He reads her well: Charlie elevates family and relations over morality and justice—not only because she has loved Uncle Charlie but also because she wants to protect her mother, who would be crushed if she were to discover the truth. Her father, too, might lose his job, she fears. The result: Charlie risks the lives of future victims, beginning with Mrs. Potter. The problems associated with elevating one's own sphere are touched on earlier when the librarian counsels Charlie about exceptions to the rule. If some seek to place themselves outside the rule of law, what happens to the rule of law? In elevating the family, Charlie contradicts the universal.[9] Even if her conflict is understandable and tragic, the elevation of family endangers others.

As Charlie studies the paper and decides to leave for the library, she lies to Ann. Charlie then tries to cross the street with oncoming traffic. She seeks to enter the library after hours. The following night, as Charlie scampers across the street, she again runs into the policeman.

Her transgressions are symbolic: she crosses beyond her traditional identity (these actions mislead or surprise others); she becomes more like Uncle Charlie. Finally, she turns into a potential murderer: "Go away, or I'll kill you myself." In not fully recognizing the value of the broader sphere and the role of the state, Charlie exhibits a dimension similar to Uncle Charlie's longing for family. Charlie wants, in some ways like her double, to elevate the family idyll. Emotional attachment to the family is both a source of great love and a restriction on its further development. Charlie's moral culpability lies not in the death of Uncle Charlie, which was self-defense, but in not alerting the police. If he were to escape, he would surely commit another murder. In her conversation with Saunders after church, Charlie refuses to hear the details of Uncle Charlie's crimes. Here she is more like Jocasta than Oedipus. Hitchcock's incestuous allusions link the restrictive focus on family and the lack of higher-order curiosity with criminality. The allusions serve more than a sexual purpose: they indicate the restrictions of a family lens that cannot see beyond itself, that elevates its own, its tribe, against a broader unity that includes difference.

Although Charlie can be criticized for resisting justice, she is willing to pledge her life for her position—so firmly does she believe in protecting the family. This suggests a potentially tragic resolution, which, however, Hitchcock avoids, as he so often does. The only possible non-tragic resolution to Charlie's dilemma, to the conflict between family and state, is that Uncle Charlie must be removed from this world, and nobody can know that he is the murderer, and this is indeed how the film ends, preserving thereby both family and justice and giving us a partially happy end.

Part of Uncle Charlie's allure is his charisma, which contrasts so visibly with the mundane aspects of Charlie's family. Uncle Charlie views his actions as a kind of mission. In his discontent with what is, he becomes an idealist. Hitchcock calls him "a killer with an ideal" (Truffaut 153). Positing an ideal, while necessary for progress, is also potentially dangerous: it can lead to discontent with the world as it is. For Uncle Charlie, a kind of fundamentalism and idealism takes over. His idealism exposes the inadequacies of reality in such a way that he is led to hate the world as it is (in its difference from his ideal); he therefore strips it of its dignity and its connection to the transcendent. Hitchcock suggests, in contrast, that we need an ideal that has room for the normal and the ordinary.

Uncle Charlie's bitter view of the world as empty of meaning contrasts with Hitchcock's more loving, if still comic, view of the characters. Comic relief is provided partly by Ann and by Joe and Herb. They exhibit an intuitive goodness, even if they are deluded. Joe and Herb are fascinated with the sinister, as is Ann with truth (but they are all presented as comic reductions). Ann has no emotional connection to her books, and Joe and Herb are oblivious to questions of motive (or depth) and focus solely on technique, that is, the shallower sphere of the how-to.

Herb is Uncle Charlie's comic counterpart. Whereas Uncle Charlie has cigars in his upper coat pocket, Herb has pencils. In one of his lower pockets Uncle Charlie hides the newspaper that reveals his crimes, whereas Herb has mushrooms and a handkerchief to tell the tale of a would-be-murder. Uncle Charlie destroys the family dinner ritual by knocking over the glass (so as to keep his identity as a murderer hidden) and by introducing alien, perverse thoughts. Herb, too, interrupts the meal, but his interruption is innocuous: Herb talks about murder, but he is incapable of murder, hate, or lying. He is like a child. He makes a silly comment about planning to kill someone by making it look as if the person committed suicide by beating himself with a club. Uncle Charlie works in the same realm (he even alludes to his own potential suicide), but Uncle Charlie commits murder; Herb simply imagines murder—much like the audience, which is lovingly ironized together with Herb. Both Uncle Charlie and Herb bring the extraordinary to ordinary dinner conversation—but in radically different ways. The camera captures Uncle Charlie at the table, holding forth. Herb, in contrast, looks diminished, as he sits off to the side.

Despite these humorous elements, each comic figure exhibits moments of insight and dignity. Ann is intuitively repulsed by Uncle Charlie; she does not wish to sit beside him.[10] Nor does Uncle Charlie impress Herb, who finds Charlie in the garage and saves her: "I figured there must be a human being in there." This echoes Charlie's earlier retort to Uncle Charlie: "But they're alive; they're human beings." Herb's and Charlie's sense of human dignity contrasts with Uncle Charlie's view of humans as "fat, wheezing animals." Further, Hitchcock recognizes the comical and the noble in these characters, which contrasts with the dismissive, even hateful, attitude of Uncle Charlie. Although Charlie and Graham laugh about Ann wanting to marry a librarian, theirs is a loving laughter. Part of the film's resolution involves appreciating the less adventurous and more mundane. The woman at the telegram office, with her lack of understanding and sensibility for telepathy, is likewise funny, but in an endearing, not a bitter way. Simplicity in this film conceals, if not depth, at least dignity.

The film's strength is ambiguity and humor. It lovingly criticizes the family. Uncle Charlie is much simpler in his views: he only hates the world. Hitchcock, in contrast, presents a sacramental view of reality.[11] Though we can criticize the world and express our discontent, and though knowledge of the world's inadequacies and alienation from it are intertwined, ultimately the world has value and is linked to the transcendent. Through that connection it has dignity. Even toward Uncle Charlie, Hitchcock exhibits a glimmer of sympathy without his backing away at all from the idea that Uncle Charlie's hateful idealism must be resisted. Critique, as Plato already knew, is very much compatible with love; in fact it is in many ways defined by a recognition that the beloved is not yet what they can or should be.

Hatred is extreme; laughter is flexible. Not surprisingly, the father notices that Uncle Charlie "takes himself very seriously." Uncle Charlie's dogmatism and ideals contrast with the elasticity of laughter, which bespeaks a love of the world. A self-reflexive moment occurs when Charlie tells Graham how grateful she is to be able to laugh again. Laughter is healthy. This is not the laughter of cynicism that drives Uncle Charlie to assert that the whole world is a joke. Hitchcock's and Charlie's laughter is not without love. In contrast to simple black-and-white negation, Hitchcock elevates on behalf of Charlie a flexibility that justly rejects reality as it is (as in many other Hitchcock films the crowd is oblivious and mediocre) but simultaneously embraces it with all its inadequacies and banalities. Charlie, who is our ultimate orientation point, is able to live in both worlds, gaining distance from the normal and mundane, but also in her development embracing that same world. In portraying Uncle Charlie and Charlie as mirrors and reversals of one another, Hitchcock sees the extent to which the world is a joke and the extent to which it remains noble.

The good arises in its battle with evil. Charlie comes to herself *ex negativo*, by not being ordinary and by not being Uncle Charlie, that is, by identifying with him, in his distance from everyday reality, and then ultimately combating and overcoming him. In the beginning, Charlie is discontent. She matures, as she recognizes, in a way that Uncle Charlie does not, the value of present reality. Charlie realizes a kind of Hegelian dialectic. The naive, thetic position is embodied in the family and townspeople; she shares a part of reality with them even as her esoteric knowledge isolates her from them. Uncle Charlie, with whom she has a deep connection, represents the antithetical position. Both Charlies recognize the world's inadequacies. But Charlie is also beyond Uncle Charlie. She is not at home in the family world, which is oblivious and predictable. She is not at home in the malign and cynical world of Uncle Charlie either. Charlie goes full circle from being an intuitive outsider to a knowledgeable one. She detaches herself from the ordinary but also distances herself from evil. What we see through the prism of Charlie is an emotional embrace of home as well as reflective distance from it, in the end, a not undesirable combination. Charlie is a synthetic figure, carrying both moments within her, a love of the ordinary and a knowledge of insufficiency and evil without giving herself over to negativity and contempt. Yet when Charlie recognizes that her uncle is horrific, her idealism loses some of its sparkle. She doesn't become the cynic that her uncle is, she does not fall prey to a view of the world as a pigsty, but she is chastened, her happiness muted.

At the end of the film, Charlie finds another person who is aware of evil but who will not kill her for her knowledge. Charlie and Graham have a special bond; they alone know of evil. Whereas Charlie is tempted to elevate family and love over community and law, Graham is a representative of the law. Graham gives Charlie an image of herself that indirectly inspires her actions: in the park, he tells her that she will do the right thing. Nonetheless, Graham lacks Uncle Charlie's charisma, which explains her hesitancy to hold him close. Charlie's appreciation for Graham is not as intense as her love for Uncle Charlie. There is no emphatic embrace or kiss at the end, no strong resolution. Charlie's inability to reach Graham on the phone symbolically contrasts with her telepathy with Uncle Charlie.

Yet while it is true that Uncle Charlie has more magnetism than Graham, the relationship with Uncle Charlie represents an immediate connection and a deep intensity that is not sustainable; it is radically altered over time. The relationship with Graham differs. Charlie and Graham begin not with an immediate connection, but with deception. Partly because Graham loves Charlie, he eventually reveals himself, although it would have been strategically wiser for him to stay silent. Whereas Uncle Charlie does not confide in others, Graham entrusts himself to Charlie. He reveals a secret, thereby risking a great deal. The relationship between Charlie and Graham develops slowly; it does not begin with infatuation or fascination, but it does evolve toward friendship. The lack of immediacy is clear. Consider the way their conversation and body language unfold in the garage. Both hold back. Instead of racing toward Charlie and violently grabbing her hands, as does Uncle Charlie in the bedroom, Graham waits. Charlie comes to him. The contrast is underscored insofar as their courting takes place in the same garage where Uncle Charlie later tries to kill her. Between Graham and Charlie is a chair, which symbolically conveys a slowly developing relationship. One sits and waits in a chair. Graham offers Charlie respect and distance.

In the end, Charlie and Graham are together. The idea that the detective represents the higher world of justice and that Charlie may be falling in love with the detective could suggest that one can develop an emotional attachment to what transcends the family. But the synthesis will not be fully realized, for Graham is himself compromised (Pippin, *Filmed Thought* 95). Graham knows about Uncle Charlie but keeps the matter private, elevating the private sphere, as Charlie has, over the state. Love and justice remain in tension, which has a disquieting, almost alienating effect presumably designed to awaken the audience.

Together Charlie and Graham may form another family, and this possibility has led scholars to criticize the portrayal of family, but there is more at play than the possibility that the child will leave the family to start another family. That Charlie and Graham will marry is not unambiguous (Hemmeter 229; Bruns 125–30). Charlie is not easily contained by the ordinary life associated with her parents' marriage. Charlie stands higher than Graham does on the steps, symbolically indicating her superior capacity to uncover and overcome Uncle Charlie. The relationship has an unconventional asymmetry. In addition, if they do become a family, the film implies that their relationship will be deeper, less banal, for they have, in contrast to the community, both transcended simplicity. They know that the world is more complex than the community imagines it to be. The town doesn't even know of Charlie's heroic battle with her uncle. Indeed, the community is so off base that the policeman actually hinders Charlie twice and openly admires her uncle. In the end, Charlie lies, she does not tell the truth or dissolve the family's or community's illusion; her self-sacrifice is heroic. As in the American Western, with which this story has loose parallels, the hero does not speak. The townspeople are criticized. It is formally positive that the community wants to honor Uncle Charlie, but the content is negative. They have it wrong. And yet the community is not excoriated; it is portrayed in both a distancing and a loving way, and that is certainly how Charlie views it.

Whereas Uncle Charlie longs for the idyllic, the idyllic folks seek adventure (through reading and imagination). This suggests that even for Uncle Charlie the common folks have a hidden dignity (after all the idealist wants to experience their life) and that an intuitive sense or possibility of goodness lies below the surface of Uncle Charlie, which Charlie and the others sense. Uncle Charlie, who was spoiled, experienced at home an unconditional love for which he still yearns. Whereas the family seeks adventure, and Uncle Charlie, the adventurer, longs for a family, only Charlie operates in both spheres, but her uniqueness also isolates her.

The question of appearance and reality is central to the film's content and technique. Is Uncle Charlie as he seems? Does the town penetrate to serious knowledge? Uncle Charlie asks, what goes on at the bank when the doors are shut? Significant here is the rhetoric of the ordinary and extraordinary. The average is in the end extraordinary. This common Hitchcock theme underscores the idea that the average and ordinary are not only to be overcome, but also somehow elevated and embraced. The ordinary are mocked. The extraordinary are elevated. But the ordinary can become extraordinary, and the ordinary has value and dignity.

Is Charlie ordinary, or is she exceptional? She is presented as both, in a sense moving from the ordinary to the exceptional and back into the fold of the ordinary. It is not surprising then that Graham, who is ordinary, calls her extraordinary, and that Uncle Charlie, who is extraordinary, calls her ordinary: "You're just an ordinary little girl, living in an ordinary little town." The film itself mirrors this dialectic of the ordinary and the extraordinary. It can be simply enjoyed, as a popular and democratic phenomenon, or it can be analyzed for its hidden meanings. Not all know, and thus the film is highly aristocratic. Yet all have dignity, and so the film is highly democratic. Further, the extraordinary comes from the realm of the ordinary. The differences are not that great in some cases, although it is clear that while extraordinary good and extraordinary evil lie close to the ordinary, there is much more of evil and good in the ordinary than most of us recognize.

The language of ordinary and extraordinary alludes to Dostoevsky's *Crime and Punishment*, a work Hitchcock knew well (Truffaut 71). While the parallels between Dostoevsky's novel and Hitchcock's film are multiple,[12] the language by which murder is rationalized offers the deepest connection. Dostoevsky's murderer Raskolnikov resolves to kill a person who is described to him as "a stupid, meaningless, worthless, wicked, sick old crone, no good to anyone" (65). He himself says: "Crime? What crime? I killed a vile, pernicious louse, a little old moneylending crone who was of no use to anyone" (518). The novel and the film both entertain the idea that people are divided into two categories, the ordinary and the extraordinary, and the status of being extraordinary gives one the right to transgress normal legal boundaries and the right, or even the imperative, to become a killer (258–61). This view, which is developed further in *Rope,* is countered here and in another film, with which *Shadow of a Doubt* has loose analogies, *Stage Fright*. In *Stage Fright* Eve expresses her love for Jonathan, who turns out to be a criminal. The relationship endangers her. As Eve recognizes his weaknesses, she develops a deeper connection to a less charismatic but better partner, Wilfred Smith, also a representative of the law, whom she affectionately calls "Ordinary" Smith. Her role-playing and dalliance with the murderer Jonathan are more fascinating, but she is at home with Smith, whose virtues the film recognizes, not least of all in his forgiving her for her deception.

The concept of loving critique is not unrelated to a view of the human being as both sinful and good. In fact, *Shadow of a Doubt* is layered with subtle religious allusions, even if many of them are modestly askew. Uncle Charlie's return perverts the story of the prodigal son. According to tradition, the gesture of tossing a hat onto the bed releases evil spirits into the house. A devil of sorts, Uncle Charlie tempts Charlie and the others with his charismatic appeal and tries to dissuade Charlie from doing what is good, namely, turning him in to the police. When Charlie observes her mother and Charlie through the window, Uncle Charlie appears to blow smoke toward a crucifix above the piano. In the Christian tradition the devil is not otherworldly but within us and among us. Uncle Charlie's expressed interest in details, which he reveals at the bank, is a subtle gesture to the idiom 'the devil lies in the details,' itself a revision of the original expression, 'God is in the details.' When in the kitchen with Uncle Charlie, Charlie stands before a cross in the windowpane and then, as she receives the ring, before a cross on the door (Figure 17). When she is rescued from the garage, she is held in a pieta pose; it is impressive that Hitchcock presents a young woman as a partial representation of Christ. Charlie's combination of being both ordinary and extraordinary is very much analogous to the idea of Christ being among us. I have stressed doubling, but the film also integrates a privileged number in the Christian tradition, three: three children; three widows murdered; three times the ring exchanges hands; three attempts on Charlie's life; three times (once the narrative begins) that we see the dancing couples;[13] three times Ann stepped on a crack (and broke her mother's back); and three times we see a rose adorning someone's hair or lapel. The rose motif itself is Christian, as the five petals of the rose were traditionally associated with the five wounds of Christ (hands, feet, and side). Rose is furthermore an anagram for eros or love, which is, along with knowledge, the highest principle of Christianity. Its significance is underscored by the film's location, Santa Rosa. In addition, the film frequently has three persons in a frame, including in several central scenes. The triadic pattern alludes not only to the Trinity but also to the three days that encompass Christ's death, descent to hell, and resurrection. Young Charlie must engage with evil in order to defeat it, just as Christ uses his power to defeat Satan. The overall reading of the film as embodying a sacramental vision and loving humor reinforces the Christian idea that despite sin, what God made is ultimately good and is to be embraced and loved.

Lover, Guardian, and Artist

In *Shadow of a Doubt*, evil wears a mask and needs to be unveiled. Uncle Charlie, who charms almost everyone, dissembles throughout. Those who see through his pretension are the lover, Charlie; the guardian, Graham; and the artist, Hitchcock. All three adopt indirect strategies: irony, lying, deception. Attentive to non-verbal communication, they observe gestures, read situations, experience telepathy, or link music with ideas. When Graham fails as a guardian, having obtained only glimmers of the truth, Charlie takes over. Hitchcock himself adopts all three roles—lover, guardian, and artist. His critique of America is a loving critique, the film alerts us to radical danger, and Hitchcock conveys both his love and his warning via a complex artistic vision.

Above I spoke of the depth in any love relationship, which involves revealing and concealing. One wishes to reveal oneself to the other but holds back, so as not to exhaust the relationship and its potential future. Subtlety and playfulness are crucial in conveying the depth essential to any love relationship. Charlie's indirect conveyance of meaning continues after her love turns to disgust. The day following her discovery of Uncle Charlie's crimes, she says that she had nightmares about Uncle Charlie: he was running away, and she was happy to see him depart. She adds that he no longer needs to play games with the newspaper. When she descends the stairs with the ring on her finger (Figure 20), she sends Uncle Charlie a message and a threat.

Figure 20 When Charlie, played by Teresa Wright, descends the stairs with the ring on her finger, she sends Uncle Charlie a message and a threat. Whereas an emerald ring traditionally symbolizes love, here it alludes to Charlie's knowledge and thus her power. *Shadow of a Doubt* directed by Alfred Hitchcock. © Universal Studios 1942. All rights reserved.

Whereas the emerald ring would traditionally symbolize love, here it alludes to Charlie's knowledge and thus her power, which now turns in her favor, much like a circle.[14] The camera moves to an extreme close-up of the ring that almost shouts out her power to Uncle Charlie (and the viewers) while everyone else is oblivious.

Not only lovers use indirection, recognize more, and hold back. Early in the film, the detectives tell the landlady that they are Uncle Charlie's friends. Graham and Saunders pretend to be surveyors and rightly surmise that Uncle Charlie has vacated his room. Saunders clandestinely keeps Uncle Charlie's photograph. Art, too, reveals truth indirectly. On several occasions—grabbing the newspaper from Charlie, mangling the paper napkin, looking at Charlie through the window— Uncle Charlie's hands reveal his intentions. Cinematic meaning is conveyed indirectly. Moreover, art dissembles and plays with ambiguity. The waitress Louise's comment, after looking at Charlie's ring ("I'd just die for a ring like that"), works on multiple levels (Figure 21).

First, Louise expresses her admiration for the ring's beauty. Second, she refers unwittingly to the widow, who did, in fact, die as a result of her having possessed the ring, and to Charlie, who could die as well, and if Louise were to fall into the role, she, too, could die. Third, the verb "to die" is a traditional reference to making love, in particular, experiencing sexual orgasm. But Uncle Charlie's sexuality is not productive or fertile; it leads to death. The film ends with a lie, a religious tribute to the beauty of Uncle Charlie's soul and the sweetness of his character, such that the director's artistic irony lingers even beyond the work.

Not only knowledge but in a different way lack of knowledge can be dangerous. Most people don't know what lurks out there. Thus, the need for the guardian, who protects, and for art, which reveals depth. The artist exhibits a love for what is, partly by recognizing its insufficiencies, partly by revealing its hidden depths, partly by embracing it in its full complexity. The artist, unlike Uncle Charlie, educates toward nuance and ambiguity. Of course not each of these three types—lover, guardian, and artist—is universally knowledgeable. We see within this chaotic family comic reductions and aberrant forms of love. Everyone speaks at once, and hardly anyone listens. The uninformed and oblivious policeman who challenges Charlie and extols Uncle Charlie is also part of this simple and comic world, hardly a true guardian. Moreover, we see reductions of art and of the reception of art: the adults' detective

Figure 21 Charlie, played by Teresa Wright, and Uncle Charlie, played by Joseph Cotton, are doubles, but Louise, played by Janet Shaw, stands between them as she studies the ring ("I'd just die for a ring like that"). Louise, as Charlie's classmate, is her darker double, and Louise's ignominious past renders her Uncle Charlie's double as well. *Shadow of a Doubt* directed by Alfred Hitchcock. © Universal Studios 1942. All rights reserved.

stories, Ann's mindless reading, and Uncle Charlie's feeble play with the newspaper.[15]

At the end of the film, we recognize a series of aesthetic ambiguities. Charlie has mixed feelings when Uncle Charlie departs. She knows that his departure causes her mother suffering, and she herself retains an elegiac sensibility. However, she knows that her life is threatened, and she wants Uncle Charlie to depart. In this scene Charlie wears black (Figure 22).

She is in mourning, a subtle identification with her mother, who despairs at Uncle Charlie's departure. Further, the black visualizes her transformation into a widow who has herself lost her lover (Uncle Charlie must leave, and Charlie's love for him has not fully disappeared). The black, widow-like dress also renders her a potential victim. Finally, the black dress unveils her darker side—the need to kill to save herself

Figure 22 Charlie, played by Teresa Wright, wears black at Uncle Charlie's departure. She mourns her mother's and her own loss of Uncle Charlie; the widow-like dress renders her a potential victim; and the color unveils her darker side, including her loss of naiveté. *Shadow of a Doubt* directed by Alfred Hitchcock. © Universal Studios 1942. All rights reserved.

and others—and with this her loss of naiveté. The darkness of the dress is essential to knowledge, to recognizing and curtailing evil, and to the substance and playfulness of art. Knowledge of danger is dark knowledge, thus not only the late visit to the library but also the discussion in the dim bar. At the station the camera's soft focus on an isolated Charlie elevates her and gives her an aura of mystery. Not only love and knowledge, but also a confrontation with the possibility of evil, of which others are oblivious, gives her depth.

Uncle Charlie is fascinated by someone who can see through him. Charlie knows of his insufficiencies ("You're my severest critic," he had said). But he despises and fears her knowledge: "I've got to do this, Charlie, so long as you know what you do about me." Indeed, if, as seems evident, there is a perversion in the way Uncle Charlie makes love to the widows and then kills them, they, too, presumably know of his inadequacies. It is a sign of Charlie's depth that she knows of another kind of inadequacy beyond the sexual. Her knowledge could lead to death, possibly hers and possibly his, thus the tension in the final scene.

At least four, not mutually exclusive readings of Uncle Charlie's death are possible.

- First, Charlie kills Uncle Charlie, exhibiting her capacity to rise to the occasion. The ordinary becomes extraordinary, and she wills herself to a higher level.
- Second, Uncle Charlie, who had earlier revealed his suicidal tendencies, takes his own life. Uncle Charlie's erasure of human dignity becomes self-destructive, and we wonder earlier why he gave Charlie the ring with engraved initials. Was he simply careless, or did he at some unconscious level want to be caught? Did he in the final scene simply give way to his death? Someone who hates life may find paradoxical fulfillment in death. As Socrates makes clear when refuting Callicles, negativity is not unified within itself but internally split; it cancels itself. This structure may partially explain Uncle Charlie's identity crisis and the doubling that occurs at the end, with the appearance of a second train. Whereas negativity destroys itself, the knowledgeable Charlie survives. Wisdom, in contrast to negativity, is a kind of good fortune (Plato 279d).
- Third, a higher power leads to Uncle Charlie's death. This could be fate or providence or God. Both suspects died in collisions with vehicles. Uncle Charlie's earlier streetcar accident foreshadows his eventual fate, and the second train arrives at just the right moment. Uncle Charlie seems possessed when he takes the newspaper from Charlie and when he grabs her on the train. His seemingly being driven by an external force is most pronounced during his dinner table address. As the camera tracks to an extreme close-up, an irrational impulse seems to speak through him. He hardly seems free. From a philosophical frame, be it Platonic or Kantian, the evil person is necessarily not free.
- Finally, the higher power that leads to Uncle Charlie's death could simply be the filmmaker. After all, Hitchcock notes that in a narrative film "the director is the god" (Truffaut 102). Indeed, Uncle Charlie is killed by a train, and we last see Hitchcock in a train (Figure 23), so the approaching train represents at some level Hitchcock

Figure 23 Hitchcock holds all the cards but doesn't reveal them. On the contrary, he deceives effectively; like Uncle Charlie, he only appears sick. We cannot see Hitchcock's face, which is symbolic, for he plays many roles, adopts various guises, and is able to identify with many persons. *Shadow of a Doubt* directed by Alfred Hitchcock. © Universal Studios 1942. All rights reserved.

himself. The film contains a number of self-reflexive moments. The doctor on the train says that Hitchcock doesn't "look very well either." The deeper meaning at play here is that Hitchcock empathizes with Uncle Charlie, who on the train also seems ill. Like the telepathic Charlie, Hitchcock understands Uncle Charlie. But Hitchcock also identifies with Charlie and ordinary life. Hitchcock holds all the cards (a perfect hand): he knows how everything will turn out, and his depth is evident in the fact that he has not revealed his cards. On the contrary, he deceives effectively; like Uncle Charlie, he only appears sick. We can't see Hitchcock's face. This is symbolic: he plays many roles, adopts various guises, and is able to identify with many persons. He knows the mind of the criminal. His holding thirteen spades connects him with death and with Uncle Charlie, whose boarding house address was thirteen. Our not seeing Hitchcock's face provides a parallel to Uncle Charlie, who has no photographs, save for one of his innocent youth. The face of evil is not easy to recognize. People don't know whether or not Uncle Charlie is good; they don't know who he is; he is elusive. But Hitchcock is multivalent as well, and this inexhaustability is characteristic not only of evil but also of art and of complex goodness.[16] By killing Uncle Charlie, Hitchcock acts out a prolepsis: he enters the plot of the film and wills the action the circumstances require.

The train is a modern counterpart to the ship of life. Uncle Charlie, who is in that train, is not alien, but an element within us. After all, Uncle Charlie is both Charlie's nemesis and an element within her. In the train of life, play is prominent, for example, the cards, but it can also become serious, dangerous, deadly. Art captures both moments simultaneously—comedy and horror. *Shadow of a Doubt* mocks the search for simple truths: the younger children, the father, Herb, and the detectives all fail to understand Uncle Charlie. Unveiling his identity requires attention to subtle gestures and ambiguities. The importance of non-verbal recognition and the multivalence of the ending, which cannot be dissolved into a singular interpretation, mock these figures and elevate instead Charlie, with her capacity to envisage multiple sides.

The various media underscore the film's self-reflexivity: the newspaper, the telegram, the radio, the telephone, photography, the detective stories, books, and of course telepathy. Charlie reads fewer books than her younger sister, but Charlie is perceptive in a different way. She understands non-verbal gestures, and the newspaper allows her to discover information about the world. The detective stories do not lead to this kind of knowledge, and the blaring radio hides the truth. Charlie's intuition is manifest early on; she has little desire for the ring her uncle gives her.

Charlie operates beyond the purely rational realm. She is shaped by her telepathy and her sensibility for music and gesture; she hears the tune that links her uncle to the murder and senses the murderer by observing his hands. The filmmaker works with music as well, also of course dance and play, and, as we have seen, Hitchcock himself exhibits a kind of telepathy.

When Graham suggests that "sometimes the world needs a lot of watching," he is speaking as a guardian. But what one watches can also include films, and the hidden meaning behind Graham's comment is that through film, we can enjoy the ordinary in light-hearted ways and learn something about evil. A lot of watching also means watching a lot of films; the comment is simultaneously comic and serious, and it is both self-reflexive and realistic, bordering on the historic. Herman Shumlin's *Watch on the Rhine*, which likewise suggests that to fight evil we must ourselves become less than passive, appeared the same year as *Shadow of a Doubt*.

An interesting aspect of the early scene on the train is that Hitchcock plays cards and appears to be a gambler. What is happening is perhaps predetermined, simply a game, but the question remains, what do we make out of the game. We can play poorly, but Hitchcock tries to guide us so that we play well. This leads to my final reflections on the film's historical resonance.

Evocative Allusion

Film is unusually rich in integrating and mirroring contemporary history. One of the first great periods of cinema, the Weimar era, reflects the trauma of the First World War along with the chaos, despair, and emerging authoritarianism that ensued (Kracauer, Kaes). But the point is universal. Cinema, unlike literature, has an economic imperative to resonate with its age. In order to be financially viable, film must draw an audience, so it tends to carry more traces of its age than less expensive art forms. Moreover, film is a collective endeavor, reflective of more than a single consciousness; its multiple creators, from the director to the writers, art directors, composers, cinematographers, actors, and editors, contribute to its meaning. This is not to say that a film is reducible to its time. Lang's *M*, in which panic is met with quick and efficient but unjust strategies, says a great deal about the attraction of ruthless and autocratic models not only during the late Weimar Republic but also beyond.

Although evil is a universal phenomenon, Hitchcock portrays it in stories that often have a contemporary political and existential interest. *Foreign Correspondent* calls on the United States to join the battle against Nazism, a turn that at the very end almost breaks the narrative; on the diegetic level, we hear an appeal to America followed by an extra-diegetic playing of the National Anthem. Hitchcock filmed *The*

Birds during the Cuban missile crisis; at a metaphysical level the film evokes the "end of the world."

Shadow of a Doubt seeks to strengthen America's sense of the not fully recognized Nazi threat. When Uncle Charlie arrives on the train, a melody with bits of American folk tunes comes into contact with notes from the European waltz (Weis 102–3). Something dissonant, but not fully recognizable, conflicts with the American spirit. Later we transition from dark music and a canted shot of Uncle Charlie, his hands acting out a strangling motion, to an appealing melody as Charlie and Graham hold hands outside. Uncle Charlie's wickedness is not restricted to the urban environment. Nor does evil lie in recognizable guises. The police don't really know what the murderer looks like. The villain may well be alluring. Hitchcock comments: "villains are not all black and heroes are not all white; there are grays everywhere" (Truffaut 153). Deceptively charming criminals populate multiple Hitchcock films, among them, Marvin in *Secret Agent*, Bruno in *Strangers on a Train*, Willie in *Lifeboat*, Tony in *Dial M for Murder*, and Rusk in *Frenzy*. As the family leaves the train station with Uncle Charlie, the music is so upbeat and joyous, it seems almost a parody. The music matches Charlie's unbridled enthusiasm at her savior's arrival. Through his actions, words, and gestures, "the charismatic convinces those who believe in him that he has access to a spiritual world for which they, dissatisfied with their own time, have long yearned in a vague way without being able to find it" (Hösle, *Morals* 360).

The desire to rid the world of what is perceived to be inadequate can appear attractive. Uncle Charlie hates the world because it does not match his ideals. Whenever we hate normalcy and long for missionary idealism, we are vulnerable to evil. There is something appealing in transcending the simple and mundane, which is necessary even to recognize evil. But as Charlie discovers, not only obliviousness, but also insight into inadequacy can be dangerous. At some level we like and understand Uncle Charlie. But we also abhor him. Uncle Charlie destroys communal life. He violates taboos. He has no moral restraint. He is a liar and a murderer.

Any society can exhibit the capacity to foster, and be seduced by, evil, but the film offers more than a universal reflection. The film is layered with historical resonance. *Shadow of a Doubt* has rightly been called one of Hitchcock's most American films. It brings together "the dark world of film noir" with "the cheery world of sentimental Americana" (Rothman, *Hitchcock* 180). But critics have yet to assess Hitchcock's picture of America in its full complexity. *Shadow of a Doubt* is about America on the eve of the Second World War. The action takes place, as we learn, fifty-three years after 1888, that is, in 1941. The first newspaper Charlie lifts off the rack has as its headline: "Tojo speaks." That year General Tojo spoke out in favor of attacking the United States, in October he became Prime Minister, and on December 7 he announced the war on Japanese radio. Germany declared war on the United States the next day, and we responded on December 11. The film was made in 1942 and released in 1943. Rothman, who has written the longest analysis of the film, notes the connection to the Second World War only in passing; in a one-sentence footnote, he comments on the sailors (360). The sailors' presence in the bar should not be underplayed, for there Uncle Charlie gives voice to the horrors that in this American community are otherwise not easily visible. In his study of Hitchcock's war films, Sam Simone doesn't even mention *Shadow of a Doubt*, and others who speak of Hitchcock's war films generally do not include *Shadow of a Doubt*.[17]

In 1941 hatred of normalcy, charismatic appeal to transcendence, denial of "freedom" and of the "rights of man," and wolves in sheep's clothing did not evoke generic evil; they signaled the Nazi threat. Uncle Charlie is blond and comes to Santa Rosa from the East. The train enters the symbolic heart of America, a small, idyllic town. Uncle Charlie dines late, drinks imported wine, wears fashionable clothes, and scorns traditional religion. Mr. Greene lauds his speech, suggesting that usually only "foreigners" speak so well. It takes the family a long time to get the telegram, that is, to realize that Uncle Charlie is really coming into their home. Like the Nazis, Uncle Charlie seeks to eradicate all who are in his eyes below the level of humanity, wheezing animals parading as something more than subhuman.

Uncle Charlie's contempt for the modern world and for ordinary people echoes the ideology of German nationalism as it developed over many years, with its hatred of the West as materialistic. Uncle Charlie is not interested in money, and he does not kill for money. He attacks the "fat, wheezing animals" who throw away money and act as parasites:

> The cities are full of women, middle-aged widows, husbands dead, husbands who've spent their lives making fortunes, working and

working. And then they die and leave their money to their wives, their silly wives. And what do the wives do, these useless women? You see them in the hotels, the best hotels, every day by the thousands, drinking the money, eating the money, losing the money at bridge, playing all day and all night, smelling of money, proud of their jewelry but of nothing else, horrible, faded, fat, greedy women . . . Are they human or are they fat, wheezing animals, hmm? And what happens to animals when they get too fat and too old?

Uncle Charlie's horrific language, with its erasure of human dignity, is the language of German anti-Semitism. Hitchcock undermines this ideology not only by making it emotionally unattractive and repulsive but also by exhibiting its internal contradictions: Uncle Charlie gets his money from the widows just as they receive their money from their husbands. Even as the threat of Uncle Charlie's sick nostalgia is layered with anti-Semitic language, he targets women. His misogynistic ideology is linked to his obsession with a world where men have the money and women are subordinate. This is also the world of Santa Rosa, as is evident when the mother expresses her ignorance of business; Mrs. Green, the wife of the bank president, asks her husband for money because she has only five dollars; and the pastor declines alcohol for both himself and his wife. For the inquisitive and bright Charlie, this ordering of society, men active and women subordinate, is called into question; it is no wonder that she becomes Uncle Charlie's nemesis.

One sees in these diverse allusions the ways in which the film evokes both universal and historical evil. Hitchcock offers historical resonance without forgoing universality. Pushing the interpretation into the allegorical would go too far. For example, what would one make of the streetcar accident? We could argue that Uncle Charlie began his life as an avid reader, but after his accident, "he had to get into mischief." By pushing the analogy, we could recognize an allusion to the land of poets and thinkers, which took an unfortunate turn after the First World War, when, to follow the film's chronology, Uncle Charlie would have been a child and would have had his accident. However, creating precise parallels along these lines misses the essential point: Nazi references resonate, but the evocation of evil is not reducible to the present.[18] One could argue that the streetcar reference arises from Hitchcock's fascination with psychology or Hollywood's insistence on clear answers (Wolitzer 31), but even these explanations do not suffice to capture the depth of Uncle Charlie's misanthropic soul. Arguably the best psychological reading of the accident comes from Humbert, who argues that Uncle Charlie cannot tolerate limits on his existence (29); the accident restricted his self-sufficiency, which he has since worked to cultivate and which appears related to his charisma. The streetcar story has yet a further dimension: it underscores the idea that the potential for evil lurks within all of us, for the story expands the links between Uncle Charlie and the three children: not only is Charlie Uncle Charlie's double, but Uncle Charlie's earlier reading links him with Ann and his having been spoiled and his subsequent restlessness with Roger.

Given the film's orientation toward evil as such, which is coupled with an array of references to the Nazi threat, it would be wise not to speak of allegory, which is not sustainable in every detail and could easily become reductionistic. Instead, we need a different category. I propose the concept "evocative allusion," by which I mean a set of allusions that create a specific resonance or sensibility that is not reducible to allegory or to a one-to-one correspondence. Echoes of Nazism are layered throughout the film, such that our sensitivity is awakened not only to evil as such but also to the specific evil of the age. The concept is not unique to film. Franz Kafka is a master of evocative allusion. His works are not reducible to allegory, but they often contain historical allusions that give his works both universal and particular resonance. As one example for many, one might think of "The Bucket Rider." Evocative allusion captures the layering of universal and particular meaning. This combination allows the filmmaker to create a more than simply tendentious work while simultaneously seeking to awaken Americans to the Nazi threat.

America's relationship to Germany, in advance of the war, was dominated by fascination or obliviousness, the very reactions that Uncle Charlie engenders. Charlie, the mother, Mrs. Potter, and most of the townspeople are fascinated by Uncle Charlie. Many, including Joe, Roger, and Herb are clueless. After the turning point in the investigation out East, even Graham and Saunders are duped. The film's title underscores the nation's inattentiveness. In the American judicial system, "beyond a reasonable doubt" is the standard of evidence required to validate a criminal conviction. The film suggests that in our ignorance, our hesitancy fully to recognize the evil in our midst, we are waiting for evidence that is "beyond a shadow of a doubt." Only Charlie moves from fascination to doubt and resistance.

The hidden meaning behind the national survey of typical American families, with which Graham tries to get a handle on Uncle Charlie, is that the film is also about America, its values and vulnerabilities. Charlie and Santa Rosa evoke America. Herb wears a small American flag on his lapel. The Bank of America and the library prominently advertise defense savings bonds: "A Share in America." Hitchcock underscored Thornton Wilder's name in the credits; Wilder, the author of *Our Town*, is the playwright of America, and this is a film about the American spirit in the early 1940s, including its contemporary threat.[19] The association between the family and America is underscored by the ways in which the home blends with the city. Twice Charlie walks out into the street without a coat, as if she were still within her home. Normally a love relationship means leaving one's family, but Charlie wants Uncle Charlie to come into the family, and Uncle Charlie very much wants to return. On a meta-level, the importance of the family, its elevation over broader universal structures, alludes to the overemphasis on nation, at the expense of the community of nations, which has marked American consciousness off and on into the present.

Germany, which is loosely evoked in the person of Uncle Charlie, became in a sense a murderer; Germany, which had hidden itself behind a curtain, had emerged. The train scene, with Uncle Charlie in a horizontal position, alludes to two of Germany's early film classics, which likewise deal with violence and have been taken to foreshadow Nazism, *The Cabinet of Dr. Caligari* and Murnau's *Nosferatu*. Hitchcock, who opposed American isolationism, was fascinated by the German threat. He followed *Shadow of a Doubt* with *Lifeboat*: there the Nazi captain shoots torpedoes at the Americans in lifeboats, and when he is rescued by them, consistently deceives and endangers them, eventually killing one of them. For most of the film, the Americans are too naive to recognize his deception. Three years earlier Hitchcock had directed *Foreign Correspondent*, a film dedicated "to those forthright ones who early saw the clouds of war while many of us at home were seeing rainbows." A central theme in *Foreign Correspondent*, which is echoed in *Shadow of a Doubt,* is that persons one loves and admires, even family members, may not be what they seem and may be contributing to widespread evil.

Uncle Charlie tries various strategies to win over Charlie and the family.

- First, with his charisma he seeks to beguile the family and the broader community. To a degree, Uncle Charlie revitalizes the family, most especially Charlie and her mother, and energizes the broader community. Charisma represents a great threat, in particular to Charlie, who longs for something beyond the everyday. The effort works until she begins to understand that her uncle seeks to obliterate the value and dignity of human beings. Still, others remain enthralled.
- A second attempt involves enticing everyone with gifts, which on the political level corresponds to opportunism and transactional relations. Ann is not pleased, and Charlie, who is searching for meaning, has no interest in material things. Later when Uncle Charlie seeks to bribe her, she responds: "We don't want anything from you." The community, however, is happy to receive Uncle Charlie's funds. On the whole, however, America is not in need of bargains and benefits, even if Uncle Charlie does make inroads.
- A third strategy is ideology. This likewise fails with Charlie and, interestingly, with everyone to whom Uncle Charlie expresses his bizarre views. Charlie has the correct categories with which to resist and refute Uncle Charlie. When he speaks of "faded, fat, greedy women," she appeals to basic human dignity: "But they're alive; they're human beings."[20] America may be oblivious to world-political events and the threat of evil, but in 1941 it had the moral categories to counter evil.
- A fourth attempt to win Charlie over is by awakening sympathy and appealing to solidarity. Uncle Charlie tells her: "The same blood runs through our veins." A social analog to the family relationship is the extent to which America in the 1940s was shaped by German blood.[21] To survive the external threat, America must in a sense murder Germany. Although Germany may not be America's father, it is its relative, its uncle, as it were. Charlie exhibits some compassion for Uncle Charlie, but sympathy ultimately presupposes a common basis, a common humanity. Uncle Charlie's appeal cancels itself.
- A final attempt is the idea that Charlie must act responsibly toward her mother. Once Uncle Charlie's charismatic appeal has been

erased, this argument has the greatest pull. In confronting her uncle, Charlie may cause her mother to despair or die. The scandal could unleash a crisis within the family or, if we consider the political analog, within the nation. Charlie waits because she doesn't want to endanger the family; that is, America delays to protect itself and its interests. Hesitation endangers the world, but acting may cause Charlie's death. A life-and-death struggle endangers lives, but Charlie is ultimately prepared to sacrifice herself, as was America in the war.

Charlie herself is for Hitchcock a counter-intuitive but appealing image of an America that needs to go to war. She has aspects of both American naiveté and European sophistication. She seems indeed to be slightly European: she is fashionable (note both her clothing and her critique of her mother's wardrobe). Though she is naive and young, an American, she is closer to the Europeans than the others are. She is smart beyond her years. (Charlie sleeps in the child's bed, but leaves it to find out the truth—she has a combination of innocence and sophistication.) To retain and gain its identity in the new world, America must engage Europe and draw on the kind of spirit that Charlie embodies, its native trust and its willingness to move beyond the status quo. Charlie must act herself. At the meta-level, this parallel seems to suggest that the community of nations is ineffective. America must act. Much as Hitchcock engenders Charlie's action, so did Britain lead America into the war.

America had difficulties recognizing that another civilized nation, a relative as it were, could be so evil. In response to the staging of the Third Reich, which is evident in films such as Leni Riefenstahl's *Triumph of the Will* and in the other arts, including architecture (Bartetzko), Hitchcock responds in kind. It is telling that Joseph Goebbels was deeply impressed by *Foreign Correspondent* (Truffaut 137). As with his other war films, in *Shadow of a Doubt* Hitchcock fights symbolically. He is the artist who is also a guardian. Nazism is not simply an aesthetic phenomenon. Hitchcock endeavors to show the real consequences of evil and to give us a contrasting value statement about the ordinary and the extraordinary, one that offers not a fanatic and idealistic hatred of the ordinary but a loving recognition of its weaknesses. Hitchcock, the artist and the guardian, is also the lover, who, like Charlie, understands, through his distance from the ordinary, the allure of Uncle Charlie, even as he, like Charlie, still loves the ordinary. Hitchcock loves America even in its weakness, though he does not hesitate to point out the deficiencies of America and of the ordinary, even as America, and the ordinary, retains its dignity.

Chapter 4

Hitchcock's Real and Apparent Gaps

Hitchcock introduced innovative formal advances, masterfully orchestrated his works, and addressed substantive themes. He is, however, not without deficiencies. This first includes his scope, including his bracketing a wide range of social issues. He devotes his attention instead to universal themes; to historical challenges, such as the Second World War; and to broad-ranging psychological and intersubjective dynamics. Hitchcock was fascinated by questions of knowledge and love. He interwove these with broad historical developments and issues of identity and human relations, including power dynamics.

Despite his otherwise wide range, Hitchcock's works do not easily fit into the now contemporary focus on social issues, including race and class, nor does he engage the challenges of developing countries, which represent one of the great moral issues of our age. Although his British films offer viewers considerable social diversity, his canonical American films take place mainly in prosperous, all-white settings. After *The Ring* of 1927 few Blacks play significant roles. In *Lifeboat* Hitchcock gives the African-American Joe some stereotypical qualities (including his playing the recorder and having a pickpocket past). Still, Hitchcock is attentive to the challenges Joe faces: Joe asks whether he'll be allowed to vote. Moreover, Joe's religiosity and humanity (in shying away from the mob's attack on Willie) are positive characteristics. In this film, Hitchcock also portrays the working-class horizon of two survivors and captures aspects of the conflict between labor and capital.

The Wrong Man is another modest exception insofar as the film shows the financial challenges of an ordinary family that lives on the edge of its capacities. The film's basis in a true story partially underscores that Hitchcock otherwise chose to film a different universe. An analogous claim can be made about the poverty in *Juno and the Paycock*. Even *Marnie*, which exhibits the social misery of the heroine's childhood, dwells instead on the upper class. When Hitchcock introduces class, he often deals with it, as in *Under Capricorn,* in terms more of identity and human relations than economic conditions. In other cases, as in *Frenzy*, it is simply part of the local color. Nonetheless, when Hitchcock presents characters who help the hero, persons who are good-hearted and generous, they are often on the fringes of society, such as the poor crofter's wife in *The 39 Steps*, the homeless person in *Young and Innocent,* or the truck driver and the circus performers in *Saboteur*. In this last work Hitchcock indirectly criticizes the upper classes: Tobin's condescension toward "the moron millions" is abhorrent. There are hints of class critique in the British films, such as *The Manxman* and *Jamaica Inn*, but the concern recedes in the later American films. Hitchcock portrayed what he knew, and with his frequent concern for the bottom line, he wanted his films to be visually appealing and uplifting so as to attract and satisfy viewers. Hitchcock's further defense, when he was asked about the social consciousness of his films, was his appeal to formalism: "Messages are for Western Union" (*Hitchcock on Hitchcock* 2.250). The response is clever, but even a formalist must choose his themes, elevating some and excluding others. A final (and very partial) defense of Hitchcock in this context would be that although he rarely addresses specific social challenges, such as race or class, he nonetheless dwells on persons who are cast out from society or placed in seemingly impossible situations.

A second concern is not one of omission. It involves the third element of the contemporary social triad, namely gender, which Hitchcock does not ignore. Indeed, gender has been the focus of considerable analysis. Laura Mulvey famously argued that Hitchcock's films evoke erotic pleasure, with women as passive objects of the male gaze: "The determining male gaze projects its phantasy on to the female figure which is styled accordingly. In their traditional exhibitionist role, women are simultaneously looked at and displayed, with their appearance coded for strong visual and erotic impact so that they can be said to connote *to-be-looked-at-ness"* (11). Male viewers of films such as *Rear Window* and *Vertigo* objectify the women, and all viewers are invited to identify with the male protagonists who exert power.

But more recent criticism has called into question this founding document of psychoanalytic feminist film theory. Tania Modleski effectively argues that the portrayal of women in Hitchcock's films is more complex than first appearances might dictate. We are often encouraged to identify with female heroes, as in *Blackmail, Stage Fright*, *Rebecca,* and *Shadow of a Doubt*, and for stretches in *Rear Window* and *Vertigo*. Women exhibit their capacities by deciphering puzzles in a number of films, including *Young and Innocent*, *Jamaica Inn*, *The Lady Vanishes, Spellbound, Strangers on a Train*, *Shadow of a Doubt*, *Lifeboat, Rear Window,* and the second *Man Who Knew Too Much*. In most of these, as well as in others, including the first *Man Who Knew Too Much* and *Notorious*, women are active and enter into considerable risk. They are also empathetic with others and invite us, in turn, to identify with them. Moreover, in *North by Northwest*, Hitchcock advances a marriage that is far beyond contemporary cliches and culminates in moments of symmetry and equality (Jenkins). One can be critical of Hitchcock, but not only critical; the director had an eye for ambiguity.

A third issue one could raise is that while Hitchcock had wonderful intuitive acumen with the psychology of trust, identity, evil, and power, when he integrates contemporary psychology, his films sometimes border on the tendentious, as with the psychological language and images of *Spellbound* and Norman Bates's split personality in *Psycho* (even if Hitchcock might defend the latter as a comic touch). At times Hitchcock's portrayals become heavy-handed, as in *Spellbound* when a close-up of the two lovers' eyes is followed by multiple doors opening. Nonetheless, it speaks for Hitchcock that he recognized the significance of the unconscious (he was always aware of the temptation of evil, the significance of fear, the complexity of identity, and the role of the subconscious), and he portrayed the challenges and difficulties of the unconscious without letting his characters indulge in self-pity. Furthermore, Hitchcock suggests that reason can be used to help those who suffer from hidden and seemingly uncontrollable weaknesses.

Still, Hitchcock's strongest psychological insights arise when he is not seeking to apply textbook psychology but instead integrates psychological ideas organically, as in *Strangers on a Train* or *I Confess*.

Hitchcock's insight into Keller's psyche in *I Confess* is subtle and deep. Keller projects fear and cowardice onto Logan when he says that Logan will turn him in to the police. Cowardice and betrayal are qualities Keller himself embodies. Logan unintentionally torments Keller by not turning him in, which increases Keller's uncertainty and fear. Moreover, because Logan's values are superior to Keller's, Logan's adherence to these values humiliates Keller. Part of Keller wants to be saved. He wants to bring forward a harmony of inner and outer. That is the hidden logic of his confession and the deeper meaning of his thinking that Logan has gone to the police. Most importantly, because Keller's sense of self-worth is comparative, he tempts Logan, trying to bring him down to his level, which would make Keller comparatively less inadequate. He cannot tolerate Logan's goodness, which reflects so poorly on his own identity, so he calls Logan out for imagined weaknesses.

The film interweaves a psychological dynamic with a theological (and philosophical) one. The greater Logan becomes in the eyes of Keller, the more diabolical Keller acts. The devil is driven crazy by the holiness of Christ's servant. Beginning with their first conversation, Keller is obsessed with Logan's goodness. For his own survival, Keller does not want Logan to betray the sacrament. Yet the priest's infinite goodness leads Keller to want the priest to fail, to share in his mediocrity. A consensus of criminality would make his crime more bearable. If the priest betrays his secret, a standard or norm of justice will blur or disappear. Keller is directed by a kind of resentment. He wants to view himself as equal with the person he values, Logan. His consciousness of self-value derives from comparison, and he recognizes that he is not as good as Logan. In this act of comparison, Keller constitutes his values. Instead of aspiring to elevate himself to Logan's position, Keller would erase his inferior value by leveling out the value difference in a negative way, by dragging Logan down to his level. This explains Keller's continuous suspicion, and hidden desire, that Logan has turned him in. Perversely, though with an inner logic, Keller would prefer to equal Logan's values (by seeing Logan weakened) than to see himself as a free man and a figure whose values and integrity society does not question. Nonetheless, the fact that Keller would compare himself with Logan and not with the common folk represents an intuitive desire on Keller's part for greatness, indeed for goodness. Whereas Keller, who is himself diabolical, suspects the worst in Logan, a deeply trusting character such as Sam in *Under Capricorn* is oblivious to Milly's machinations.

After the relative neglect of race and class, the complexity of Hitchcock's gender portrayals, and the occasional heavy-handedness of his integration of psychology, a fourth issue arises: Hitchcock's plots sometimes seem to lack organic structure. Hitchcock was aware of the issue and not overly concerned about probability. He did not care as long as the audience was enthralled, but non-integration of part and whole, including issues of motivation, is an aesthetic weakness. The plots may be fun, but they are not always woven into an organic whole, a problem not restricted to a thematically incoherent film like *Champagne*. In what is often considered Hitchcock's best film, *Vertigo*, Elster's anticipation of how to kill his wife, a central plot element, borders on the absurd. Some films, such as *The 39 Steps* and *Saboteur*, have the kind of improbable and episodic structures Aristotle rightly found to be inferior to more organic plots, even if one could make the case that the theme of the hero on the run demands such a form and that richly hidden connections exist in *The 39 Steps:* repetitions, modulations, inversions, foreshadowing, and thematic links. The strongest films, such as *Shadow of a Doubt* and *Notorious*, are tightly interwoven. *North by Northwest* is a fascinating case, for, while it seems picaresque, the diverse parts are effectively integrated (Wood 131–41). That is part of Hitchcock's genius: with a light touch, he gives us great artworks. In truth, only one film, *Number Seventeen*, has such a confusing plot that it truly weakens the work's reception. A related issue is that in his desire to pit good against evil, his works are not always nuanced, even if this problem is modestly rare. Some of the works do fall into melodrama, as with *Saboteur*. An occasional lack of nuance can also help ensure accessibility for the non-esoteric viewer: consider the connection between darkness and ignorance and light and knowledge in *The 39 Steps*, where at key moments of realization, brighter light is visible, and at the very end when the whole truth is revealed, the stage is fully lit.

Chapter 5
Hitchcock and Beyond

Hitchcock was not simply an entertainer. His films illuminate reality. Moreover, they awaken empathy with those who suffer, those who combat evil, even those who contribute to chaos. In Hitchcock's eyes, we are all fragile beings—"people are unaware that catastrophe surrounds us all" (*Alfred* 44)—and each of us is capable of evil. In *Rear Window*, Jeff watches apartment life across the courtyard almost like a cinema audience enjoys a movie. Jeff observes his neighbors initially out of boredom and idle curiosity. He wants to escape, but he eventually becomes active himself, partly through others, especially Lisa, and partly on his own. Lisa's entering the cinematic world, so to speak, changes his view of her. What happens in Thorwald's apartment symbolically fulfills Jeff's desire to be rid of Lisa, and Jeff reacts with horror (Wood 104). He recognizes that Lisa is courageously willing to sacrifice herself for the truth, such that he binds himself to her in new ways. To see cinema as mere entertainment is to fall as low as Jeff at his shallowest point. *Rear Window* supports the idea that art uncovers the truth.

Although the Nazi threat and the Cold War were the dominant foci of Hitchcock's age, his analyses of evil are sufficiently broad as to be applicable across time. Hitchcock's recurring theme of superior and inferior beings, evident in *Shadow of a Doubt*, *Rope*, and *Strangers on a Train*, indirectly illuminates America's racial caste system, which presupposed a concept of superior and inferior beings (Wilkerson). The system's enshrinement in the legal system lasted into the 1960s. Its residue remains with us, not least of all with voting rights and with unjust policing and sentencing.

Fear is one of our most primal emotions, and its cultural resonance has not diminished since Hitchcock elevated it. He understood that emotions move people for good or for ill. In Nazi Germany and in the Soviet Union, arousing fear was a dominant political strategy. Franklin Roosevelt in contrast elevated "freedom from fear" as one of his "four essential human freedoms." Nonetheless, a string of recent political campaigns in the United States and Europe have elevated fear, division, and xenophobia. This phenomenon is not unrelated to the wrong man motif or in its sociological extension the scapegoat phenomenon. Although Hitchcock understood that fear can grip the soul, most of his characters respond by taking risks and exhibiting courage, which brings forth further confrontations, adventures, and danger. Though Hitchcock awakens fear in his audiences, on the screen he shows its suitable response: improvisation, courage, and hope.

Hitchcock's films bridge two otherwise opposed modes of thinking: on the one hand, a fixed view motivated by fear and oriented toward safety and, on the other, a flexible perspective open to the world and new experiences (Hetherington and Weiler). Though Hitchcock understands fear and anger as motivating forces, he is not drawn, as are most persons who emphasize threats, to simple answers. Hitchcock insists that to counter threats, we need knowledge. He looks for nuance, which in fact contributes to his avoidance of hate and his embrace of human dignity. The Hitchcock characters we admire most trust one another. They are not consumed by fear, which undermines openness and trust. In his films Hitchcock foresaw how trust can be eroded.[1] When mistrust and confusion override knowledgeable engagement, then in the face of genuine threats—be they from a pandemic or climate change, to take two current examples—little progress can be made. We require trust, even as institutions need individual acts of heroism to help restore our faith in institutions and in ideals.

Hitchcock's films may be the best artistic representation of one of philosophy's first great insights—that consensus is no guarantee of truth. Hitchcock repeatedly dramatizes the problems of a consensus theory of truth: in its predication of guilt and innocence, the crowd is almost always wrong. Hitchcock recognizes the dangers of disinformation and our inclination to believe what we want. In his contribution to *Memory of the Camps*, a documentary of Nazi horrors, Hitchcock ensured the inclusion of wide establishing shots in order to counter any potential claims that the evidence had been staged (Rogow). He also introduced maps to underscore the proximity of the death camps to towns: he thereby made clear that ordinary Germans were not in the dark. Readers immersed in social media and aware of disinformation campaigns, as with the American elections of 2016 and 2020 and their aftermath, can recognize how far-reaching Hitchcock's understanding of disinformation was. Anyone who is overwhelmed by such disinformation could easily succumb to cynicism, but Hitchcock provides a counter-narrative defined by ferreting out the truth and resisting an ill-informed majority.

Hitchcock's heroes are engaged in the world because they are thrown into predicaments that demand action. They do not have the freedom to sit back with unsullied hands. They must exert power to survive, but they do not elevate power as its own end. That is a lesson for today. The contemporary world's embrace of power as an end in itself reversed a mid-twentieth century emphasis on human dignity. Much of American foreign policy this century has elevated power positivism at the expense of values. The result: unjust wars, torture, neglect of human rights, overly restrictive borders, and support of autocrats. Even as Hitchcock recognizes that we must understand power structures, he cautions us about uninformed, capricious, and corrupt government actions.

Why has the ideology of power positivism increasingly gained acceptance? First, power positivism follows from the increasingly widespread idea that all moral values are simply constructed. We do not seek to discover objective moral norms. Instead, we invent them. As such, they are not binding. Second, we increasingly think that any interpretation of reality is so skewed to personal interests that the idea of objective facts and a common reality recedes from view. Hitchcock's elevation of classical virtues and his fascination with knowledge counter both of these views. For Hitchcock, we must learn to know and understand the world, and we must measure it against an ideal. A society that loses its relation to either the descriptive or normative realm is in delusion or moral crisis. Pity the country that has lost both an acceptance of objective reality and a guiding moral vision of what should be.

Despite Hitchcock's critique of power positivism, he unveils evil in its complexity. The persons who seek to enact evil are more often than not interesting and ambiguous. They embody formal virtues, often charm and a certain warmth, at times kindness toward family, which remind us that as humans they have dignity, even as they provide a cautionary tale about the need for vigilance. In portraying evil in this way, Hitchcock avoids a black-and-white dichotomy and reminds us that we can have a complex relation to our opponents. What is evil must be sought out and fought, but the battle need not eradicate our humanity; indeed, it can help shape and form us. This is one reason why Hitchcock's thrillers are so often interwoven with love stories. For Hitchcock love is the truth of hate and hope the answer to despair.

Hitchcock's concept of loving critique should appeal to a culture that oscillates between blind affirmation and bitter alienation. Hitchcock criticizes what is but does not relinquish optimism. Harsh criticism and a sense of alienation need not mean abandoning idealism. Hitchcock trusts in the individual's capacity to shape history even as he recognizes challenges to the self and elevates positive forces that transcend the individual. Adopting such a double lens can help give a culture resilience. Hitchcock does not hesitate to criticize his nation, even in the midst of war: consider the portrayals of Americans in *Shadow of a Doubt* and *Lifeboat* and of the American government in *Notorious* and *North by Northwest*. We should be alienated by deviations from the ideal, even when they are part of our collective identity, for if the ideal is to be made real, its realization presupposes critique of deviations from that ideal. In the United States today our sense of patriotism and our collective identity have not sufficiently integrated this form of love that allows for, and demands, critique. Even though Hitchcock did not address race in any prominent way, his view of patriotism as including moments of critique, his integration of the wrong man motif, his suspicions of unjust authority figures, his recognition of the gap between law and justice, and his suggestion that the individual can help contribute to shaping history do give us connections to the present moment.

Not only *Shadow of a Doubt* thematizes America's collective identity. The MacGuffin in *North by Northwest* is nothing other than a film of government secrets. As Cavell argues, *North by Northwest* seeks to become a monument to, and interpretation of, America, but we can add multiple elements not named by Cavell. First, Mt. Rushmore as a tribute to America is static, whereas film, a temporal and linguistic art, can better integrate change and critique. Hitchcock suggests that an art that seeks to capture America's spirit must be dynamic, as the country has evolved over time and continues to do so, thus the film's historical allusions, which range from the Christian era to modern architecture and music. *North by Northwest* is also spatially expansive, reaching beyond monumental leaders and encompassing the nation from New York to Prairie Crossing and on to South Dakota. Moreover, Hitchcock suggests that "sculpture" (a term with which Thornhill mistakenly describes Eve) does not capture the complexity of emotions we recognize in film. The shot on Mt. Rushmore of Eve's and Thornhill's hands reaching for one another reimagines Michelangelo's *Creation of Adam*: Hitchcock underscores not an asymmetrical relation between God and man, but an intersubjective act of love, and a coming together, not a release from one another, that must contend with evil, in this case, Leonard's brutal attempt to crush Thornhill's other hand.

Courage, which is evident in Thornhill's final actions and prominent in virtually all Hitchcock films, is arguably the classical virtue most lacking today. The need for physical courage naturally recedes in an age defined by institutions set up to ensure justice, both domestically and globally. In politics, where we have traditionally found leaders, civic courage has likewise diminished. Politicians have become cautious, subservient to public opinion and keen to stay in power. Social media, polarization, and money in politics only exacerbate the challenge, which can lead to defeatism. And so, the need for intellectual and psychological courage continues unabated. When institutions fail, individuals need to act. We need persons who do not despair, but act confidently with trust in the future, who can be motivated by a vision of goodness and not dissuaded from realizing that vision, despite attacks from vested interests and ignorant onlookers. We need and benefit from heroes who pursue a worthy path despite lacerating challenges to their reputations and livelihoods. Recently courage has been mistakenly ascribed to the simple act of challenging and breaking norms, but courage is a virtue; therefore, courage truly exists only when it is combined with knowledge and wisdom (Roche, "Courage").

Despite his deep warnings about evil and mediocrity, Hitchcock tends to offer at the end of his films, if not also along the way, glimmers of hope in a redemptive universe. Such faith carries with it considerable risks, which most Hitchcock heroes, in pursuing goodness, are willing to undergo. The hero's confidence seems to derive from a belief that ultimately, they can prove their innocence and that the world is just. But even as the enormity of the threats and the incompetence of the police and other authorities make manifest the need for a hero, Hitchcock's universe is hardly individualistic. Hitchcock's heroes are driven by a vision of the whole. They depend on help from others and equally enough on chance or moments of undeserved grace and providence that allow them to reach their telos. This arc, which applies to almost all Hitchcock films, cannot be captured by the dichotomy of tragedy and comedy. The sober implications of evil in *Shadow of a Doubt* cannot be erased even when the film ends with a glimmer of poetic justice. Whereas the drama of reconciliation captures works such as *The 39 Steps* and *North by Northwest*, Hitchcock tends simply to beckon toward reconciliation without giving us a fully realized happy end. This structure of gesturing toward reconciliation encompasses films such as *Shadow of a Doubt* and *Marnie*. The ambiguous gesture fits our times and gives meaning to Hitchcock's combination of suspense and comedy, of goodness triumphing but only at great cost.

Notes

Introduction

1 Rohmer and Chabrol occasionally note Catholic moments, such as images that echo Christ on the cross and concepts such as guilt and redemption, grace and providence. Although they rightly stress Hitchcock's ambiguity, their concept of "the *interchangeable guilt* of all mankind" elides concepts of differentiation and responsibility that are prominent in Hitchcock, who seems to work with a unity of unity and difference (149, emphasis in the original). To say, as Hitchcock does, that the temptation toward evil is in all of us or "the devil is in each of us" (*Alfred* 40), is not to say that our guilt is the same. Since this French study from the 1950s, the literature on Hitchcock and Catholicism has been sparse, as one might expect, given trends in film criticism. Exceptions include Hurley and Alleva, who publish in non-film journals.

2 Some actresses, such as Ingrid Bergman (as hostess to the AFI Life Achievement Award for Hitchcock) and Grace Kelly (in her preface for Spoto's *The Art of Alfred Hitchcock*), praised Hitchcock profusely. However, Tippi Hedren, who had the lead roles in *The Birds* and *Marnie*, had a different experience: she criticized Hitchcock's behavior as both obsessive and abusive. Besides Hedren's autobiography, see Spoto, *Dark Side* 450–79. Spoto's charges have been much discussed. For a balanced review of his book, see Paul Thomas, who rightly observes that Spoto's claims, however one is to assess them, fail to shed light on the films themselves.

3 It was once necessary to address the question whether film and philosophy should intersect at all, but today the question is only, in what meaningful ways can film become productive for philosophy and philosophy for film analysis. It is telling that the journals *Film and Philosophy* and *Film-Philosophy* have each now been in existence for twenty-five years or longer.

4 *Hitchcock on Hitchcock* 2.192. The comment is not isolated. "Content, I am not interested in that at all. I don't give a damn what the film is about. I am more interested in how to handle the material so as to create an emotion in the audience" (*Alfred* 89; see also *Alfred* 78–9, 160, 183 and

Truffaut 282). However, Hitchcock concedes that the content of *Shadow of a Doubt* is not insignificant (*Alfred* 139). Certainly, some dimensions of content are less interesting, such as the MacGuffin, an object the characters chase after, but which is relatively unimportant to the audience (see, e.g., *Alfred* 109 and Bogdanovich 502), but searching for the MacGuffin can trigger complex intersubjective relations and rich moral issues, such that the films represent more than formal achievements.

5 Philosophical books do not dominate Hitchcock criticism. Jane Sloan's critical survey lists six major trends, none of which could be called philosophical. However, because the philosophical resonance of Hitchcock is not easily avoidable, some of the most illuminating Hitchcock books, for example, those by Wood and Brill, raise philosophical issues even when they have no overt philosophical orientation. Two books, one by Robert Pippin, which emphasizes unknowingness, and a theory-driven anthology edited by Katalin Makkai, address the philosophical significance of *Vertigo*, a work I discuss briefly, but on which I do not dwell. Two other anthologies exist: *Hitchcock and Philosophy* and *Hitchcock's Moral Gaze*. No common thread exists within either volume, and in many cases, contributors relate a given work to a particular philosophical theory or use isolated scenes as catalysts for philosophical rumination without seeking a meaningful interpretation of the work. In a few cases, however, as with Carroll on *Vertigo*, the readings are rich. Even though many of the essays fall into jargon or employ the films as visualizations of philosophical topics instead of using philosophy to illuminate the films, all of them underscore the extent to which Hitchcock evokes philosophical issues. Drumin and Yanal are closest to my study in offering single-authored works that explore in broad terms Hitchcock and philosophy.

Chapter 1

1 As Hitchcock likes to tell the story, if the audience knows that a bomb is under the table while the actors chat with one another innocuously and the audience wants to scream, the appropriate category is suspense, and it can last a while (e.g., Bogdanovich 529). If, however, a bomb goes off, and the audience knew nothing about it, then the appropriate category is surprise. Knowledge drives suspense. Suspense, with its different levels of knowledge, offers the greater incongruity.

2 See Hösle, *Die Krise* 213–19 and *Morals and Politics* 158–62. Hegel's realms are essentially threefold: idea, nature, and spirit. Spirit, however, is best split into subjective and intersubjective spirit. Popper's worlds are comprised of the worlds of (1) physical objects; (2) feelings and thoughts; and (3) products of the human mind, including mathematical and scientific theories, engineering constructions, languages, works of art, and social institutions. Popper's third world needs to be differentiated into intellectual products that have a relation to a normative realm, such as laws that embody justice and philosophical claims that are true (Hegel's realm of the idea), and intellectual products that fall into the purely descriptive realm, such as social scientific theories, business organizations, and the central principles of the Nazi party.

3 The laughter of superiority has been articulated by Hobbes, Vico, and Baudelaire, among others, the laughter of relief by Spencer, Freud, and Bakhtin, among others, and the laughter of incongruity by Hegel, Schopenhauer, and Kierkegaard, among others. Many theorists (e.g., Kant and Bergson) focus on particular kinds of incongruities. Monro anomalously discusses a fourth theory, the ambivalence theory: "we laugh whenever, on contemplating an object or a situation, we find opposite emotions struggling within us for mastery" (210). I consider this definition a variant of the incongruity theory, a particular kind of contrast, though here, as with the other reception theories, in the recipient, not in the object.

4 Despite the voluminous literature on Hitchcock and the rich presence of comedy in his films, works on the comic are relatively modest, and as yet no definitive study exists. Comedy surfaces off and on in Brill's book on romance and irony. And it is touched on by Leitch, whose primary focus is playfulness; Smith, whose predominant interest is tone; and Naremore, who stresses the mingling of humor and suspense. The most detailed study is Gehring, who underscores Hitchcock's dark comedy. However, because Gehring does not recognize any connection between comedy and religion (he sees Hitchcock as "not religious" 150), Gehring misses the combination of critique and embrace of humanity that I elevate below under "humor."

5 Sullivan's analysis of music in Hitchcock's corpus is superb, on a level with the best general books on Hitchcock, those by Wood and Brill, and the excellent study of women by Modleski.

6 A brutal example of non-comic iteration is *The Wrong Man*. Here, too, it betokens an almost endless battle, which in this case comes close to triggering complete despair.

7 As a classical philologist, Nietzsche of course knew *Gorgias* and *Republic* I, where Thrasymachus also advances the idea of justice as the right of the stronger. The German philosopher's originality lies more in his cultural criticism and psychological acumen than in his ethics, for Nietzsche on good and evil can be traced back to Plato's literary creations even if Nietzsche adds a new and inflammatory moment, his attack on Christianity.

8 Yanal views the Professor as a surrogate for Hitchcock (78). In terms of manipulating the action, the Professor is indeed a surrogate director, but he is also deeply unethical. Ethics plays a lesser role for Yanal, whose study ignores *Rope*, about which he says, it "did not strike me as having philosophical implications" (2).

9 Wartenberg makes the very good point that even though Eve is primarily saved by Thornhill, they need the aid of the government, such that we see at the end a synthesis of two positions, the individual and the collective.

Chapter 2

1 I include here not every difference between theater and film, but only those that elevate film's distinct capacity for expression. Balázs, for example, highlights the unity of film versus the two layers of theater, the writer's work and its interpretation on the stage (17–18). Bazin further notes the extent to which in theater the human being is invariably primary, whereas in film the human being can be an accessory to a setting (*What* 1.102).

2 Camera work is of course part of the mis-en-scène, such that the three categories of camera, editing, and mis-en-scène can be considered distinctly but also partly overlap, as one would expect in an organic artwork. One could say that they can be noted separately but not imagined separately. Only the combination of all three elements gives film its distinction. The settings in *Rope* and *Dial M for Murder* do not expand greatly beyond theater, but the camera work makes manifest cinematic reality.

3 Arnheim emphasizes that film offers not a mechanical reproduction of reality but an expression that diverges from the given by opening up new angles on reality. It would be metaphysically wrong to suggest that the reality shown in a film is exhausted by empirical reality. Film can also convey a higher reality of ideas. Relevant here, if we can draw an analogy to another art form, is Hegel's argument that a portrait should be more like the real person than the person themselves (15.104).

4 For a helpful analysis of sound and silence in the first *Man Who Knew Too Much*, see Weis 77–86.

5 The broad movement toward film reception has diverse strands, among them film phenomenology, affect theory, and cognitive film theory. For an example of a cognitive approach to film analysis that is marked by clarity and enriched by examples from Hitchcock, see Plantinga.

6 The idea that Hitchcock's self-reflexive strategies are philosophical is present in a few critics, such as Abrams, but Abrams and Danto, on whom Abrams draws, overlook the extent to which self-reflexive art predates modernity and is evident as far back as Homer, even if modernity accentuates it.

7 Fawell explicates much of the self-reflexive banter in *Stage Fright* and offers a compelling interpretation. One quibble: Fawell agrees with Thompson (153–4) that Smith is "incapable of lying" (33), but Smith certainly deceives Jonathan toward the end (so that he can arrest him outside of Eve's house), thereby protecting Eve and her family. In doing so, Ordinary Smith, as Eve calls him, becomes extraordinary.

8　Hösle introduced the concept of a director's drama (*Praktische Philosophie* 84). Hagens has written an insightful essay on the topic. To my knowledge the topic is not the focus of a Hitchcock study, though it would certainly merit one. Occasionally critics use the concept implicitly, for example, Allen 22–3 and Pappas 37–8. Noting the need for characters to improvise, Brill speaks analogously of some characters, such as Hannay, Tisdall, and Kane, as "screenwriters within the movie" (44).

9　For a fuller discussion of tragedy and reconciliation in *I Confess*, see my *Tragedy and Comedy* 264–70.

10　Rothman is right to call Hitchcock's *Vertigo* a tragedy but mistaken to call it "his only tragedy" ("Scottie's Dream" 67).

11　Singer is wrong when he claims that *The Trouble with Harry* is Hitchcock's only "outright comedy" (51).

12　Still, even with his comic embrace of the larger collective, Hitchcock mocks the deputy, Calvin Wiggs, who is obsessed with making money and catching law breakers and unable to keep up with the artist. As in the comic tradition, those who are loveless and cast shadows (as he does literally when he arrives at Jennifer's house) are expelled from harmony.

13　See Rohmer and Chabrol 113. I have elsewhere argued that Catholic cultures lend themselves to the cultivation of comedy, where, unlike in Protestantism, we see less emphasis on the individual qua individual and greater stress on the larger whole in which the individual finds fulfillment ("Hegel's Theory" 425).

14　In his essay on *North by Northwest* Cavell loosely includes *North by Northwest* among comedies of remarriage, as the two figures unite, do battle, and then reconcile. Hitchcock's fascination with the theme is also evident in *The Ring*, which likewise moves toward remarriage, not, however, as a comedy, but as a drama of reconciliation.

15　Among critics who understand ambiguity to be a central element in Hitchcock, I would name especially Allen.

16　I give a lengthy analysis of the drama of reconciliation, with literary and cinematic examples, in *Tragedy and Comedy* 247–89.

17　Keller's final confession moves the work to a drama of reconciliation. In contrast, Alice's not confessing and Frank's discouraging confession render *Blackmail* a problem play.

18　The beauty of this scene is missed by Wood, who views the film as "a failure" (82) and writes: "Anne Baxter's final withdrawal with her husband, leaving the man she loved in a situation of extreme peril, showing neither concern nor interest, is very awkward and indeterminate in aim" (83).

19 On our sight of Larrue's single eye, see Brill 100. On opticality as a motif in the film generally, see Pomerance 170–213.

20 If the choice were only tragedy or comedy, then comedy would certainly be the correct designation, but since Hitchcock's films contain elements we tend not to see in comedies, such as the potential for wrongful conviction or death, we need to extend our vocabulary. This is especially the case with darker works, such as *Notorious* and *Marnie*, but the principle applies more widely.

21 Negri sees the resolution as mere chance, which certainly fits our modern aesthetic, but this postreligious aesthetic is not compatible with the resonance of the Christ image and the eventual clearing of Manny's name, nor does it easily accord with Hitchcock's biography or parallel passages in his corpus. Still, Godard's use of the term "miracle" may be overly strong, especially given Manny's statement when his wife remains beyond help: "I guess I was hoping for a miracle."

22 See Spoto (*Art* 257), who does not even mention the film's religious moments. Beyond the more obvious elements above, Christopher Emmanuel Balestrero contains a double allusion to Christ, and given Christian iconography, even the name "Rose" alludes to Christ.

23 Wood points out the moral ambiguity of Mark, including his virtues (173–97 and 388–405). Wood writes: "It is partly this acceptance of necessary moral imperfection that gives him his maturity—seen as a willingness to accept responsibilities and follow them through whatever this entails" (186–7).

Chapter 3

1 On *Shadow of a Doubt* as Hitchcock's favorite film, see *Hitchcock on Hitchcock* 2.82; 2.150; 2.249; Cavett; O'Connell 119; Raubicheck 50; Chandler 147 and 212; and Perry. In one interview Hitchcock denies the claim; see Truffaut 151. Elsewhere he calls the film one of his best, for example, *Alfred* 34 and 187; Bogdanovich 475 and 511; and Bazin, *Cinema* 152.

2 The doubling has been noted in various publications; for two of the more impressive lists, see Spoto, *Art* 120 and Carson 349–50. Freedman writes: "it might well be difficult to name another movie in which the number two is more prominently featured" (94).

3 This sequence, first with Uncle Charlie above the stairs, then Charlie below, casting a long shadow, fits within a powerful array of Hitchcock shots that capture dialectical tension via vertical space. Zirnite, who analyzes spatial tension, notes that the singular figure above tends to represent darkness and "deceptive charm," whereas the figures below often embody "a precarious sense of decency" (4). The first shot echoes the earlier scene where Uncle Charlie looks out over the tenements after having eluded the detectives; the difference here lies in Charlie's knowledgeable return gaze and her formidable aura (she is backlit by sunlight).

4 In his interview with Truffaut Hitchcock discusses the movement from love to hate, stating about *Shadow of a Doubt*: "You destroy the thing you love" (111). He cites as his source Oscar Wilde, a reference to Wilde's "Ballad of Reading Gaol."

5 Saint Peter's Basilica and Bernini's colonnade together form the image of a keyhole. In front of the Basilica is the statue where Saint Peter holds the keys to the Church. Inside the Basilica, the coat of arms of Pope Urban VIII features the keys to the kingdom of heaven. Keys represent the Church, the path to the kingdom of heaven, and of course love—thus their significance also in *Notorious*, where Alicia steals a key from Sebastian and gives it to Devlin.

6 As an example of this reduction, see Gordon. Another form of psychological reductionism arises in Spoto, who views Hitchcock's films from a production-aesthetic perspective, interpreting them in the light of Hitchcock's personal predilections and psychoses (*Dark Side*).

7 Among the small number of scenes with either shallow or soft focus, none are of Uncle Charlie. Charlie is notably captured in soft focus in a close-up just before she hears that the other suspect has been killed and the search concluded and in a medium close-up at the train station when she is ready to send off Uncle Charlie (Figure 22). In both these shots and in what immediately follows Hitchcock presents her as both alluring and strong.

8 The marriage of Charlie's parents, the film suggests, had become boring. The gift of a wristwatch to the father suggests retirement: the father is being replaced by Uncle Charlie, who assumes the head of the table. Both the arrival scene and the announcement of Uncle Charlie's departure underscore the love relationship between Emma and Uncle Charlie, including its incestuous dimensions, even if the mother seems unaware of them. It was Uncle Charlie all along who had the charisma the father lacks. And yet, when Uncle Charlie learns of the survey, in his self-interested misogyny he calls even Emma a fool.

9 Family, primarily the conflict of family and independence, including the oppression of women, has been much discussed; see McLaughlin, Hemmeter, Kay Sloan, Carson, and Simpson. None of these writers address the dialectic of the family and the universal. This neglect may derive from the tendency to reduce the objective evil of Uncle Charlie to the psychological and to view the relationship with Graham as movement toward a new family life, thus overlooking the complexity of their relationship.

10 The best account of Ann, and of the domestic scene generally, is Michie; for some good comments on Roger, the son, see Carson 355–6, and for some occasionally insightful comments on both, see Rothman, *Hitchcock*.

11 Hitchcock's Catholicism is most pronounced in works with profound religious imagery, such as *I Confess* and *The Wrong Man*, but it is evident, in subtler ways, throughout his films.

12 Oddly, the literature does not comment on these connections, though Bazin briefly notes that the film has "strange echoes of Faulkner and Dostoevski" (*Cinema* 113). Both works open with the murderer wondering if he will meet his enemies on the street (3). Both contain allusions to counting steps (5). The murderer is alienated from, and drawn to, his family. The murderer becomes physically ill, and according to Raskolnikov's theory, murder is always accompanied by an illness (258). At some level the murderer seems to act without freedom (62, 70). A cat-and-mouse game with the police arises. Love turns into hate (275). Each work refers to redirecting blood money for a hospital (65), which both undermines the idea of goodness and hints at a moment of atonement. Hitchcock makes a direct reference to "crime and punishment" in *Rope*, which also wrestles with the idea that superior beings, the privileged few, have the right to take the lives of ordinary people: "the lives of inferior beings are unimportant."

13 We see the dancers after Charlie receives the ring and recognizes the initials; after she reads the newspaper article that links Uncle Charlie with the murderer, at which point she takes off the ring; and after Uncle Charlie dies.

14 The ring circles through the story. Charlie receives it as if it were a kind of wedding ring. Uncle Charlie puts it on her, then takes it off. When Charlie reads the initials, he offers to take it back, yet she puts it back on. She takes it off at the library when she learns the truth. At the pub she pulls out the ring, which Uncle Charlie then takes and hides. In the end, her locating the ring and placing it on her finger is a statement of power that leads to his departure, but it also elicits his third and final attempt to murder her. Not surprisingly, the ring is an ambiguous symbol, representing, on the one hand, marriage and symmetry and, on the other, evil and power—as it points to the murder of the widow. In both cases, it has also a sexual connotation. In Hitchcock's *The Ring*, the concept of the ring is likewise ambiguous; it refers not only to the circular bracelet, and so to love, but also to a cycle (or wheel) of who is dominant and who is weak and, finally, to the boxing ring itself and the circular drum that calls out the rounds (and thereby the battle).

15 Uncle Charlie tries to turn the newspaper into a house (for Ann) and a barn (for Roger). The idyll is only imagined; Uncle Charlie cannot fully return home, not least of all because his crimes and further machinations, which partly through the paper have entered the family idyll, make home unavailable to him. In destroying the father's newspaper, Uncle Charlie further displaces Joe. The father only reads, whereas the paper records Uncle Charlie's deeds. Two later connections are drawn to this scene: the revelation in the library when Charlie reads the newspaper and the scene in the bar when Uncle Charlie twists a paper napkin as if he were strangling someone. He cannot undo his crimes, he can only repeat them.

16 San Juan and McDevitt recognize the extent to which Hitchcock identifies with many of his villains, but they do not see that Hitchcock is not exhausted by his villains. Instead, he identifies with a full range of characters.

17 An exception is Wood, who in his essay on fascism recognizes that *Shadow of a Doubt*, like *Rope* and *Vertigo*, tells us a great deal about fascism. Hantke, too, recognizes the historical moment, but his essay has two limitations: it recognizes in Uncle Charlie's words and actions only discord within the nation, not an allusion to Nazism, and he presupposes a dichotomy or tension between wartime engagement and cinematic artistry, when in fact Hitchcock beautifully interweaves the two.

18 I would be cautious about any allegorical reductionism. Perez, for example, sees in *Shadow of a Doubt* an "incest allegory" (264), and Greven reads the film as "an allegory to feminism and queer theory" (55). Not only is it difficult to sustain a one-to-one correspondence in all particulars, the concept of allegory excludes the other, very rich themes that animate such a multivalent film.

19 The role that the ordinary and the extraordinary play in American life, all the way to the present (one need only think of the fascination with the normal person who becomes a hero or celebrity), underscores that the film is about America and that Hitchcock had a wonderful capacity to capture some of the nation's central characteristics.

20 Cf. in this context Hitchcock's critique in *Rope* of the master race concept, with its "contempt for humanity," and the filmmaker's corresponding elevation of "the right to live."

21 Even today, as the US Census Bureau's 2017 American Community Survey data tell us, German is the most common ancestry in 21 of our 50 states, and 43 million Americans claim to have German heritage, more than any other national ancestry; the figures would already have been dramatic in the 1940s, for the greatest waves of German immigration stretched from 1844 to 1854 and 1872 to 1892 (*Historical Statistics*, Table Ad 106–20).

Chapter 5

1 In recent decades trust has decreased globally. The annual Edelman Trust Barometer reveals a global drop of trust in institutions. Recent surveys from the Pew Research Center show declining trust within the United States.

Credits

Works Cited

Abel, Richard. "Stage Fright: The Knowing Performance." *Film Criticism* 11.1–2 (Fall–Winter, 1986–7): 5–14.

Abrams, Jerold J. "Hitchcock and the Philosophical End of Film." *Hitchcock's Moral Gaze*. Albany: SUNY Press, 2017. 211–33.

Ackroyd, Peter. *Alfred Hitchcock: A Brief Life*. New York: Doubleday, 2016.

Alfred Hitchcock Interviews. Ed. Sidney Gottlieb. Jackson: University Press of Mississippi, 2003.

Allen, Richard. *Hitchcock's Romantic Irony*. New York: Columbia University Press, 2007.

Alleva, Richard. "The Catholic Hitchcock: A Director's Sense of Good and Evil." *Commonweal* (July 16, 2010): 14–19.

American Community Survey 2017. C04006. People Reporting Ancestry. United States Census Bureau. https://data.census.gov/cedsci/table?q=American%20Community%20Survey%202017.%20C04006.%20&tid=ACSDT1Y2017.C04006&hidePreview=false. Accessed January 7, 2022.

Arnheim, Rudolf. *Film as Art*. Berkeley: University of California Press, 1957.

Balázs, Béla. *Early Film Theory: Visible Man and the Spirit of Film*. New York: Berghahn, 2011.

Bartetzko, Dieter. *Zwischen Zucht und Ekstase: Zur Theatralik von NS-Architektur*. Berlin: Mann, 1985.

Bazin, André. *The Cinema of Cruelty: From Buñuel to Hitchcock*. New York: Seaver, 1982.

Bazin, André. *What Is Cinema?* 2 vols. Berkeley: University of California Press, 2005.

Belton, John. "The Space of *Rear Window*." *MLN* 103.5 (1988): 1121–38.

Bogdanovich, Peter, ed. *Who the Devil Made It*. New York: Knopf, 1997.

Braudy, Leo. *The World in a Frame*. New York: Doubleday, 1977.

Brill, Lesley. *The Hitchcock Romance: Love and Irony in Hitchcock's Films*. Princeton: Princeton University Press, 1988.

Britton, Andrew. "Hitchcock's 'Spellbound': Text and Counter-Text." *CineAction* 3/4 (Winter, 1986): 72–83.

Brooks, Peter. *The Melodramatic Imagination: Balzac, Henry James, Melodrama, and the Mode of Excess*. New York: Columbia University Press, 1985.

Bruns, John. *Hitchcock's People, Places, and Things*. Evanston: Northwestern University Press, 2019.

Carroll, Noël. "The Paradox of Suspense." *Suspense: Conceptualizations, Theoretical Analyses, and Empirical Explorations*. Mahwah: Erlbaum, 1996. 71–91.

Carroll, Noël. *The Philosophy of Horror or Paradoxes of the Heart*. New York: Routledge, 1990.

Carroll, Noël. "*Vertigo* and the Pathologies of Romantic Love." *Hitchcock and Philosophy: Dial M for Metaphysics*. New York: Open Court, 2007. 101–14.

Carson, Diane. "The Nightmare World of Hitchcock's Women." *Michigan Academician* 18 (1986): 349–56.

Cavell, Stanley. "North by Northwest." *A Hitchcock Reader*. 2nd ed. Oxford: Wiley, 2009. 250–63.

Cavell, Stanley. *Pursuits of Happiness: The Hollywood Comedy of Remarriage*. Cambridge: Harvard University Press, 1984.

Cavett, Dick. "Interview with Alfred Hitchcock." *The Dick Cavett Show* (June 6, 1972). https://www.youtube.com/watch?v=xh9llXHHClk. Accessed January 7, 2022.

Chandler, Charlotte. *It's Only a Movie: Alfred Hitchcock; A Personal Biography*. New York: Simon, 2005.

Cohen, Hermann. *Ästhetik des reinen Gefühls*. 2 vols. Berlin: Cassirer, 1912.

Danto, Arthur C. *After the End of Art: Contemporary Art and the Pale of History*. Princeton: Princeton University Press, 1997.

Dolar, Mladen. "Hitchcock's Objects." *Everything You Always Wanted to Know about Lacan but Were Afraid to Ask Hitchcock*. New York: Verso, 2010. 31–46.

Dostoevsky, Fyodor. *Crime and Punishment*. Trans. Richard Pevear and Larissa Volokhonsky. New York: Vintage, 1993.

Drumin, William A. *Thematic and Methodological Foundations of Alfred Hitchcock's Artistic Vision*. Lewisten: Mellen, 2004.

Dürrenmatt, Friedrich. *Problems of the Theatre*. New York: Grove Press, 1966.

Durgnat, Raymond. *The Strange Case of Alfred Hitchcock, or The Plain Man's Hitchcock*. Cambridge: MIT Press, 1974.

Dynia, Philip. "Alfred Hitchcock and the Ghost of Thomas Hobbes." *Cinema Journal* 15.2 (1976): 27–41.

Edelman Trust Barometer. 2020. https://www.edelman.com/trustbarome ter. Accessed January 7, 2022.

Fawell, John. "*Stage Fright*: Alfred Hitchcock's Fear of Acting." *Film Criticism* 26.1 (Fall, 2001): 25–41.

Ficino, Marsilio. *Commentary on Plato's Symposium on Love*. Dallas: Spring, 1985.

Freedman, Carl. "American Civilization and Its Discontents: The Persistence of Evil in Hitchcock's *Shadow of a Doubt*." *The Cambridge Companion to Alfred Hitchcock*. New York: Cambridge University Press, 2015. 92–105.

French, Tony. "Your Father's Method of Relaxation. Hitchcock's *Shadow of a Doubt*." *Cine Action* 50 (1999): 43–45.

Gehring, Wes D. *Hitchcock and Humor: Modes of Comedy in Twelve Defining Films*. Jefferson: McFarland, 2019.

Gilmore, Richard. "Hitchcock and Philosophy." *A Companion to Alfred Hitchcock*. New York: Blackwell, 2011. 493–506.

Godard, Jean-Luc. *Godard on Godard: Critical Writings*. London: Secker, 1972.

Gordon, Paul. "Sometimes a Cigar Is Not Just a Cigar: A Freudian Analysis of Uncle Charles in Hitchcock's *Shadow of a Doubt*." *Film Literature Quarterly* 19 (1991): 267–76.

Gottlieb, Sidney. "Early Hitchcock: The German Influence." *Framing Hitchcock: Selected Essays from the Hitchcock Annual*. Detroit: Wayne State University Press, 2002. 35–58.

Greven, David. *Intimate Violence: Hitchcock, Sex, and Queer Theory*. New York: Oxford University Press, 2017.

Hagens, Jan Lüder. "Forging a Link between Stage and World: The Genre of Director's Drama." *Essays on Twentieth-Century German Drama and Theater*. New York: Lang, 2004. 46–52.

Hantke, Steffen. "Hitchcock at War: *Shadow of a Doubt*, Wartime Propaganda, and the Director as Star." *Journal of Popular Film and Television* 44.3 (2016):159–68.

Hedren, Tippi, with Lindsay Harrison. *Tippi*. New York: Harper, 2016.

Hegel, G. W. F. *Werke in zwanzig Bänden*. Ed. Eva Moldenhauer and Karl Markus Michel. Frankfurt: Suhrkamp, 1978.

Hemmeter, Thomas. "Hitchcock the Feminist: Rereading Shadow of a Doubt." *Hitchcock Annual* (1992): 12–27.

Hetherington, Marc, and Jonathan Weiler. *Prius or Pickup?: How the Answers to Four Simple Questions Explain America's Great Divide*. New York: Houghton, 2018.

Historical Statistics of the United States: Earliest Times to the Present. Ed. Susan B. Carter. New York: Cambridge University Press, 2006.

Hitchcock, Alfred, director. *The Birds*. Screenplay by Evan Hunter. Universal Pictures, 1963.

Hitchcock, Alfred, director. *Blackmail*. Screenplay by Alfred Hitchcock and dialogue by Benn Levy. British International Pictures, 1930.

Hitchcock, Alfred, director. *Foreign Correspondent.* Screenplay by Charles Bennett and Joan Harrison and dialogue by James Hilton and Robert Benchley. United Artists, 1940.

Hitchcock, Alfred, director. *I Confess.* Screenplay by George Tabori and William Archibald. Warner Bros., 1953.

Hitchcock, Alfred, director. *Juno and the Paycock.* Based on Seán O'Casey's *Juno and the Paycock.* Adapted by Alfred Hitchcock. Scenario by Alma Reville. British International Pictures, 1930.

Hitchcock, Alfred, director. *Lifeboat.* Screenplay by Jo Swerling and story by John Steinbeck. 20th Century Fox, 1944.

Hitchcock, Alfred, director. *The Man Who Knew Too Much.* Screenplay by John Michael Hayes and story by Charles Bennett and D. B. Wyndham-Lewis. Paramount Pictures, 1956.

Hitchcock, Alfred, director. *Marnie.* Screenplay by Jay Presson Allen. Universal Pictures, 1964.

Hitchcock, Alfred, director. *Murder!* Screenplay by Alfred Hitchcock, Walter Mycroft, and Alma Reville. British International Pictures, 1930.

Hitchcock, Alfred, director . *North by Northwest.* Screenplay by Ernest Lehman. Metro-Goldwyn-Mayer, 1959.

Hitchcock, Alfred, director. *Notorious.* Screenplay by Ben Hecht. RKO Radio Pictures, 1946.

Hitchcock, Alfred, director. *Rear Window.* Screenplay by John Michael Hayes. Paramount Pictures, 1954.

Hitchcock, Alfred, director. *Rope.* Adaption by Hume Cronyn and screenplay by Arthur Laurents. Warner Bros., 1948.

Hitchcock, Alfred, director. *Saboteur.* Screenplay by Peter Viertel, Joan Harrison, and Dorothy Parker. Universal Pictures, 1942.

Hitchcock, Alfred, director. *Shadow of a Doubt.* Screenplay by Thornton Wilder, Sally Benson, and Alma Reville. Universal Pictures, 1943.

Hitchcock, Alfred, director. *Spellbound.* Adaptation by Angus MacPhail and screenplay by Ben Hecht. United Artists, 1945.

Hitchcock, Alfred, director. *Strangers on a Train.* Adaptation by Whitfield Cook and screenplay by Raymond Chandler and Czenzi Ormonde. Warner Bros., 1951.

Hitchcock, Alfred, director. *The 39 Steps.* Adaptation by Charles Bennett, continuity by Alma Reville, and dialogue by Ian Hay. Gaumont British Picture Corporation, 1935.

Hitchcock, Alfred, director. *To Catch a Thief.* Screenplay by John Michael Hayes. Paramount Pictures, 1955.

Hitchcock, Alfred, director. *Vertigo.* Screenplay by Alec Coppel and Samuel Taylor. Paramount Pictures, 1958.

Hitchcock, Alfred, director. *The Wrong Man.* Screenplay by Maxwell Anderson and Angus MacPhail. Warner Bros., 1956.

Hitchcock and Philosophy: Dial M for Metaphysics. Ed. David Baggett and William A. Drumin. New York: Open Court, 2007.

Hitchcock on Hitchcock: Selected Writings and Interviews. 2 vols. Ed. Sidney Gottlieb. Berkeley: University of California Press, 1995–2015.

Hösle, Vittorio. *Hegels System. Der Idealismus der Subjektivität und das Problem der Intersubjectivität.* Hamburg: Meiner, 1987.

Hösle, Vittorio *Die Krise der Gegenwart und die Verantwortung der Philosophie. Transzendentalpragmatik, Letztbegründung, Ethik.* 2nd ed. Munich: Beck, 1994.

Hösle, Vittorio. *Morals and Politics.* Notre Dame: University of Notre Dame Press, 2004.

Hösle, Vittorio. *Praktische Philosophie in der modernen Welt.* Munich: Beck, 1992.

Hughes, Rowland. "Shadows and Doubts: Hitchcock, Genre, and Villainy." *The Devil Himself: Villainy in Detective Fiction and Film.* Westport: Greenwood, 2002. 107–19.

Humbert, David. *Violence in the Films of Alfred Hitchcock: A Study in Mimesis.* Lansing: Michigan State University Press, 2017.

Hurley, Neil P., S.J. "Soul in Suspense: The Catholic/Jesuit Influences on Hitchcock." *New Orleans Review* 17.4 (1990): 44–52.

Hurley, Neil P., S.J. *Soul in Suspense: Hitchcock's Fright and Delight.* Lanham: Scarecrow, 1993.

Hyde, Thomas. "The Moral Universe of Hitchcock's *Spellbound.*" *A Hitchcock Reader.* 2nd ed. London: Wiley, 2009. 156–63.

Ingarden, Roman. *Ontology of the Work of Art: The Musical Work, The Picture, The Architectural Work, The Film.* Athens: Ohio University Press, 1989.

Jenkins, Jennifer L. "The Philosophy of Marriage in North by Northwest." *Hitchcock's Moral Gaze.* Ed. R. Barton Palmer, Homer B. Pettey, and Steven M. Sanders. Albany: SUNY, 2017. 253–69.

Kaes, Anton. *Shell Shock Cinema: Weimar Culture and the Wounds of War.* Princeton: Princeton University Press, 2009.

Kleist, Heinrich von. *Sämtliche Werke und Briefe.* Munich: Hanser, 1977.

Kornhaber, Donna. "Hitchcock's Diegetic Imagination: Thornton Wilder, *Shadow of a Doubt*, and Hitchcock's Mise-en-Scène." *CLUES: A Journal of Detection* 31.1 (Spring, 2013): 67–78.

Kracauer, Siegfried. *From Caligari to Hitler: A Psychological History of the German Film.* Princeton: Princeton University Press, 2004.

Lee, Sander. "Existential Themes in the Films of Alfred Hitchcock." *Philosophy Research Archives* 11 (1986): 225–44.

Leitch, Thomas M. *Find the Director and Other Hitchcock Games.* Athens: University of Georgia Press, 1991.

Makkai, Katalin, ed. *Vertigo.* New York: Routledge, 2013.

Mann, Thomas. *The Coming Victory of Democracy*. London: Secker, 1938.

McGilligan, Patrick. *Alfred Hitchcock: A Life in Darkness and Light*. New York: HarperCollins, 2003.

McLaughlin, James. "All in the Family: Alfred Hitchcock's *Shadow of a Doubt*." *A Hitchcock Reader*. Ed. Marshall Deutelbaum and Leland Poague. Ames: Iowa State, 1986. 141–52.

Mead, George Herbert. *Mind, Self, and Society*. Chicago: University of Chicago Press, 2015.

Michie, Elsie B. "Unveiling Maternal Desires: Hitchcock and American Domesticity." *Hitchcock's America*. New York: Oxford University Press, 1999. 29–53.

Miller, D. A. *Hidden Hitchcock*. Chicago: University of Chicago Press, 2016.

Modleski, Tania. *The Women Who Knew Too Much*. 3rd ed. New York: Routledge, 2015.

Monro, D. H. *Argument of Laughter*. Notre Dame: University of Notre Dame Press, 1963.

Mulvey, Laura. "Visual Pleasure and Narrative Cinema." *Screen* 16.3 (1975): 6–18.

Naremore, James. "Hitchcock and Humor." *Hitchcock: Past and Future*. New York: Routledge, 2004. 22–36.

Negri, Sabrina. "I Saw, Therefore I Know? Alfred Hitchcock's *The Wrong Man* and the Epistemological Potential of the Photographic Image." *Film Criticism* 41.1 (February 2017): n.p.

The New Oxford Annotated Bible with Apocrypha. 4th ed. Ed. Michael D. Coogan. New York: Oxford University Press, 2010.

Nietzsche, Friedrich. *Werke*. Ed. Karl Schlechta. 6th ed. 3 vols. Munich: Hanser, 1969.

O'Connell, Pat Hitchcock, and Laurent Bouzereau. *Alma Hitchcock: The Woman Behind the Man*. Berkeley: University of California Press, 2003.

Palmer, R. Barton, Homer B. Pettey, and Steven M. Sanders, eds. *Hitchcock's Moral Gaze*. Albany: SUNY, 2017.

Pappas, Nickolas. "Magic and Art in Vertigo." *Vertigo*. New York: Routledge, 2013. 18–44.

Perez, Gilberto. "Hitchcock's Family Romance: Allegory in *Shadow of a Doubt*." *Understanding Love: Philosophy, Film, and Fiction*. New York: Oxford University Press, 2014. 251–70.

Perkins, V. F. "I Confess: Photographs of People Speaking." *CineAction* 52 (2000): 28–39.

Perry, George. "Hitchcock on Location." *American Heritage* (April–May, 2007): 58.2.

Pew Research Center. "Trust and Distrust in America." July, 2019. https://www.pewresearch.org/politics/2019/07/22/trust-and-distrust-in-amer ica/. Accessed January 7, 2022.

Pippin, Robert B. *Filmed Thought. Cinema as Reflected Form*.
Chicago: University of Chicago Press, 2020.

Pippin, Robert B. *The Philosophical Hitchcock: Vertigo and the Anxieties of Unknowingness*. Chicago: University of Chicago Press, 2017.

Plantinga, Carl R. *Moving Viewers: American Film and the Spectator's Experience*. Berkeley: University of California Press, 2009.

Plato. *The Collected Dialogues*. Ed. Edith Hamilton and Huntington Cairns. Princeton: Princeton University Press, 1978.

Pomerance, Murray. *An Eye for Hitchcock*. New Brunswick: Rutgers University Press, 2004.

Popper, Karl R. *Objective Knowledge: An Evolutionary Approach*. Oxford: Clarendon, 1972.

Popper, Karl R. "Three Worlds." *Michigan Quarterly Review* 18.1 (1979): 1–23.

Pudovkin, Vsevolod Illarionovich. *Film Technique and Film Acting*. New York: Grove, 1976.

Raubicheck, Walter. "Working with Hitchcock: A Collaborators' Forum with Patricia Hitchcock, Janet Leigh, Teresa Wright, and Eva Marie Saint." *Hitchcock Annual* 11 (2002/2003): 32–66.

Roche, Mark W. "Courage as an Intellectual Virtue and the Puzzle of President Trump." *Telos*. 27 September 2017. http://www.telospr ess.com/courage-as-an-intellectual-virtue-and-the-puzzle-of-presid ent-trump/. Accessed January 7, 2022.

Roche, Mark W . "Hegel's Theory of Comedy in the Context of Hegelian and Modern Reflections on Comedy." *Revue Internationale de Philosophie* 56 (2002): 411–30.

Roche, Mark W. "Idealistische Ästhetik als Option für die heutige Ästhetik und Literaturwissenschaft." *Idealismus heute: Aktuelle Perspektiven und neue Impulse*. Darmstadt: Wissenschaftliche Buchgesellschaft, 2015. 271–89.

Roche, Mark W. *Tragedy and Comedy: A Systematic Study and a Critique of Hegel*. Albany: SUNY, 1998.

Roche, Mark W. *Why Literature Matters in the 21st Century*. New Haven: Yale University Press, 2004.

Roche, Mark W. and Vittorio Hösle. "Religious and Cultural Reversals in Clint Eastwood's *Gran Torino*." *Religion and the Arts* 15 (2011): 648–79.

Roche, Mark W. "Vico's Age of Heroes and the Age of Men in John Ford's Film *The Man Who Shot Liberty Valance*." *Clio: A Journal of Literature, History and the Philosophy of History* 23 (1993–4): 131–47.

Rogow, Faith. "Memory of the Camps." *Frontline. Public Broadcasting Service*. n.d. https://www-tc.pbs.org/wgbh/pages/frontline/teach/ camps/memoryofthecamps.pdf. Accessed January 7, 2022.

Rohmer, Eric, and Claude Chabrol. *Hitchcock: The First Forty-Four Films*. New York: Ungar, 1979.

Roosevelt, Franklin D. "State of the Union (Four Freedoms)." January 6, 1941. https://millercenter.org/the-presidency/presidential-speeches/january-6-1941-state-union-four-freedoms. Accessed January 7, 2022.

Rothman, William. *Hitchcock the Murderous Gaze*. Cambridge: Harvard University Press, 1997.

Rothman, William. "Scottie's Dream, Judy's Plan, Madeleine's Revenge." *Vertigo*. New York: Routledge, 2013. 45–88.

San Juan, Eric, and Jim McDevitt. *Hitchcock's Villains: Murderers, Maniacs, and Mother Issues*. Lanham: Scarecrow, 2013.

Scheler, Max. *Wesen und Formen der Sympathie*. Bonn: Bouvier, 2005.

Schroeder, David. *Hitchcock's Ear: Music and the Director's Art*. New York: Continuum, 2012.

Simone, Sam P. *Hitchcock as Activist: Politics and the War Films*. Ann Arbor: UMI Research, 1985.

Simpson, Philip. "Jack the Ripper and the Merry Widow Murderer: Blood Brothers in Hitchcock's *Shadow of a Doubt*." *Clues* 18 (1997): 45–76.

Singer, Irving. *Three Philosophical Filmmakers: Hitchcock, Welles, Renoir*. Cambridge: MIT Press, 2004.

Sloan, Jane E. *Alfred Hitchcock: A Filmography and Bibliography*. Berkeley: University of California Press, 1995.

Sloan, Kay. "Three Hitchcock Heroines: The Domestication of Violence." *New Orleans Review* 12 (1985): 91–5.

Smith, Susan. *Hitchcock: Suspense, Humour and Tone*. London: British Film Institute, 2000.

Sontag, Susan. "Theatre and Film." *Styles of Radical Will*. New York: Anchor, 1991. 99–122.

Spoto, Donald. *The Art of Alfred Hitchcock: Fifty Years of His Motion Pictures*. 2nd ed. New York: Anchor, 1992.

Spoto, Donald . *The Dark Side of Genius: The Life of Alfred Hitchcock*. New York: Da Capo, 1999.

Sterritt, David. *The Films of Alfred Hitchcock*. New York: Cambridge University Press, 2003.

Sullivan, Jack. *Hitchcock's Music*. New Haven: Yale University Press, 2006.

Thomas, Paul. "Review of *The Dark Side of Genius: The Life of Alfred Hitchcock*, by Donald Spoto." *Film Quarterly* 37.1 (1983): 34–7.

Thompson, Kristin. *Breaking the Glass Armor: Neoformalist Film Analysis*. Princeton: Princeton University Press, 1988.

Truffaut, François, and Helen G. Scott. *Hitchcock*. New York: Simon, 1984.

Vest, James M. "Phones as Instruments of Betrayal in Alfred Hitchcock's *Bon Voyage* and *Aventure Malgache*." *French Review* 72.3 (1999): 529–42.

Vico, Giambattista. *The New Science*. Ithaca: Cornell University Press, 1984.

Wartenberg, Thomas E. "Ethics or Film Theory? The Real McGuffin in *North by Northwest*." *Hitchcock and Philosophy: Dial M for Metaphysics*. Open Court, 2007. 141–55.

Weis, Elisabeth. *The Silent Scream: Alfred Hitchcock's Sound Track*. Rutherford: Fairleigh Davidson University Press, 1982.

Wilkerson, Isabel. *Caste: The Origins of Our Discontents*. New York: Random, 2020.

Wolitzer, Meg. "Shadow of a Doubt: Fat Man and Little Girl." *The Movie That Changed My Life*. New York: Viking, 1991. 25–33.

Wood, Robin. "Hitchcock and Fascism." *Hitchcock Annual* (2004/2005): 25–63.

Wood, Robin. *Hitchcock's Films Revisited*. New York: Columbia University Press, 2002.

Yacavone, Daniel. *Film Worlds: A Philosophical Aesthetics of Cinema*. New York: Columbia University Press, 2014.

Yacowar, Maurice. *Hitchcock's British Films*. 2nd ed. Detroit: Wayne State University Press, 2010.

Yanal, Robert J. *Hitchcock as Philosopher*. London: McFarland, 2005.

Zirnite, Dennis. "Hitchcock, on the Level: The Heights of Spatial Tension." *Film Criticism* 10.3 (1986): 2–21.

Žižek, Slavoj. "In His Bold Gaze My Ruin Is Writ Large." *Everything You Always Wanted to Know About Lacan but Were Afraid to Ask Hitchcock*. New York: Verso, 2010. 211–72.

Index